GW01145360

Welcome to Mollywood

Novels by Molly Parkin

Love All
Up Tight
Full Up
Love Bites
A Bite of the Apple
Breast Stroke
Write Up
Fast and Loose
Up and Coming
Switchback

Welcome to Mollywood

Molly Parkin

For
Dear Susie
love from
Moll xxxx

First published 2010
www.beautiful-books.co.uk

Beautiful Books Limited
36-38 Glasshouse Street
London W1B 5DL

ISBN 9781907616020

9 8 7 6 5 4 3 2 1

Copyright © Molly Parkin 2010

The right of Molly Parkin to be identified as
the author of this work has been asserted by her in accordance
with the Copyright, Designs and Patents Act 1988.

All rights reserved. No part of this publication may be reproduced,
stored in or introduced into a retrieval system, or transmitted, in any form,
or by any means (electronic, mechanical, photocopying, recording or
otherwise) without the prior written permission of the publisher.
Any person who does any unauthorised act in relation to this
publication may be liable to criminal prosecution
and civil claims for damages.

A catalogue reference for this book is available from the British Library.

Cover by Molly Parkin.
Cover photographs by Anthony Lycett.
Queen of Bohemia, painting by Darren Coffield.
Jacket layout by Ian Pickard.

Printed and bound in the UK by CPI Mackays, Chatham, ME5 8TD.

"No one is useless in the world who lightens the burden of it for anyone else."

Charles Dickens

"Be kind, for everyone you meet is fighting a hard battle."

Plato

*"Now is the time to understand
That all your ideas of right and wrong
Were just a child's training wheels
To be laid aside
When you finally live
With veracity
And love."*

Hafiz

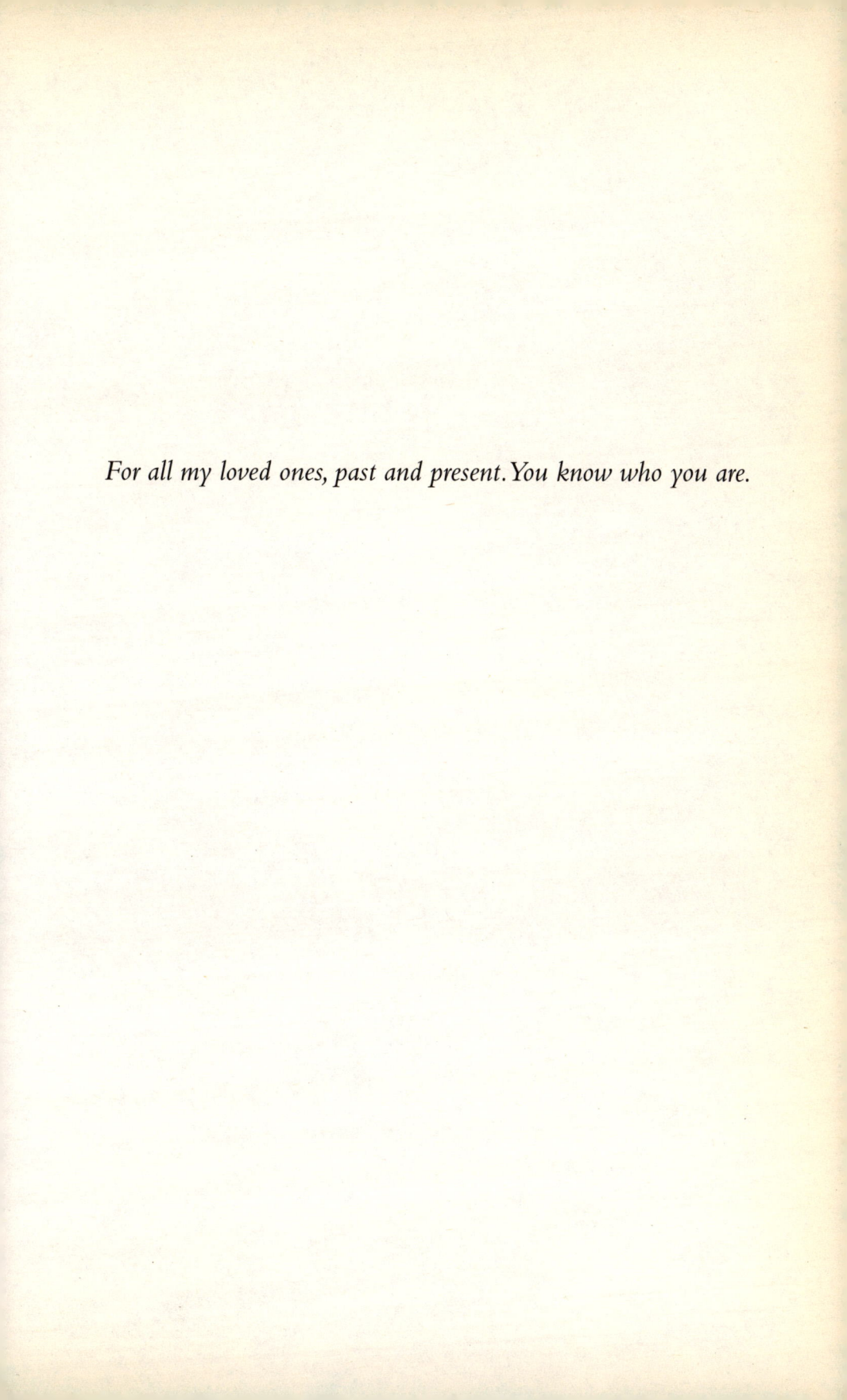

For all my loved ones, past and present. You know who you are.

Rodents made off with my teeth
before Christmas.

Thus affecting the rest of my entire life, the short span that remained of that life, for I would be celebrating my 78th birthday soon after Christmas. Leaving only two more years before crash-bang-walloping into my 80th, when I determined to kick the bucket and move on, feeling I'd done it all brilliantly by then. Time to depart.

It was late last year, 2009, October 1st, a Thursday, my favourite television viewing night, and I settled down to watch my three regular BBC programmes.

10pm: *News*.

10.35pm: David Dimbleby's *Question Time*.

11.35pm: *This Week*, with Andrew Neil, joined by MP Dianne Abbott and former MP Michael Portillo.

For this treat I opened a packet of ill-fated, seldom indulged, Cadbury Chocolate Eclairs, cramming four into my mouth, two in both cheeks, waiting for the chocolate goo to ooze through the encasing toffee. These four friends roamed my orifice, free spirits dispensing pleasure, herded ineptly by my tongue, resulting in a conglomerate knot, stuck to the ceiling of my false teeth, a comparatively recent acquisition.

I eased this denture from my mouth, placing it on the low table beside my reading armchair, carefully, not to spill the mouth-warm cargo of congealed toffee midst melted chocolate.

I looked forward to extricating the toffee knot and licking it clean later. In dizzy anticipation of this I closed my eyes, to savour the sublime coating of my saturated tongue and gums and my very own original lower molars.

When you've been reared in a succession of sweetshops throughout adolescence, even the whiff of a single Chocolate Drop, sold loose from a glass jar, can nudge dawdling nostalgia. For me, few perfumes arouse like the scent of confectionery.

I must have dozed into a deep sleep, for I awoke to the chorus of dawn. It was already 5am, my TV programmes were long since gone.

And so were my teeth.

The Carribean Pest Control Operative, Ossie Thomas, paid me a visit that same day, after my frenzied search for the missing dentures revealed acres of unfamiliar 'droppings'.

Coal black in colour and miniscule, the size of microscopic moon landings. Strewn singly at random around areas where eating took place or food was prepared. Such as the kitchen, and ominously, my TV viewing and reading and chomping armchair. The cultural and creative haven where I shape and handstitch my stylish chapeaux and deliberately Bohemian garments.

Where I scribble poems, and pontificate when filmed as a National Treasure, or when interviewed by the likes of the *Sunday Times*, *Time Out*, and this latest, the first British magazine on death, *Eulogy*.

Welcome to Mollywood

The site for the making of miniature paintings, of planned outsized abstracts, of delicate drawings, of prolonged conversations with overseas buddies and loved ones back home; of receiving intricate instructions from Virgin engineers (inexplicably in India) as to which knobs to twist or turn when the television falters. This hapless, shapeless, broken-springed, multi-cushioned, all-embracing, blueprint of my body, drenched in my D'n'A for the past 40 years, now playing host beneath and behind to a thriving community of MICE.

I say thriving community, but I should reiterate and re-term, outpost to the rodent City of Kitchen. There the sooty calling cards, some in urgent need of a dusting, were revealed to me in their tens and twenties, hundreds and thousands, multiplying toward the million mark.

I wondered if they were set out in mouse morse code, actual messages relaying the good news on an hourly basis, such as spilled porridge oats or unwashed plates with tasty remains.

Or arranged in hieroglyphic order, warning of danger afoot, from the me, their landlady, the alien inhabitant's blundering bathroom visitations sometimes more than once in the night. Or actual invitations to unexpected sugar-treats, like the gnawed remains of my silver seal-wrapped sheet of anti-reflux medication.

My blood had not run cold, my heart had not hammered, I was still capable of speech, at the appalling evidence of just how many uninvited flatmates were sharing my abode. But given alternatives, I would certainly not have chosen to live with a species dedicated to such enthusiastic defecation.

Domestic pets, the most popular, respond to rules laid down by the devoted owner.

Dogs attune their bowels to regular voidings, certainly when reared in cities. Usually at the end of a lead, when walking the park. Rewarded with a biscuit whilst the owner, wearing rubber gloves, gulping revulsion, scoops the offensively steaming canine offering in specifically designed plastic bags complete with sealing device, placing it carefully into the nearest rubbish bin.

I have never owned a dog, but I speak from experience having dog-sat my daughter's whilst she and her family were off on holiday. On my return home I missed the sanguine company of fellow dog-walkers on Primrose Hill, each smiling sympathetically in sunshine and hail, as we followed the same dog-defecation procedures.

I know of no similar club for the arse-wiping of mice. Though doubtless before my days are done, there will be disposable nappies aimed at the animal kingdom, marketed by the same brand who so ably service the private hazzards and public humiliations suffered by incontinent senior citizens.

I have chosen to live alone for the past 30 years, since the end of my second and last marriage. Despite the popularity I have basked in all my life, I am in essence a loner. I thrive in the solitude essential to the artist. Though vivacious in company, laughing and talking non-stop, a social device of the semi-stone deaf who follow conversation in an agony of non-comprehension, I blossom in silence.

My favourite places are the deserted edge of the ocean or the empty top of the mountain. But I also adapt to inner cities, exchanging smiles with strangers, whilst smoothly passing on. I identify with the crowd, with the mass communication, whilst marching in protests against wars inflicted upon an unwilling nation.

So this intrusion upon my home by the uninvited was never the plan for my advanced years.

And why would this mice-kingdom have chosen to crown me as their sovereign?

Me, the vegetarian with the non-dairy lifestyle. No cheese. No meat. No alcohol for their celebrations, I am now in my 24th year of sobriety. No cakes, no biscuits, no bars of chocolate. No tubs of ice-cream, no bread, no milk, no yoghurt. None of their favourites, not one.

Just fruit and veg and tinned tuna, or sardines or mackerel for brain food. Fish, ordered by my doctor as brain food, when I'd asked why I hadn't been able to recall my sister's name when I had known her for over 70 years. I got my memory back in a fortnight. But I can't stomach fresh fish flesh in my kitchen.

And how would the rodents even recognize the space as a kitchen? Apart for the giant fridge, sprayed scarlet to be invisible in the totally scarlet setting. More night club, more musical stage-set, utterly gaudy, camp glamour. Crammed to the bursting gills with the accoutrements of colour-production.

For this kitchen was my studio, where running water secured clean, brilliant acrylic shimmerings on brushes held beneath taps, between applications of paint. It's where I headed first thing every morning to release the images in my head which built up during dreams to an intolerable pressure, awaiting release.

Ballet dancers have told me, athletes too, that muscles need stretching every day for peak perfomance, and for writers and poets and painters it is the same, you have to keep your hand in to nourish the Muse.

When Ossie Thomas arrived to shoo away the rodents, he showed no surpise, or critical aversion to the state of the crammed kitchen. He referred to it as necessary creative clutter, given my calling. He was a kind man, and a handsome one. At an earlier stage of my life, long since passed, I would have made it my business to dress up to the gaudy gills in preparation for his visit, if I had bothered even to dress at all, and sprayed the entire place and myself with seductive French perfumes.

And confide in him flirtatiously that if we two were to marry I would be reverting to my maiden surname, which had been Thomas, and what a ring to it. I would have continued, hell-bent on an outcome, what harmony on introduction, Molly and Ollie Thomas. But this would have been wishful thinking, on the first visit.

Later, I was corrected, his name was not Ollie, but Ossie. Not the same ring to it.

Instead, circumspect now, I watched him without interference, placing granules in containers, which warned the rodents to retreat.

Retreat and never return. The advice he gave me was to clear as many free surfaces as possible.

We stared steadily into each other's eyes, when he said that. He, to emphasis what he had just uttered. Me to check if there was any means of escaping the necessary tidying, a chink for me to wriggle through. I tried a twinkle in the eye, without going as far as a saucy wink. But Ossie remained unsmiling in the face of it. He was there to carry out his duties, just doing his job. Kind but firm.

It occurred in a blinding flash that this was the sort of man most women the world over would choose as a husband.

Not me, but most.

A sensible and caring rock of a man, who would always know best. There to look out for his wife and his family in fair weather and foul. Obviously with such a stalwart at the helm, my home, or rather our home, would never have been invaded by rodents. The steady force of his presence would have held them at bay. Quite apart from the fact that as a pest control official the word would already have been spread, underground as in criminal circles, that here was a chap not to be challenged.

So I dropped my gaze, along with the misplaced defiance, and promised to do my best. Even going so far as to say, this just for effect, that I'd roll up my sleeves and get on with the clearing right away. Pronto.

I blitzed the entire space. I started as soon as I was alone. I reclaimed my territory. And felt cleansed.

I cleared all the paints away and put them in a cupboard. And stacked the canvasses in the open plan living and sleeping area against the wall. The rest I hung with barely an inch between them up on the walls. The brushes and papers, and palette knives and art books, plus the general paraphanalia of artistic utensils, I squashed beneath tables and behind the sofa.

Then I did what I had meant to do since my final visit to India, which I'd been visiting for 12 years on a two- to four-monthly basis. I constructed a shrine in the kitchen of all my three dimentional religious artefacts; arranged incense and candles around the fluorescent pink Budda from Bancock, garlanded the full length Madonna from France, tenderly placed the carved BC prostrate devotee on the kitchen table, before the hanging image of my deceased Indian guru, Ramana, and tokens of inspirational visits to the Egyptian Pyramids, Mexico City, Arctic outposts, the deserts of Dubai, the Great Wall of China, Cuba's Havana, pre-tsunami New Orleans, Gaugin's South Seas, Van Gogh's Provence, the Hollywood Hills, the gambling dens of Las Vegas, the Couture confines of Paris, Turner's Venice, Giotto's frescoes of Assisi, the sun-baked soil of Uganda and coral seas of Ceylon.

Long after my exotic locations for fashion shoots as Fashion Editor were no more, I became a travel writer for up-market magazines such as American Express Gold Card, and The *Telegraph*'s Sunday supplement to assuage my hunger for roaming the globe.

This overwhelming appetite for the unknown has never ceased to simmer. My Romany blood raising the zeal of the nomadic Celt. Once I counted 54 homes in my adult years, before giving up. Roaming the dusty corridors of memory can prove a strenuous pursuit for me these days; as taxing as summoning up reliable statistics on sexual shenanigans, from which I emerge shaking with mirth.

I would only wish that those partners were still alive to recall those shambolic couplings together. Anything for a laugh. Now in my scarlet kitchen, I had cleared the space to spark off the memories. Reliving my former life all over again.

Thank you Ossie Thomas. Bless.

Before Ossie Thomas had departed I had asked the burning question. Where were my teeth?

He seemed genuinely surprised by my stupid ignorance, my inability to put an obvious two and two together.

'The mice took your teeth. I've had enough experience of their group behaviour to know that. Rodents can't resist chocolate. The word gets around, they will journey the length of London for the taste. They would have been drawn by the chocolate on the teeth and working as a team whilst you were fast asleep in the chair, they would have eased the dentures from the low table to their nest, where they would have had a communal feast with their family and friends.'

'Under the table? In the corner?' I was struggling for comprehension, yet I'd watched enough Walt Disney cartoons with

Mickey Mouse antics to know what he was talking about.

'No, no, no! The mice don't live here. There are no puddles. And they pee all over the place with an extremely strong odour. Their nest is elsewhere. That's where the celebration took place.'

I looked in the mirror when I was alone again; truly alone.

I was assured by Ossie that the mice would not return. He, himself, would come back to check this in three weeks' time.

I rang my dentist, to arrange a re-fit for a new top denture. She informed me that they would take three weeks before I was able to collect them. This time I requested a back-up. If I'd had a replacement, I wouldn't now be in this awkward spot.

I was compelled it seemed to cancel two forthcoming poetry performances within the three-week time-slot, which I had been anticipating with great pleasure. One with my valued friend—poet, musician, painter Mike Horovitz—and the other with the esteemed poet, Tim Wells.

I smiled at myself, toothless, to assess the effect.

Grotesque.

I was reared within a family where a full view of gum was quite normal. The pain of adjusting to false teeth proved too painful, so they just didn't wear them. The married relatives persevered in deference to their partners. Spinster aunties couldn't be bothered, so treated their false teeth as table ornaments set out on lace handkerchiefs, upon a patterned plate or bestowed pride of place on top of the mantelpiece. That way they knew where they were at all times, should the need ever arise.

If a single, marriageable male appeared on the horizon, for instance. Or a lambchop smelt delicious enough to be nibbled. Plenty of the village menfolk tucked their dentures in the top pocket of their waistcoats when out on a spree, for chewing purposes at the end of the evening. My own mother only ever put her teeth in her mouth as she was leaving the house. They went with the high heels, which replaced the bedroom slippers, which we all wore indoors to protect the carpets from undue wear and tear.

The dramatic transformation of my mother never ceased to thrill me. She dropped years and became a sensual young beauty again. In later decades I would relive that same excitement, watching ordinary girls transform beneath the skill of trained beauticians and hairdressers, emerging as stunning models from another realm, posing and preening in garments I would have chosen for them, prepared for the artistry of the photographer. With these at hand, anyone could be a model.

My own mother had proved that to me before the age of ten. And all she had needed were the teeth and the heels, given her natural assets.

But to disguise my now, to me, offensive gums I played around with yashmaks and draped chiffon, tying it over, then under the nose. And thought I could just about get away with it, carry it off. Playing the class clown.

Then decided, for once in my life, to resist.

Viagra and *Cock-size*, both recently written comic erotic verses, could have sustained themselves with the yashmak for amusing effect. But not *Babel*, a political contemporary comment.

All these recent poems of mine had been seriously reviewed. Why wouldn't I now honour them and myself with the same respect?

I stood in front of the mirror in my nightie, reciting them in the bathroom, yashmak in place to judge the effect upon my audience.

Viagra

I went to my doctor for Viagra,
two years and a bit before my 80th birthday.
She suggested I may not care for the side effects,
a chronic headache at the base of the skull
for a full week,
and (here's where she put me off)
uncontrollable, incontinent, diarrhoea
meaning to say that I could expect
a shit in the middle of the shag.
'I graciously decline, doctor,' I said.
'Wise decision, dear,' she replied with a smile.
'You've already pleasured the male population
of entire continents, and how!
What about giving others a crack of the whip now.'

I'd gone on the suggestion of a young taxi driver
who was servicing an elderly lady, former fare
from Belgravia to Brixton, where
he'd dropped her off at her toyboy,
a teenage drummer from Illinois.
She was on Viagra, so the taxi driver

got in on the act, on hearing that fact.
Now the two of them have made the pact,
the Welsh driver and the Belgravia dame
torrid screws around the clock.
But a firm friendship, all the same.

He's tried his own Viagra share
a stiffie up for a fortnight,
a fucking nightmare,
trying to fit it under the steering wheel,
firm as rock, hard as steel!

But, as for me, I've lost the sexual urge
since my Las Vegas screw, the final splurge.
My doctor says it's diminishing hormones
and I did sense sediments showering my shoes
where these hormones must have exited my extremities,
leaving no stain of former hedonistic excess,
rendering me impervious to the opposite sex.
Such that even David Beckham with his
show-off, lolly-popper-chopper
wouldn't find a welcome in my now-single bed
my chosen companion being cocoa instead.

It seemed to me that the yashmak added to the reading, actually enhancing the comic turn, by lending eastern modesty. Encouraged, I read other poems, head high.

Cock-size

Much too much fuss is made about size
when it comes to sex
one of the very best times
I've shared with an ex
was when he wiggled his prick
(the length and width of a matchstick)
round my orgasmic clit
by-passing the stroll
up my cunt's larger hole,
easing four fingers instead
past the old maidenhead,
having licked on each tit,
at the nipples' outer-tip.

Good lovers with petite pricks
learn to pick up these tricks
transforming straightforward pokes
into shared, glorious jokes

whilst cocks hung like a horse
can feel brutally coarse,
relying mainly on force
propelled by male ego at source.

Bedroom Behaviour

I used to regard violence
as evidence of passion
I used to mistake jealous rage
for mad love.

I sported black-eyes and bruises
and broken teeth as badges
weaving humorous tales
as to how they'd been acquired,
whilst painfully, pitiably, perishing inside.

When I got better,
many decades later
I came to understand
from a wise soul
close at hand
that we had been drawn to each other
these bully boys and me.
Both marriages
mirror images
of mutual anger inside
stuff that from childhood
we'd been struggling to hide.

But when I meet up
with these ex-husbands now
sweetly, sedate, charmers in old age
each of us reaching our own final stage

what I feel for them is fondness
profound love and respect.

Yet still curiously elated,
in calm senior citizen repose,
at having punched both sexy bastards,
so often in the bedroom,
so hard on the nose.

Babel

I reside in the Tower of Babel
At the Chelsea area, World's End
The council dumped me
On this once-savage estate
As they had Christine Keeler
When she was at a low-ebb
Meant as a punishment for two good-time girls
She for bringing down
The Tory government in the sixties
by shagging Profumo,
The Foreign Secretary,
And a Russian spy
Both at the same time
During the Cold War.
And me, for being bankrupt
for not paying my taxes
Choosing to spend the cash

Boozing all day, every day,
With Francis Bacon and the like
At The Colony, instead.
Which I would do all over again given the choice,
seeing it as the essence of my creative education
For the conversation alone
Celt to Celt with Francis
And being cuddled and called Cunty
So tenderly by Muriel, my mentor
And as for the punishment
I've been whipped with a string of pearls
And am utterly in my element
Here in what's
Termed Sheltered Accommodation
For the Elderly and Infirm
With my very own garden,
Where I've planted palm trees and bamboos
And fragrant bushes of lavender,
And bee-seducing honeysuckle
And crimson roses, crying to be plucked
Heavy under their own weight,
Like young women with child

I have shy global refugees as neighbours,
None of us knowing what the other is saying
Passing in corridors, spilling from elevators
So smiling instead and saying it all,
With a gentle look in our eyes
Of caring about each other,
Men and women and children,
Infants and ancients,

Mourning families back home
And those left for dead in political strife
The displaced going through it.
Sharing life on an inner London council estate
Which unless you've done it, you can't possibly know it
Every politician should be forced to try it
Like taking a pleasure cruise on the Titanic
It unexpectedly brings
Human beings, homo-sapiens, closer together
Whether they share the same language or not
Like the huddling of penguins in arctic blizzards
And I'm old enough to remember
That's how it was in the London Blitz
With enemy bombers overhead

So we exchange a brief embrace,
A twinkle in the eye
Or a fleeting brushing of fingers
Feeling comforted and understood
Using this kind of language
With sentences left unsaid.

My sacred shrine gave me the answer.
  CANCEL!
  And the confirmation of this came the very next day attending a routine medical check-up on the Fulham Road around the corner in Chelsea.
  I had blood tests taken with a sequined gauze wrapping my entire head, necessarily slit for eyes and mouth. Rather fetching, stylish in the extreme, I'd thought.

But as I entered the confines of the Chelsea and Westminster Hospital I noticed other patients averting their gaze, as if out of respect. And even sick children, openly sniggering.

'Can I actually spare all that blood?' I asked the male nurse, conversationally. 'You've just syringed enough cocktails for a Convention of Vampires!'

'We have many tests to perform on you,' he replied warily, as if my cowled appearance denoted dementia.

'Mice made off with my teeth,' I whispered, leaning into him, gesturing to my yashmak as explanation of my appearance.

He registered distaste and called for the next patient.

The last time I'd had tests done about ten years ago, in this particular hospital, they diagnosed cancer with the same lack of sensitivity. That shocked me so much that I'd taken refuge in the hospital prayer room for the rest of the day. Attendants removed me.

The reminder put my present predicament into proportion.

The mice had only tootled off with my teeth, easily replaced. They hadn't gnawed off my nose. That was the good news.

And more was to come when the results of these hospital tests came through. My doctor's clinic asked me to come in for the news.

Excellent in every department of my body, they said. Of all their patients, I was one who they judged had another twenty more years left, actually two more than that, taking me all the way to a hundred.

But by the time that news was given to me I had already been prepared, making plans of my own. Apart from cancelling all my poetry performances, I had decided to view the disappearing dentures as a sign, a signal telling me to change my life. To take a different tack.

I had decided to hibernate all the way to Christmas and maybe even beyond, all the way through 2010. I'd informed my loved ones, my family and close friends that at long last I had decided to retire. Retirement, meaning that I no longer wanted to lead the life of a driven person. Creating, creating, creating, asleep and awake. Driven to ultimate madness like Van Gogh. Van Gogh and my own mother.

My decision was accepted without any questions. Whatever makes you happy, is what they said. As simple as that!

Now, however, this medical pronouncement of a further 20 years handed over to me altered everything, absolutely.

That and the advent of Christmas.

My daughter Sophie had bought me amongst other Christmas presents, a copy of *What's The Bleeding Time*, the biography of my first lover, James Robertson Justice.

The author, James Hogg, had interviewed me on the telephone whilst researching the book. It was published in 2008 and widely reviewed, with mentions of our affair, but I still hadn't chosen to read it myself.

It would have been too painful to revive those memories of my romantic entanglement with the love of my life, the mentor who I still considered to be my most formative influence.

This was before my first marriage to Michael Parkin, when I was still Molly Thomas, fresh from art school and teaching Art to under-privileged girls at a Secondary Modern School in Elephant and Castle.

I was still a virgin at 22, until I met James who was 30 years older. He had telephoned the Earls Court basement flat I shared with an art-school friend from Brighton. And was intending to invite her out to dinner, having promised her father, his own friend, to do so if ever in London.

But she had gone home for the weekend. So he invited me out instead.

Thus our lives change by chance accidents of fate.

To the rest of the world James Robertson Justice was one of the leading lights of the British film industry. A compelling presence, on screen and off. A bosom pal of Prince Philip, a keen practitioner of the art of falconry. An enormously popular anarchist currently enjoying prestigious personal publicity as the bearded, witty, irascible, eccentric Sir Lancelot Spratt in *Doctor in the House*. It was a larger-than-life character that he barely had to bother to act, requiring little effort, for Sir Lancelot was James Robertson Justice.

The cultured growl, full of jocular humour, on the telephone was exactly the same. My stomach leapt to my throat. Transported, I dropped the receiver, it slithered out of my sweaty hand. But the voice was still there when I picked it up. I had to sit down to stop my knees from shaking.

He would be round to pick me up within the hour.

From thenceforward that would be my reaction every single time James telephoned me, every time I heard his name or saw his face on a cinema poster, or set eyes on him whenever we met. In recent years, now sober, I have allowed myself the intense pleasure of watching James in television re-runs of his old movies. I can do that now without lapsing into maudlin sentimentality, without indulging in churning emotions and taking a further drink to quell deep-felt regrets.

For James was married and loved his wife, Dilys, dearly. They had supported each other through the tragedy of his drowned son, an only child. The question of divorce never arose. But, almost immediately, he wanted to set up home with me in London, to buy me a house and start a family together, so that I could give him another son.

Instead of feeling overjoyed by this proposal, it triggered off an unsettling anxiety. I felt guilty enough about having an affair with a married man, married to a Welsh wife, what's more, which made my deception and treachery to another female even worse. I didn't enjoy the secrecy of our relationship.

I couldn't brag about James to my family and friends, about the full depth and passion of the relationship. And how important that was to me.

I was ashamed, in the core of me, of the hole-in-the-corner aspect of the affair, as if I was betraying myself and everything in the Welsh chapel that I'd been brought up to believe. My inner voice told me what my pious granny would have said, that this man had no respect for me, or he wouldn't be making such immoral suggestions.

But I had nobody to tell, no one anywhere to consult. Least of all James. I couldn't confide these feelings to him. How pathetically parochial, how nauseatingly naive I would have sounded to such a wordly man. I would lose him forever.

He had already been teaching me to think for myself, encouraging me to read more widely. He'd given me copies of Dylan Thomas's *Under Milkwood*, and Frank Harris's *Memoirs of a Victorian Gentleman* for my journey to work, on those mornings when he couldn't drive me in his scarlet sports car, a pillar-box red Karmann Ghia.

He claimed that poetic prose and pornography were the perfect travelling companions, in life as on a journey. And if there was any grain of wisdom to be learned from his experience, I was always to remember the vital importance of satisfying the equal demands of the soul and the senses.

I welcomed reading any book on public transport in the

morning. I dreaded him driving me to school anyway. But my reaction to this too would change. The very first time he did, dropping me off on his way to Pinewood Studios, where he was filming, I pleaded with him to draw up around the corner.

I didn't want anyone seeing me with a man at that time of the morning, let alone with the famous James Robertson Justice.

They might jump to all sorts of conclusions and think there was something going on.

He ignored my pleas, throwing his leonine head back and gaffawing at my obvious discomfort. He filled the sports car to capacity with his six-foot bulk and abundance of energy, I looked at him, my eyes ate him up. Over 50 already, but at his peak, in his prime. I thrilled to the potent male power of the man. And—let's face it, the sheer gut-churning glamour of sitting in a sports car with a film star. Fuck what people would say!

I was learning fast.

He put his foot in its lemon-yellow sock on the pedal. Building up speed so that when he slammed on the brakes, the streak of scarlet metal screeched to a halt, halfway up the kerb at the very edge of the school playground. I cringed at the contrast between this absurdly swish car, this expensive symbol of affluence, and the rubbish-strewn, broken pavements of these impoverished streets.

The intensity of the colour, like a concentration of geraniums, attracted a swarm of gaping girls who flung themselves and their satchels all over the gleaming bonnet. It felt like being inside a hive covered by buzzing bees.

James honked the horn to scare them away, but this only attracted more, which delighted him. We were surrounded, like visiting royalty. James was used to this kind of situation with autograph hunters, but I had never been the centre of such attention before. And it set off a spiralling anxiety in me, praying that Mrs

Macmillan, the headmistress, couldn't see this. She was a committed member of the Communist Party and would view the whole incident as a corruption of minors, in which case I could well be out of a job.

I slipped out swiftly to escape James's farewell embrace, deep-throating it with his tongue, which I just knew he was planning for the over-excited audience. I broke through the throng and gave a brisk wave from the school gates as he swung the car around and zoomed off down the Walworth Road. The girls squealed with delight. They made a nightmare of my whole day. From thenceforth I chose to travel by public transport. I just couldn't trust him.

When James insisted otherwise, cuddling me close, whispering tender endearments, 'obstinate little cunt', I accepted the lifts to work but hopped out of the showy vehicle at Elephant and Castle traffic lights, preferring to walk the rest of the way.

Sometimes he chose to kerb-crawl, yelling obscenities to command my attention and make me laugh, until a patrolling policeman interrupted the proceedings, warning him off for making himself a public and unwelcome nuisance to an innocent young lady. From then on I only travelled to the school by London Underground and bus. But still with James's choice of reading matter, the sauciest wrapped by me in brown paper.

On our very first date we dined in chandelier'd elegance at the legendary Ivy Restaurant, with stars of stage, screen and radio at every table. And there within inches of everyone, James had one hand in my Marks and Spencer underwear throughout the meal. It had been a bold move on my part to dispense with my roll-on, an all-in-one reaching halfway to the knee, complete with elasticized gusset, known as passion-killers. We all wore them, as a way of remaining virgins. Now I see them on sale again, which I never, ever thought could happen. Though no longer worn as chastity belts, or even solely as fetish garments, but articles of high fashion to ensure flat stomachs and lean flanks beneath skin-tight clothing, such as the fashion label of Victoria Beckham.

After the Ivy we spent our first night in the Cadogan Hotel. I suffered acute embarrassment walking past the desk clerk. Wise and white-haired, discreetly lowering his eyes as we passed. At first glance he resembled the favourite chapel preacher of my youth.

I had the guilty urge to turn around and run away. But as soon as we were in the lift James started kissing me and I astounded myself by responding with a passion equal to his own.

We couldn't stay apart, magnetized together by an electrical current demanding the physical contact of flesh on flesh. He tore my knickers off in the corridor and tossed them into the scarlet, sand-filled fire bucket.

Later, when I sneaked out to retrieve them, they had been stolen. I was puzzled, shocked, concluding that a male pervert had purloined them, fragrant crotch to the nostrils. But now it is more apparent that one of the female housekeeping team would have fished them out of the bucket, wearing rubber gloves, swilled them through, dried them out, and worn them back home. They were a choice article, first time on and typical of a 'fifties virgin, white broderie anglaise cotton, edged with lace. Five decades later I still lament the loss.

Inexperienced in matters of the world, as I then was, that single experience gave me a sense of the avid social underbelly beneath a seemlessly smooth surface, however urbane, despite the sophistication, and cloaked in grandeur. This was Belgravia.

The passionate process of my thorough de-flowering took

James fully five hours. I had not so much surrendered my cherry, but gratefully bestowed upon him with total abandon the whole bowlful of cherries. Years of sexual restraint and self-denial. Of frustration and ignorance. Of forbidden fruits. Of shyness, self-consciousness and youthful hesitation, face-to-face with ardour.

James peeled the layers away, tenderly, with practiced precision. Forcefully but with immense fondness.

He tunneled his way with sublime sensitivity into my heart, into the very soul of me until I surrendered my all, aroused now to a level of sensuality that I had never been aware of before.

This was my introduction to the transformation of carnal lust into the purest devotion. With a hefty helping of base humour to enforce the flow.

James had kissed me halfway through the earliest caresses, claiming to worship and adore me, that if we were not careful we we would devour each other to extinction.

Once inside our suite, we had started off on the floor just inside the bedroom door. The carpet flush got up my nostrils, so I sneezed my way to the supreme importance of my first orgasm. But there was something so pleasing about the informality of the position, down there viewing the undersides of all the chairs, that it didn't matter. Indeed, James said, without even having knowledge of my frigid history, that the sneezing would have helped release hovering tension.

Next we attempted intercourse in the bath and flooded the entire bathroom floor. Which had me on my knees mopping up with dripping towels. James was driven to frenzy by me in this position. He claimed I had the most erotic arsehole this side of the Arabian Desert.

He asked me if I understood what he was talking about and, unlike my true self, I took the decision to come clean and be honest. I said no. So he took a toothbrush, smothered the handle with soap and stuck the tip of it up my bum. When he asked if I was enjoying it I took the honesty even further and admitted that I was not.

Not at all. Not one bit.

He said that's the Welsh bloody chapel for you, and to beware of the puritanical, that it could destroy an entire life.

And removing the offending toothbrush, he left it at that. I didn't feel that I had pleased him as much as I would have liked. So much for my honesty. I'd best beware of the destructive effects of that from now on.

When we eventually got into bed, having wrecked the entire room in our fervour, James licked my love-swollen lips, saying he had a final treat for me. He extracted the neon-strip lighting from the bedside lamp and inserted it into me, telling me not to move or cough, or sneeze, just to continue breathing as gently as possible.

I lay there petrified. Recalling the Hollywood scandal of film star Fatty Arbuckle accused of causing the death of the young woman he had infiltrated in this same manner, with a champagne bottle. Which had splintered. I sure as hell needed my chapel faith now to see me through.

But James was proud of me now, for being so obliging. He withdrew the sixty watt light with a genial twinkle so that I saw it all as good fun. A way, as he'd explained, of familiarizing myself with every orifice. He encircled the width of the bulb with his fingers.

'This is your capacity in cubic inches,' he said lovingly. 'If you ever feel less than sexually satisfied, you know where to reach from now on.' He replaced my latest lover in the light socket.

We cuddled up to together, and satiated, fell fast asleep.

Fifty-five years later, in the first week of this year, 2010, this romantic tale of lustful abandon hit the newspaper headlines, involving the censorship by His Highness Prince Philip of the raffish details in the biography of his good friend James Robertson Justice, to which he had penned the Foreword.

This resulted in the lead article in the *Telegraph*, involving the unbeatable combination of Royalty, Prince Philip, National Treasure (moi) and one of the most popular film character actors of his time, James Robertson Justice.

I had never read this biography, playfully entitled *What's The Bleeding Time*, the famed catchline of the character, Sir Lancelot Spratt, the charismatic surgeon played by James in the first film of the *Doctor in the House* series.

I had been interviewed by the author, James Hogg, who professed to be delighted by the raffish nature of the material I had related about James and myself.

He rang to apologise on publication of the book, that the juiciest of my material had been censored by Prince Phillip, who, as a close friend of James, had provided the prologue.

To my surprise, gratification and chagrin an entire chapter was devoted to our affair, entitled, *Hello Molly*. Though brutally truncated, which caused my chagrin.

'All the fucking spunk has been sucked out of it, all the fun and the frolics with tooth brush and strip lighting!'

I complained to the celebrity blogger Madame Arcati, aka my present fiancé, still in his 40s, qualified barrister, award-laden journalist, published novelist, psychic satirist and astrologer, Victor Olliver.

His posting on the internet, was picked up by the *Telegraph* and is now permanently on my entry for all to peruse, via Google.

James would certainly not be pleased. He despised censorship in any shape or form, for whatever reason. Prince Philip excused his censorship in defense of 'good taste', certain that James would wish to keep his sexual activities private.

When I was told that I exploded. As would James.

It made me question the friendship and just how well the Prince actually knew his 'close friend'.

But the entire episode has brought James Robertson Justice roaring back into my life. He arrived first in the séance held by my medium, Lealah Kay, at the Spiritualist Church, in Eaton Square. She described his appearance and the extraordinary charisma right away and then went on to claim that he was and remains still, the most formative influence in my life.

I silenced her. 'I know exactly who you mean.'

Since then he visits almost daily. Sometimes assuming the shape of a blackbird, with a bright yellow beak, who taps on my French Windows leading out to my garden, perching on the brick wall besides.

The very first time he did that, I burst out laughing. It was so typical of James. Other times, in the gardens of the Chelsea Arts Club, he flutters around me in the guise of a Robin Redbreast.

My dining companion questioned the visitation. 'That will be James,' I replied, still eating. The companion was astonished.

'His idea of a joke,' I went no further than the perfectly adequate explanation. This was my first meeting with this person. There have been no further lunches.

James, as Robin, had achieved his objective.

Following my announcement of planned retirement, he thundered back to me: 'Thomas! Thomas!' Molly Thomas was my maiden name before marriages. 'What the hell is happening here!

Get back to those canvasses. Start writing again! More poems, more prose. Complete those memoirs you started in Mexico. Life is for living, hurl yourself into it. Painters and writers don't retire!'

And he has entered my dreams again, not only my waking hours. Sometimes I ride into the dawn on the crest of the orgasm that James has induced.

And I have no explanation for that, when I claim that I have lost all interest in sex, that my hormones have now withered on the bough.

In my 70th year

I had dramatically dysfunctional sex with a former lover, a once legendary stallion. He had proved to be impotent. Viagra was out of the question since he was on medication for a heart condition. But I was unaware of that crucial information until later, when shock at the news and the near miss of tragedy could well have voided my atrophied bowels.

Had I known earlier I would have treasured this lover with the tender solicitude and patient attention to detail he deserved and expected from me, an intimate friend for years and femme fatale of experience. Instead, wildly misjudging the situation and in scant possession of facts, I whacked into the proceedings with the combined energy of jolly hockey sticks aiming for goal, and an impatient houri paid for pleasure by the half-hour, with a long queue of clients lining the corridor.

'Abject apologies, my darling girl, exhausting flight.' That was how he excused himself. Bless him.

But I was not without my own difficulties. I was unnervingly aware of dislodging my recent upper denture and as a result was shamefully inept at oral sex now. That was a hard one for me to swallow, since it had been my global speciality in the previous century. Of course, the obvious answer would have been to remove the false teeth and attack with renewed relish, no doubt achieving excellent results.

Sexual connoisseurs do claim that gum jobs are superlative. Indeed there is an African tribe whose custom it is to remove the central top and bottom teeth of virgins due to be brides. This is to ensure greater pleasure to the nervous groom on his first night of nuptials.

Had this been a tried and true marriage, we both would have overcome our mutual hurdles, allowing humour to save the situation. But the hideous visual impact of me without my top teeth is apparently not as amusing as I seem to find it myself. The critical view being that it is disturbing enough to induce instant coronary in the enfeebled. Or those with an unreliable heartbeat.

My grandchildren clamour for the sight, reduced to shrieks of hysteria, it's their very favourite thing in the world, particularly as delaying tactics before bedtime. But their youthful nervous systems can survive it.

I was hesitant to take the risk with this mature lover. And thank goodness I didn't, for at that precise stage I was unaware of his heart condition.

So I soldiered on, spluttering and gagging in excruciating discomfort, the defiant denture parting company with my upper gums, eager to make the acquaintance of this unfamiliar intruder.

But merciful reprieve was imminent. I finally gave up, raising a haggard countenance, saliva slavering my chin, satin lipstick shot to buggery. I had surely aged a half-century. And just how glamorous was this look, the knackered hag out of Hades. A sad crone who can't cope with oral sex.

I did think wistfully how much more fun it would have been

in my flat with an episode of *Sex and the City*, watching Carrie Bradshaw and her chums relishing this kind of thing. I had to remind myself that there was certainly a forty-year gap between those raunchy girls and myself. Wasn't I just as avid at their age?

Well maybe at their age, in my thirties. But in my early twenties, when all my friends were most sexually active with youngsters their own age, most of the chosen beds I found myself in were occupied by grandfathers the age of my present lover. Even my youthful nubile charms couldn't raise an erection, which was just how I liked it and why I was there. I preferred their conversations to sexually athletic youths, by far. So why should I expect this lover to be any different now, just because we shared such a long and passionate history?

I relaxed and let go of the cold, uncooked sausage. I allowed it to fall by the wayside. Perhaps now we could get back to safer ground and share some good laughs, forget about sex.

My lover patted my head affectionately, as you would an educationally sub-normal bloodhound who'd been hanging on in there for grim life, believing there was some sort of medal at the end of it. For perseverence, if nothing else.

'Out of practice, precious? Never mind, I still adore you.' As if it was my fault. Men do that.

He'd hit the nail on the head there though. Out of practice, indeed, at coaxing life from the living dead. This was unfamiliar territory for me. I had never shared a bed with a limp prick before, not when we were both there with the express purpose of sexual congress. But we two had not done this kind of thing together for fifteen years. We'd not even seen each other in that length of time, living on separate continents, in or out of collective marriages.

Our timing, as with Dietrich and Hemingway, had always been out of kilter. We were fated never to wed each other either. Ours had been an essentially torrid affair, glamorous, discreet, guilt-ridden, conducted in private against the backdrop of international hotels and the more adrenalin-fuelled for that.

Our mutual appetites were insatiable from the first sly-eyed glance at a fashionable dinner party in the 'sixties. The recognition was in place. I was in the early throes of my first divorce. He was there with his second wife of seven months. We had been inextricably linked ever since, for over forty years. On and off. Off and on. On and off.

His telephone call came early in May. Our affair had started in the month of May, all those moons ago, so it was always special for us. We regarded *Spring Fever*, from the musical *State Fair*, as our song.

We were the only two people we knew who had ever seen that film. Dana Andrews. Jeanne Craine. Flame haired songstress, Vivien Blaine. And the hearthrob crooner, Dick Haymes, who outstripped the popularity of the bobbysoxers' idol, Frank Sinatra. Later, Haymes became Mr Rita Hayworth, following her divorce from Orson Welles and Ali Khan.

My weekly film fan magazine, *Picturegoer*, kept me up to date with all this. How could any serious cine-fan not know that glorious '40s Technicolour extravaganza?

But we two had myriad inconsequential things in common, despite the yawning chasm of our backgrounds. His priveleged, mine not.

It was early on a Saturday morning and I had picked up the receiver after only one ring.

I'd been expecting a call from one of my four grandchildren, an enchantingly rougish small boy who had fallen irrevocably in love with Barbie, the cute doll from the television advertising campaign. He wanted me to buy her for his birthday. I had asked if he'd like Ken, too.

'Who is Ken, Granny?'

'Barbie's boyfriend, my angel.'

I could have bitten my tongue out. I was an insensitive adult, the harbinger of heartbreaking news.

His voice was suddenly full of tears. 'I'd thought I was going to be her boyfriend, Granny.'

'Well, you will be, darling heart. Once we buy her, she's all yours. That will make you her boyfriend.'

So are false romantic hopes planted in the hearts of the young male by the mendacity of the foolish ancients. May my own flesh and blood, when on the brink of manhood, forgive me for misleading him into believing that money buys the love and fidelity of young ladies.

My deceit went even further. I was undermining the parental control of his own parents. We had secretly planned to buy Barbie, then house her in my home, since his parents disapproved of the doll, even for their smaller daughter, let alone their son. Soon it would be his birthday. We were to arrange what time I would take him to Hamleys, the toy emporium, ostensibly to buy him a Spiderman outfit, a truck and a football. Suitably boyish stuff like that. But we'd smuggle Barbie and her change of clothing into my own bag.

'Hello, my darling girl.'

This wasn't the decibel of a child on the telephone. The sound of my lover's voice, theatrical, enthralling, dry, deep, witty, was still enough to quicken my blood. Nobody else ever addressed me as 'my darling girl', only ever him. Mr Big, Carrie Bradshaw's lover from *Sex and the City*, is the closest I can get to describing him.

If I'd even imagined that sex upstairs would be the outcome of dining downstairs at the Ritz, I would certainly have given more thought to my underwear. I'd drifted in this previous decade to a self-serving single syndrome, of comfort for comfort's sake, when it came to underpinnings.

Though my outer facade was an amethyst chiffon, '20s antique vision of sophistication, beneath it I was wearing a pair of delicately frayed granny knickers, high in the waist and long in the leg to prevent inner thigh-chafe. They were soft, oft-scrubbed old favourites which had always brought me luck.

As to any uplift, I'd dispensed with support moons ago. So many women I lunch with can't wait to get home to take off their brassieres. Others, I know, sleep in theirs to keep their shape. But I'd dispensed with mine, allowing my bosoms to swing free as a pendulum on a grandfather clock.

I'd been influenced by the natural silhouette of female elders in rural India. They bent over, breasts dangling free of restraint, shrouded in home spun cottons. Their tiny grandchildren slept, strapped to their backs, as they picked rice in the paddy-fields.

They smiled at me as I walked by and beckoned me to them. Many had shaved their heads and presented their flowing locks to the temples in an act of piety. They looked utterly, unselfconsciously, beautiful.

This was more than acceptance of the ageing process, this was celebration.

That year I returned from Southern India I dispensed with all my Rigby and Peller brassieres (Corsetierres by Royal Command), and requested an astonished Keith at Smile Hair Salon on Chelsea's

Kings Road to do a skinhead job on my scalp. The young trainee dumped my fringe and frayed ends in the rubbish bin. It would have been an affront to offer them to the Indian temple on my return the following year, the waist-length wasn't there for a start, and I just knew my Welsh chapel wouldn't be interested. There's no call for coiled hair in the valleys.

But I'd also plagiarised the profile of the veteran film luminary Gladys Cooper in *My Fair Lady*. I admired her performance as the haughty mother of Professor Higgins, but most particularly her proud frontage resting so elegantly on her waistband.

However, my lover had known me in a different body. In past decades I used to appear in public and particularly on television discussing my latest paintings, my novels, my stage performances, with high breasts hoisted so much higher they endangered my own eye-sight.

Everything was on offer. Necklines slashed to the nipple. An arresting sight which certainly helped boost sales and ensure further regular income from never-ending chat-show appearances. These mammaries, my individual dress sense, my supernatural vodka-fuelled vivacity, my Welsh way with words—especially four-lettered—the juicy details of my sex-life (a cast-list of hundreds), these supported my one-time high public profile. Thus my popularity. My celebrity status.

Once a celebrity always a celebrity. However outdated the image, sullied the reputation, preserved the privacy, whether relegated or not to the lower echelons ranking from A List to X, Y or Z. There will always be someone in a restaurant, a store, a secluded beach, who hares over to tug a sleeve.

'You are who I think you are, aren't you? What are you up to now? We thought you were dead. We used to love you on the television, the outrageous things you used to come out with. You made us laugh, all dressed up in your sexy outfits. It is you, isn't it—or are you having me on?'

But cleavage belongs to youth. The spell of seduction is cancelled out by an auxiliary ordnance survey of creases and crinkle. A mesmerised granddaughter, remarkable for her candour and curiosity, studied me undressing one overnight visit.

'Granny?'

'Yes, little one?' This is the tiring aspect of small children. They first establish your attention before posing the question. Everything takes twice as long. But I have fathoms of patience now.

'Granny, will I be wearing my nipples right at the bottom of my titties, peeping out from underneath, when I'm gone past caring what people think, like you?'

'Life is all about choice, sweet thing.' I smiled.

Satisfied, she grinned back at me with an expression of affectionate understanding. Then she shut her eyes and went straight to sleep.

If I had anticipated sex at 70 with anybody at all, I certainly would have taken a tube of lubricant, some trusty KY Jelly. My own juices are just not up to the job.

The sap is no longer on the rise. A gardening term.

The oil well is empty. Industrial jargon.

An Indian doctor, who had practiced in Paris, told me that in time Western women would come to embrace the Eastern acceptance that Nature has a biological plan for the human body. There is a season for every kind of activity. When the sexual frenzy of an orgasm is pursued beyond the allotted years, post-menopause in fact, the body must restore the amount of moisture lost in the act. A severe headache is the outcome, starting below the cranium, at the back of the neck, from the top of the spine.

'Christ! What the hell!' my lover had exclaimed on our second night.

I'd squeezed the KY tube of jelly over-enthusiastically. It was as though I'd upturned a tub of hair-gel between my thighs. I scooped a handful and waddled, knees together, to retrieve a towel from the ritzy Ritz bathroom.

'Best put this towel beneath me,' I soothed, as to an infant, on my return to the bed. 'The jelly will do it. You'll be gliding in now like a hand in a slippery glove, sweetheart.'

This particular lover had always responded to my kind-nanny, course call-girl endearments. But the thought occurred, even as I was murmuring so-softly, that none of these activities could have encouraged a tired and timid erection.

And, alas, the visuals were sadly lacking. Shuffling off, bare-arsed to the bathroom like that, with the man taking in the back-view from a rumpled bed was more the comfortable behaviour of a long established marriage. With the wife tootling down to the kitchen to bring back the cocoa, and the alternate choice of grilled sardines on hot buttered toast or cold pickles and cheese, as a nice little pillow treat.

This was meant to be a glamorous, hot-desire-enhanced boudoir reunion, here at the Ritz. Was I utterly, stark-staring, fucking bonkers? Me, who'd been proposed for the International Sexual Olympics more times than I could remember.

I'd obviously lived in solitary bliss for far too long. Nude nocturnal trips to the lavabo, relieving bladder or bowels depending on midnight-gluttony, were certainly normal. But, though I never bothered to study my backside these days, I knew for certain that the rear view of me alone wasn't what it had once been.

The last time I was fitted for swimwear at Peter Jones in Sloane Square several years before, I was truly astonished to note in the rear-view mirror that I was carrying the extra accoutrement of cellulite, rippling like the ebb-tide from my buttocks to the back of my knees.

Where the hell had all this ruched flesh-curtaining come from, it wasn't there when I last looked! Should I request an ambulance? Or was it merely the pig-awful strip-lighting in these fitting rooms, evolved by some sadistic mother-hating male?

Since then I've made it my business to make a study of the onset of cellulite. Few women escape this, all shapes, sizes, nationality, and age. It isn't just me. I've noted this with profound satisfaction and joy in my heart, on sublime seashores and around sumptuous swimming pools all over the world.

Waddling back to the bed, towel-trussed like a nappy, my breasts tap-dancing over my two umbilical hernias, wasn't, let's face it, what my lover had been used to from me. Where was the allure of old?

'Was he still an Adonis?' my older sister had snorted, when I'd described my mortification. That made me feel better, because of course not, he wasn't. Everyone ages more or less, at the same rate. But just when do women no longer expect to be the object of desire? When they, themselves, experience freedom from desire.

If I had even imagined that my lover may still want me physically I would have applied more consideration to which handbag I'd taken to dinner. The Duchess of Windsor diamante shoulder-purse, containing the barest of social essentials would have been better replaced by an old fashioned trunk, the sort that children are packed off with to boarding school. That would fit the bill for romantic overnights these days. I had become a high-maintenance filly.

But concerns of how I might appear first thing in the morning to a lover without my war paint, these were dispelled by the events of the night. This lover had mellowed. Youthful lust had been replaced by a tear-inducing tenderness. I had been made to feel cherished. I know that he felt the same.

There in the cuddling and all-concealing darkness we had exchanged feelings, infinitely more profound than the sexual record-breaking, endurance-testing passions of the past.

We fell asleep, purring in each other's arms and stirred around dawn, still holding on. He kissed and caressed my face on the pillow, as a young mother may kiss and caress her first-born from joy and with wonder.

And the purity and power of the love that was bestowed upon me caused emotional tears to spring beneath my closed eyelids.

'Beauty,' he murmured, before we both dozed off again.

I was precociously sexualised

at infancy on the lower steps of the staircase leading up to my bedroom. Forced to endure my mother's pounding piano behind the locked door of the parlour, I suddenly stopped squirming in my Daddy's lap, though I was still desperate to escape his imprisoning arms.

I had become aware of a rigid presence between his legs, pressing into the back of my new floral nightdress.

Though it was considerably shorter than the adjoining ones I must have accepted this intruder as Daddy's friendly third limb. So it seemed perfectly natural when he spun me around to face him, lifting the front of my nightdress, parting my legs and pressing his clammy third limb between them. It was just to get better acquainted.

I reached up and tried to stretch my arms around my Daddy's neck to show how very much I loved him, as a way of saying not to mind about Mama locking herself away with her piano so often now.

But Daddy pulled me back down and perched me more securely with my little skinny legs around his third limb, placing my fingers around the pink stem, moving them up and down, up and down. It seemed to like this and reared up as a puppy dog does when it is being stroked.

I laughed, I think I must have enjoyed this game, too. I know I didn't want to stop because Daddy was kissing my face now and squeezing me so hard against him that I thought I'd never catch my breath again. But it still felt like fun.

Except suddenly it was all over. There were no sounds of piano from the other side of the door. Only the harsh grating of the key turning in the lock and Mama's angry voice following Daddy and me as we disappeared up the stairs.

'That child should be fast asleep in bed by now. I just can't trust the two of you together, can I?'

That was the start of the game. The start of the secret that Mama must never, ever, discover. And nobody else either. I had promised my Daddy on his own father's leather bible. Which meant that it must be forever.

I broke the promise in my mid-sixties, when the right moment presented itself. Then I told my older sister.

'What was the trouble between you and Daddy?' she'd asked, mulling over memories of childhood, long after the death of both parents. 'There was always such tension there, as if you loathed him. You'd never even stay alone in the room with him. And the way you looked at him, the contempt in those eyes of yours sent shivers down my spine. I couldn't understand it at all. He had his faults but he was such a lovely man, the perfect father.'

So I unburdened myself.

It had started not to feel like the same uncomplicated fun any more when my father began teaching me things. Things like how to ride my three-wheeler bicycle, and soon enough my new two-wheeled one. How to swim all alone down to the deep end of the swimming pool. How to read out loud without making mistakes, from the library books that he'd chosen for me. How to sit still for hours at a time in front of John Constable's *The Haywain* in the National Gallery, relishing the brushwork, living in the landscape.

All of these pursuits afforded me the greatest pleasure. Even in early childhood I was a natural athlete, scholar, performer and artist. It was his tuition which made me uncomfortable. The blatant physicality of his methods, coupled with the very real awareness that there were people around who might see what he was doing and publicly denounce us both.

This confusion was complicated with the need to please my Daddy, to continue our games. To make sure that I was still the most special one in the world to him, because that's what he said.

But when his open palm and inviting fingers remained on the leather saddle of the bicycle, after lowering my white cotton crotch onto it, smiling into my eyes, brushing my cheek with a kiss, there in the park with everyone watching, I wanted to run away.

His hand held me in place there between my legs as he wheeled the bike under the tall trees far away from the pathways. We were alone now, completely alone so I began to relax. Nobody could see. If they glanced this distance away, to them it was just another devoted parent spending quality time with his child.

I was using the pedals on the tricycle, getting the general hang of things, there was no need for his hand any more. I raised myself up from the saddle, legs stiff. He let go of me and I found myself riding round and round the trees, in and out, back and forth. Pedalling beautifully, totally in control. Nothing could stop me now.

'You've had enough? You want to stop? Come to me now, there's a good girl.'

He held out his arms and usually I'd have flung myself into them. But I didn't want to stop. I wanted to go on, and on, and on. All by myself.

But when I looked at his face I couldn't say so. I knew what he wanted to do.

He knelt down beside me so that we were on the same level. He was gentle and loving, and whispered to stand very close to him with my arms around his neck whilst he took my knickers off. It was easy to be obedient, to do as I was told when somebody was this nice. Instead of putting the knickers in his pocket as he used to do, he laid them carefully on the grass, as if I'd had an accident and they needed to dry in the sun. That would be his excuse if anybody came. He explained that to me when we'd done this kind of thing last time.

We lay down together under the low, leafy boughs of the trees. He drew me into the crook of his left arm, and brought my knees up to my chest. Then he began fingering me from the back, under my short Shirley Temple summer dress. My skinny legs fell apart and his index finger and thumb came round the front. The stroking was so soft and so soothing that I must have closed my eyes and fallen asleep, there in the dappled shade. This was the kind of game we both loved, in the warmth of the sun, with the heady scent of cherry blossom and the blackbird song up above, just the two of us on our own. My Daddy and me.

I awoke in clean pyjamas tucked up in my own bed. He must have put my knickers back on and carried me home from the park, it was no distance at all. It had been a long and exciting day for me. I had learned to ride my three-wheeler in one afternoon with my Daddy's help. Not every little girl my age could claim that, he whispered, nibbling my ear.

Perhaps things were not so bad after all. All I needed now were some more coloured wax crayons and a box of paints with a brush to make my life perfect. Daddy would buy anything for me, after some more games. That's what he'd said before the tricycle appeared. These were my thoughts as I dozed back to sleep.

A week later in the swimming baths however, I resolved to learn even the dog-paddle as swiftly as possible. I really needed to get away from my father's probing fingers beneath the transluscent turquoise surface. The sparkling surface was rippled by other swimmers too intent on their own strokes to wonder what was going on with this man and child.

I hated it when he'd hold me facing him, wrapping my legs around his lower torso, forcing my shoulders into the water under the guise of practicing a back-stroke. I could feel the bulge beneath his swimming trunks growing harder the longer we spent in that position, with the water getting in my eyes, up my nose, down my throat. The more I yelled and struggled the better he liked it. Then without warning he'd toss me into the air and I'd land with a splash, squealing with excitement, as often as not to see a faint milky substance swirling away from him. The bulge was already subsiding.

He'd carry me in his arms out of the pool then, though I was perfectly capable of scrambling up on my own. I would have preferred it. There was a sense of achievement in hauling yourself up over the side with the strength of your own puny arms, then sprawling like a jelly fish, getting in everyone's way, whilst you recovered your breath.

But if there was any chance of my father carrying me anywhere in those years, he would, usually on his shoulders with my legs each side of his head. This way easier to tease me by mock-biting my bare thighs, then kissing them better as I protested. And he'd place me there and lift me off by holding firmly on each buttock and between. Every part of my body presented endless pleasure. That's how it felt. As if I was a pet, to be stroked and fondled and shaken and cajoled.

He'd take me into the dressing cubicle and peel my wet swimsuit down my slippery body and help me step out of it and leave me there, shivering, teeth chattering. Then he'd lower his own trunks and the two of us would be naked. Naked and dripping.

'Two drowned rats,' he'd laugh, and tickle me without mercy until I lost control in hysteria and peed all over his toes. He'd pretend to be cross and smack me hard on my bottom. Then he'd comfort my tears with salt kisses and lick the stinging to ease the pain.

I'd try to concentrate on the thought of the ice-cream cone that he always bought me after such interludes. But the anxiety flowed through me that passers-by would glance in and see us. Practising caution he'd sit down on the narrow bench and pull me to him with a large bath towel which concealed us both. His penis hung down between his open legs, already twitching with another incipient erection.

I remained a virgin until I was in my early twenties and had intended to remain so forever. That was the plan. Even the thought of a penis was repugnant to me. I was popular, the prettiest girl at the party, the belle of the ball, but with the reputation of Fort Knox, strictly no entry. I'd had enough of the male member in one childhood to last me a lifetime, that's what I thought then. But love has a way of changing everything.

The learning to read out loud was marginally less fraught, since mutual nudity had no place in this pursuit. But it was agonising enough with the family seated around the fire in the same room. My father and I would be poring over my book at the mahogony table in the window, behind their backs. The table was covered with a woven chenille cloth for protection, a rich red with tassels which reached to the carpet.

Neither my mother, nor my sister, nor any visiting aunt or neighbour could see what was going on behind and under the table. They'd be listening to the wireless, or reading a newspaper, or simply gossiping over tea and Marie biscuits. Whilst my father's fingers crept higher up my bare thigh, seeking discreet entry into my warm gusset. Or his trousers gaped open, his clenched fist inside enclosed around mine, working the flesh. And he'd tilt my chin with his free hand and wink at me as if in glorious conspiracy, making funny faces to force a giggle as the cream spurted into the huge handkerchief, there at the ready.

The risks taken were madness, permutations were endless on any given evening. But they always ended the same way.

'I'll get this nipper up to bed now. Don't you disturb yourself, I'll read her a goodnight story. You keep warm by the fire.'

There was no story, no time for those. Not with the games going on.

But just sometimes there was nothing, only cradling me in his arms and humming into my hair, rocking to and fro as if I was still a baby that had to be lulled to sleep. But my handsome Daddy's face, I could see in the opposite wall mirror, was the saddest face I'd ever seen, with shiny eyes as if tears were close. And my heart would leap up to my throat in a painful twist. I would have done anything then to make him happy.

My sister had recently returned to live with us in London. I hadn't even known there was an older sister until the arrival of this smiling, well-behaved, stranger. She'd been sent to live with our grandparents in Wales on my birth. Our mother simply couldn't cope with two children, so she claimed. Now our grandparents felt it was time for this older child to be with her immediate family.

I welcomed her presence, feeling that perhaps my father's attentions may shift to her. Or at least she could take a fair share in my involvement. It was not to be. In fact my father's need for me appeared more urgent, the risks of discovery ever greater. It was as if he was gambling on being found out. I dreaded the day, feeling the fault lay at my door. There must be something about me that goaded him on, I began to ponder, especially when he left my older sister, such a calm and pleasant girl, mercifully unmolested.

My memory had erased my father from the childhood experience of studying Constable at the National Gallery. So I thought. But when I first went there as a 17-year-old Art Student I was physically sick down in the cloakroom.

Returning to my tutor and the group, still shaky, I moved on with relief to the Turner seascapes and to my further delight, the Rubens nudes, both painters with no past history for me.

My father and I would visit on a Saturday. I can't imagine why my mother and sister were not with us, they were probably prowling the shops. And I was considered the Daddy's girl then, though later the reversal took place and I was much closer to my progressively eccentric mother. I could identify more easily with her behaviour than my father's brutality towards me now.

Saturday afternoon is an important one in the theatres of any city. That's when the theatres run their matinee performances, before the evening ones. So there are two shows that day.

My father was as obsessed with the stage as he was with art, with a capital A. He was an artist manqué, totally blocked from producing a painting, a novel, a stage or screen performance. He died a deeply frustrated man because of this. The more so because by the time of his death I was, to his absolute chagrin, leading the very life as an artist that he had always envisaged and yearned for himself.

But at that time his only offering of value to that world of high bohemia was this younger daughter, still to prove her talents in the artistic arena. But there was something about me and my extreme youth that he thought may be pleasing to an actor's eye.

He'd lead me away from the National Gallery and position me outside every stage door, week after week, before the start of the matinee. We'd await the arrival of the stars, the leading actors, hurrying into make up and costume.

My father would bar their way, doffing his trilby. Resolute. Implacable.

'Excuse me, could you kindly spare a moment?' The actor would attempt to brush past. 'Shame on you, sir.' My father's voice would have reached the back of the stalls. 'You deny a moment for a budding thespian.'

He'd point at me, thrusting me in the beleaguered performer's path. The actors acquiesced and granted me an autograph. But nobody invited us around to their dressing rooms, or slipped a card into my father's gloved hand, murmuring to get in touch and to bring the lovely child along.

Time was running out for my father. I was growing older every day. That was his failure, the inability to stop the march of time. With my age came the unexpected for him, my defiance. And distaste. Then polite distance. But my hatred had already taken over by then.

That was the true domestic tragedy in the toppling emotional structure of our home.

The first violence began after the failure to find a theatrical paramour or a protector, or frankly a paedophile, to share his daughter. One who might change the family fortunes for the better.

He'd read somewhere that Errol Flynn had a penchant for young girls, the younger the better, and began gambling a portion of his wages on a weekly basis to raise the fare to Hollywood for me and himself. For there were always financial crises in our household, made worse now by this.

That and the strain of coping with two daughters instead of one was getting my mother down. Her husband was rarely there now, certainly not in the evenings. He'd come home from work, change and go out again, not returning until well after we were all in bed. None of us knew where he went.

'He'll be window shopping, up west.' That was my mother's lame explanation. 'Or having his political say in Hyde Park, supporting Oswald Mosely and his Fascist Party up at Speakers' Corner. That's more than likely.'

Within weeks, after men clothed in black arrived at our house goose-stepping up the garden path pushing fascist pamphlets through the door, my mother issued an ultimatum. Mosely or us. She threatened to leave, taking us girls back to Wales with her. My heart leapt with joy at the possibility.

But it was not to be. My father promised, no more Blackshirts. But his adulation of Mosely never diminished. Supporters of that doctrine were men such as my father. Life's frustrated failures. Bullies. Tormentors of the vulnerable, the aged and the children.

All this was beginning to tell on my mother. It was me in

particular who wore her down the most.

It was my constant chatter. My exuberance. My singing and laughter. She used to lament on a daily basis.

'You're wearing me out! Why can't you be more like your sister, nice and quiet.'

Then it was, 'Wait until your father gets home! He'll see to you, little demon.'

That was the threat for the frailest misdemeanour, for chipping a saucer, for dropping a lighted candle on the carpet and making wax stains, for spilling gravy on the tablecloth. The list was endless, and the punishments were on a weekly basis. She was giving him carte blanche, if only she'd known it. Playing straight into his hands to do with me what he may, in the privacy of his own home. Behind locked doors, bedroom doors.

My bedroom door faced the very top of the stairs in this suburban house bought for us by my grandfather. My sister says now that she has perfect recall of crouching on those top stairs listening to my screams. She and my mother, arms wrapped around each other sobbing, would cry out for my father to stop beating me, behind the locked door.

It is still painful for me to hear that. I can't even find the words to question why they couldn't have removed the bedroom lock for easier entry the next time it happened. Or called a neighbour to break the door down the first time.

But they wouldn't have done that. Domestic violence carries such shame, it certainly did then and remains marginally unchanged to this day. Whichever the state or nation it has to be kept secret, and in the family.

He'd beat me whilst I was beneath the bedclothes so that there would be no telltale bruising. A cunning ruse. But it hurt all the same and was easily the most frightening thing that had ever happened to me in my short life. My father's rage was terrifying and there was no stopping him when he was in the grip of it. He'd become unrecognisable, as if he had actually lost his mind or was another person once the first blow was delivered. The rest rained down the full length of my body, though I'd hide my head beneath my pillow I still felt it there. It seemed to go on forever.

My sister confirms this. But the worst part, according to her, was after my screams died away and she and my mother didn't know if I was dead or alive.

'We seemed to be sitting on the stairs for hours in total silence. What on earth was he doing with you in there for so long?'

'Breaking my spirit,' I'd answer dully, in those decades when I was still bound by my promise.

Within the year I would be rushed to hospital with acute mastoid, a dangerous process of the temporal bone behind the ear. I was afflicted in both ears, leaving me with permanent deafness in the right one.

'Has this child suffered a blow to the head?' my mother was asked up at the hospital. My father never came. He refused to co-operate or even talk to the doctors. He was the same with the teachers at my schools. He wasn't interested.

She shook her head, as though affronted. 'Absolutely not, doctor!'

Everything changed when I reached the age of eleven. I began menstruating and my father lost all sexual interest in me now that I'd reached womanhood and was sprouting breasts. Even the beatings ceased. He couldn't be bothered.

There was no friendship there, no connection at all. He didn't congratulate me on passing the dreaded Eleven Plus exam, which decided the future of every schoolchild in Britain then.

When I passed from my grammar school on a state scholarship to become an art student, he turned his back and went out to prune the roses.

When I was in my fifth and final year at Brighton Art School, aged about twenty one, my sister had her first baby. My mother paid her a visit to her home now in Wales, to help out with the new baby just at the start. I was on my third fiancé by then, all art students. But so far they had only been allowed to kiss me goodnight, no more than that. I had the reputation of a heart-breaker, who wouldn't give an inch. I wore safe panty-girdles with long-leg gussets made of re-inforced double elastic, which reached almost to the knees. If a prying finger ever strayed inside it would have snapped on the vice-like grip of my underwear. Thus was my purity kept intact.

When my mother went to my sister's, it left my father and me alone in the house for the first time ever. His health was getting steadily worse as the smoking of the shop profits had begun to affect his lungs. So much for Dr Brighton's famous fresh air. He was worse than when we had lived in London. But he held no terrors for me now.

The night before my mother's return however, I was awakened in the early hours of the morning by an earth-shattering crash. My heart leapt to my throat. The crash had come from the shop immediately beneath my bedroom. I got up in the dark and hurried downstairs.

I could make out two bodies, one on the floor unconscious, the other clumsily trying to lift him up. My father, comatose in drink and Cliff, his Welsh drinking companion, the publican, equally pissed.

My father's false teeth lay at my bare toes, the top denture snapped in two. The entire front shelf of sweet bottles had smashed to the ground. The mess was unimaginable. My heart sank. It would be up to me to restore this to some sort of order before my mother returned later today. My father was due to travel to London to meet her at Paddington, so that they could enjoy a pleasant day up there together.

Cliff, a rugby six-footer, was so inebriated that it took the two of us to drag my leaden father up the stairs to bed. He had passed out completely, was as if in a coma. Cliff said we had to undress him and leave him to be completely naked in the bed. I averted my eyes at the sight of his withered genitals, so unlike the proud set of my childhood. But Cliff was impatient at my modesty.

'Fetch a bedpan for the diarrhoea, there's a good girl.' His words were slurred, but his tone was kindly. 'You can expect to stay up all night with your Da, now, because we don't want your Mam coming back to any mess on the sheets. He's likely to soil the bed from all ends of him, see, bach. So you'll be needing a bowl for the vomit, and a bottle for the piddling, apart from the bedpan. Oh, and fetch some towels for the mopping up.'

Then he held my face between his hands and came so close that I went dizzy from the alcohol fumes. He said that the most important thing in the world right now was that the shop should be cleaned up by me and that my mother must never, ever know about this little business. Otherwise, and he emphasised this, there would be absolute hell to pay. Then he went home, saying that he'd have hell to pay from his own wife, as it was.

I was left alone with my naked, utterly incontinent father.

I had never seen male genitalia other than my father's before, but that was years ago. Our male models at Art School always wore posing pouches in those days. Though just once, travelling on the back of an empty bus in our valley, an elderly gent had sat beside me and tried to aquaint me with what appeared to be a lolling lump of beige putty in his lap. I thought it was easily the most revolting object that I had ever seen. I certainly would not have counted that as male genitalia.

The image sprang to mind now. The sporadic baldness of the entire region, the uncontained area of utter devastation, the sagging scrotum. I had to sort out which bit of it all to place in the mouth of the bottle, studying to see just where a possible hole might be within the flaccid melange. I was bewildered until a helpful dribble began. I almost vomitted guiding the boneless mess into the vessel.

But worse was to come, heaving my father's withered flanks onto the bedpan and then wiping him clean with lavatory paper. Before holding the bucket to his face for vomit, just in time. The heartless light of dawn arrived just a few hours later, the action had subsided. But I couldn't take any chances so my vigil continued.

No thoughts entered my mind then. My brain was completely empty. I seemed to be performing some kind of penance. But for what, I couldn't explain. Except that I had waded in these murky waters with my father before, but this time I was in command of the situation. I didn't feel like the victim, hadn't felt like it for years.

The next morning he was prostrate with hangover and gagging even over a cup of tea. I helped him try to stick his upper denture together with glue. It didn't work. He went off to meet my mother, without his top teeth, trembling in alcohol withdrawals, desperate for a hair of the dog, but scared she may smell it and put two and two together.

I scrutinised the bed after he'd gone. Spotless. I would have made an excellent nurse, or ward-orderly. I opened the window wide to let some fresh air in, swilled out and scoured the bedpan, bucket, and bottle. Splashed my own pale face with cold water.

Then set about restoring order in the sweetshop below.

By the time of their return, nothing appeared out of the ordinary.

My father and I never mentioned the incident. Nor did Cliff, the Welsh publican, save by a sly wink the next time we met.

My mother continued to question me until the day that she died. I never betrayed my father. To do so would have been the first step to unlocking Pandora's Box. She went to her own grave never knowing.

But on his deathbed in hospital he asked my mother to stop bringing me in with her at visiting time, claiming I made him feel uncomfortable.

'Your talented daughter sold a painting today. First of many, I expect,' my mother had told him with pride. 'What do you say to that?'

'I say pour me a glass of water, I'm really thirsty.'

He died in the night, a broken man. He died of heart failure, taking a part of mine with him.

It is claimed that all men marry their mother and conversely, that girls marry their father. I married my father twice, in that the thread of violence continued throughout both those marriages. It was familiar territory for me. I knew where I stood, how to provoke and what to expect. Swings from passionate rage to passionate love making, the very tenderest and as sensually inventive as there could ever be. Which was why I have always advocated married sex as being the best, and the main reason both those marriages lasted as long as they did.

But I was a different person then. Now I cannot conceive of remaining with a man after a first blow, or even being drawn to someone with that unseen agenda beneath the surface. Why would I have visited the same scenario, not once but twice? Like a murderer needing to visit the scene of his crime, or a mangy dog returning to snuffle the sour remains of a devoured carcass.

I've been told since, that I was full of pent-up rage myself, that it had been curdling for years awaiting combustion. And I accept that completely.

However, neither of my husbands were personal, social or professional failures, like my father. Quite the reverse. The allure was their confidence and popularity, their sensitivity and scholarly intellect, their fine physique and handsome features. It was their aura of success that drew me to them both.

But my rage needed expression and they provided me with that. My own behaviour and language, exceeding the bounds of propriety, quite literally must have driven both clever husbands to utter distraction (distraction.n, perplexity: agitation: madness.).

Elizabeth Taylor's favourite marriages were her most violent (excluding the first to Nicky Hilton, where she didn't know how to fight back). She enjoyed physical fights with Mike Todd and Richard Burton. Most of all, she and they loved the reconciliations.

I was the same, it wasn't one sided. I wore my black eyes, my broken nose, my splintered teeth with pride, not shame. They would not have been out of place on a gypsy encampment, and I do boast gypsy ancestry. I was able to sport them as badges of achievement, a testament to my disturbing power to infuriate. It seemed to me to be mission accomplished. All these superficialities could be mended and were.

On my second divorce, two of my favourite Welsh aunties, school cleaners, took me aside.

'You can relax now, retire from this business of marrying English. You've done your part for Wales. In fact you deserve a bloody medal, you do, for making life hell on earth for two of our Norman bastard Conquerers. Congratulations, let's open the Christmas Egg-Nog!' Anti-English racism is the obligatory lesson taught on emergence from the womb, in my Welsh valley.

But from that first marriage I was given two loyal and loving daughters, half-English, half-Welsh, who have survived their upbringing to become exemplary mothers themselves. Their father continues as a constant and loving presence in their lives. There has been no history of violence in their own choice of relationships, none at all. Praise be. My darling son-in-laws have been as the sons I would have chosen for myself. My four irresistible grandchildren remain the rejuvenating lights of my life. I shall always be there to be twirled around their little fingers.

When I stopped drinking almost twenty years ago and found my life turning around immediately, certain suggestions were made to ensure that it would continue to do so. Top of the agenda was the practice of forgiveness, starting with self, then gradually working down a deeply considered list.

My father's name was at the bottom of that list. That is where I chose to place him. It has taken almost twenty years for me to drop my judgements and replace these with compassion. I learned facts about his own childhood and the domestic violence there. I've been able to stand outside my own suffering as a child and understand the misery that he must have been enduring himself. I've recalled the one time I saw that acute sadness on his face as he was rocking me to sleep, and how much it had moved me then. My compassion is so profound now that I can embrace the ghost of my father, and enfold us both in the devotion that we were actually meant to bestow upon each other.

I can do that with both my ex-husbands, though the two are far from ghosts. I want them to know how much I value their influence and artistic support in my life, and accept my total share and more, of the eventual strife which tore us apart. We were together as long as we were meant to be. I will always treasure the mutual enchantment and laughter we shared in the best of those years.

I would like to express my appreciation and fondness, now that the sap is no longer on the rise, for every single one of all my gloriously generous lovers, wherever they may be, in the celestial chorus or still here on earth. They were lusty couplings and full of the greatest fun, various in duration, from snatched moments of pure bliss to lengthy decades of gentle intimacy.

I loved you all boys, you know that, just as you loved me.

It is what you didn't do that you regret, rather than the things you did.

I regret not giving into the unexpected moment of unadulterated lust when I was seventy-two, and invited 'round the back', by an exquisite and amorous Mexican eighteen year-old, on the Island of Cozumel. Please forgive my lack of fiery resolve.

I regret not accepting Cary Grant's offer of an evening out in London, when he was flying back to the States the next morning. As my daughters still lament. 'A night with Cary Grant could have meant a childhood for us in Hollywood.' Sorry, darling girls!

I regret declining to dance with divine Sean Connery, understanding only too well what it would certainly lead to, on a party-yacht moored in the middle of the Thames. I had recently undertaken vows of fidelity. Thanks for the invitation anyway, Sean.

I certainly regret not finally getting it together with Omar Shariff, all the times that we almost did.

And I'd like to say to the late Orson Welles, Lee Marvin, and

Walter Matthau, more than any of the pretty boys of Hollywood, 'Make mine a large, I'm on my way, lads. Line up, there's plenty of time.'

P.S. James Robertson Justice, my sexual Svengali. I owe you everything for starting me off.

I have outlived my pussy.

Also my ability to ponder words without spectacles, masticate my food without plastic molars and now the latest, to listen without a hearing aid.

I could correctly be described as existing in the MOT stage of my life, like some ancient and much-loved old automobile, a banger held together with straw and water, not quite as road-worthy as once was. Best kept, clean and well-cared for, in the garage. Alongside the outdated perambulator of the first-born, the toddler toys, the paraphernalia of camping holidays, the bikes and roller-skates, the excruciatingly inept attempted home-made wines and general detritus of family life, outlived, no longer necessary, yet each saved as talismen of former times.

I know of these things only because they have become familiar through friends and members of my Welsh family, who have this satisfying kind of solid lifestyle. And I've seen them in films, the heroine or hero climbing those steep wooden stairs which unfold from the attic. Spending pleasurable hours re-reading favourite passages from treasured volumes. Unlocking trunks, and trying on before dated, bevelled swing-mirrors, party garments which had been worn on first meetings with partners who later became bridegrooms. Or outfits with matching hats and shoes, now too tight, worn at chistenings and other family nuptials.

Sally, my own sister has, or had, those.

But I never have.

Drawn to the maxim of the rolling stone gathering no moss, I have lived most of my life more or less permanently on the spur of the moment at express-train high speed. Propelled by an animal instinct of preserving every second of being alive, fully alive, squeezing each single drop out of corruscating collective experience. Before slithering snakelike onto the next.

But everything changed when I gave up the alcohol. Total and absolute sobriety slows you down.

As does celibacy. Or so I had thought.

But for me, at almost 25 years of both, with occasional lapses from celibacy, but never, ever from sobriety, the ensuing serenity has revealed a stillness akin to silence in me as spellbinding as the glorious giddiness of my former years.

The rich tapestry of my present life is the amalgam of both.

I have come to accept the concept of garage and attic, as integral to my personality, without having owned either.

At 73, I shagged a 23-year-old surfer in Las Vegas. We met in the gambling casino of the Bellagio Hotel, where I was staying with some friends for Christmas.

Favouring black silk, satin and diamonds, I was done up to the nines, in tune with the festivities, albeit 3.30am, having just arrived off the plane from London.

'Christ Almighty, you're gorgeous! Any chance?'

That was his opening gambit. Later, after the carnal stuff, when I told him my name and got to know his, Laban, over breakfast, before he caught his plane back to Melbourne, he told me he shared his birthplace with the other Kiwi charmer, Errol Flynn. Their Mother's Milk must have contained magic potion.

This boy was as iconic as Errol. Blond crew cut, bronzed body, blue eyes. There is something about the way surfers carry the ocean with them. An unfathomable quality of fresh air, and sea-breeze and spume. And high energy.

Yet I had been cruelly chilly on his first approach.

'Any chance?' I'd repeated his words. 'Any chance of what exactly?'

'Any chance of a fuck?' His eyes warm with anticipation.

'Absolutely not!' I was icier now. And stern. 'How old are you? Because I am 73, going on 74, and a fuck is out of the question!'

It seemed to whet his appetite. I was a challenge now.

'I am 23 going on 24. And you may be 74, but I bet it's warm and juicy down below.'

'Quite the contrary! I've been celibate for years and it's as cold as a toad and as dry as a moth's wing!'

'Now I'm aroused,' he said, and tilting his face to mine, he urgently added, 'gimme a kiss!'

Looking at him, I saw my 18-year-old grandson's features for a brief second. But dismissed it from my mind and planted a chaste peck on the cheek.

'Lips, on the mouth…' There was even greater urgency now.

I pressed my lips together for a dry kiss.

'French, I want French, with tongues.'

I opened my mouth to say that enough is enough. And he seized the opportunity to slither his tongue inside and press against my own, his aroused young body pulsating with penis.

It seemed like forever since this had last happened, and had an extraordinary effect on me.

As if the ardour of this astonishing youth had fanned fresh energy on the dying embers of an ancient fire, bringing it back to life.

My clitoris jumped to attention, into a dance of its own. That sliver of gristle, which had long-since retired, was suddenly raring to go. I found myself kissing him back (French with tongues).

The question of taking him up to my suite arose, but I told him I was not entertaining him there. The reason being that the harshly unsympathetic lighting system had not been designed with mature ladies in mind. And in any case, as I explained and he understood immediately, which drew us closer, that sex in an ordinary double bed seemed too mundane for this explosive magnetism we had discovered between us.

'I'm an alley-cat, Kid,' I'd explained. And that I chose to live spontaneously and would as much enjoy shagging, just for the fun of it, up against a wall, any wall. We couldn't find the wall. Now we were equally rampant with sexual frustration!

Since his plane was returning to Melbourne in under two hours, time was of the essence, so we scuttled into the Gents, after being refused entry in the Ladies and headed for the large cubicle at the very end, which would have accommodated a wheelchair.

Once inside the locked privacy of the space, I prepared to restrain the youthful ripping off of my garments. Instead he skillfully slid one leg out of my underwear, after freeing it from my satin trousers, mercifully on an elastic waistband, which stretched for the onslaught, leaving the other half of my lumber regions still fully clothed.

At 73, almost 74, I had never been so swiftly or so seductively semi-undressed, ever. Not ever. And this endeared me now to this total stranger, so that to facilitate easier entry, I planted my left foot atop the lavatory seat, cover down. Such that with every sensual lunge, an automatic response like the pulling of a chain to expel the contents of the lavabo occurred, as loud as a symphony concert.

We whooped in unison, roaring together, brimming with this added humour unexpectedly enhancing the occasion, bent double but still attached by our genitals. This boy was a sublime lover!

The orgasmic rapture was speeded up by the sounds of the cleaner approaching; clanging an enamel bucket and thrusting his mop under the door when it failed to open. We could barely contain our laughter, but contain it, we did. Mesmerised by the action, to and fro, of the mop, we both climaxed together in silence. The atmosphere was electrifying. The cleaner retreated, banging the exit door behind him.

My lover kept coming. I had forgotten just how much spunk young men produce. Had I still been fertile, I would have conceived sextuplets or more, from that single insertion.

It gives me a profound satisfaction to declare that this had been one of the more invigorating of my many sexual encounters. One I still hold dear to my heart, which to this very day, writing this now, still brings a wide smile to my face. Proving indeed to be my sexual swansong. We always recall so easily, the first and the last.

When we embraced on his departure to the airport, his blue eyes shone with unshed tears.

And conversation was limited, my throat was so choked.

I recovered enough to explain that what had happened between us was the outcome, a closure of the previous relationship we had enjoyed in our former lives. And he understood absolutely. Being a surfer. A creature of the eternal elements.

We are still in contact from opposite sides of the globe.

The fleeting romance yet lyrical connection was meant to be. It brought me back to life, as I live it now and have ever since.

On my return I paid a visit to the local sexual health clinic, since our spontaneous coupling had not incorporated condoms. I was tested and reassured that everything was clear. I was in excellent health.

The doctor had enquired as to what had brought me to the clinic. I was several generations senior to the youngsters, whey-faced teenagers, who worriedly sat there awaiting results of the tests for HIV they had undergone.

I related the entire Las Vegas saga, including the cleaner's mop in the Gents. The doctor and nurse, neither in the first flush of youth themselves, seemed mesmerized. Well, speechless. I broke the silence, asking if they considered such behaviour outside the norm, possibly unacceptable?

To my relief, well, not actually relief because I couldn't have cared less, quite frankly, what their opinion may have been… Drop the judgements, sweeties! I may well have said if the response was in the negative.

But it wasn't. They were all smiles. In fact the doctor murmured a few words to the nurse, who left, then returned fo the surgery with a carrier bag full of condoms.

The doctor presented me with them. 'We applaud your adventure and encourage our senior citizens to pursue a sex life, even unto death. It not only keeps them healthier, but it means they are a bloody sight more cheerful. These condoms are a gift from us to support your spontaneous lifestyle!'

My forty-year-old fiancé came into my life as a result of my poem *Las Vegas Lay*, which I performed live in an evening of poetry and jazz, organized by my poetry mentor, Michael Horovitz in Paul Pace's basement jazz club, The Spice of Life, in Soho.

A person present in the audience contacted Madame Arcati, suggesting she/he interview me.

We met in the flesh after several years of getting to know each other by remote contact, on the internet.

Internet romances are very low maintenance. No need to shave limbs or underarms. No panic over delayed re-touching of roots. No last-minute rush to catch the dry cleaners. Or to stock up on snacks. Or maintain spotless bed-linen and soft, fluffy clean towels. Less concern over odours, halitosis, anal emissions, solid or wind. Next to no worries about guzzling and resultant tightness of clothing. No attention wasted on diets, mind-improving, general home maintenance, restoring order in kitchens, bedrooms, bathrooms, sitting room.

I could continue, the benefits are endless. And I can see that, yes, you miss the kisses and yearn for the hugs. Even someone like me, who now says no to the fucking (though I can see that could change!). But all in all, I am 100 per cent for the internet romance. It brings a smile to the lips.

It transforms you into a love object, whilst gifting you with one in return.

Arcati, aka Victor, and I met in the flesh finally. We danced together in the Green Carnation Club in Soho. I had accepted the offer of one night a week as DJ there following the unexpected demise of the legendary resident transvestite, Tallulah.

I agreed on the inclusion of my daughter, Sophie and 18-year-old granddaughter, Carson. We called it The Parkin Lot, embracing three generations of females. I'd thought it would prosper for roughly six weeks, in fact it drew crowds for 12 months. We ended it there. Sophie got married, Carson was offered another club and I was fulfilling the invitation to hold an exhibition of large canvasses in Croatia.

I understand that we created a precedent with The Parkin Lot by representing a multi-generational club in the very heart of the West End of London where all ages were welcome to drink and dance on their very own, in the knowledge that they would receive the warmest of Welsh welcomes. A unique concept indeed in these youth orientated times, at the rare cost of £5 entry. We were crammed out every week, from 9pm until 3am, with a scintillating mix of artists, writers, film-makers, students and pensioners.

Indeed, one week Age Concern brought along a coachload of 80- and 90-year-olds, who all took to the dancefloor with admirable alacrity. No evidence of arthritics or lumbago there. In truth it turned out to be one of our jolliest evenings, playing, as we did evey week, a medley of music from the '40s through to the present day. The one sure get-up-and-dance disc remained throughout our annual run, Michael Jackson's *Billie Jean* from the *Thriller* album. Oh, yes, and the Andrew Sisters' Second World War smash hit, *Boogie Woogie Bugle Boy of Company B*. Both are two of my favourite recordings of all time. When I play them as I rise in the mornings I can't help but dance.

BBC TV arrived to film our opening night, following up on a piece written for the *Times* by my Sophie.

She and I were interviewed on Breakfast TV the following morning, having only just been to bed at 4am that very morning. Carson wasn't with us. We'd sent her home early the previous evening. She was at school sitting her A Level examinations. I know she was there, she refused to miss the opening night.

So this was the setting for the very first meeting between Madame Arcati, aka Victor Olliver, and myself.

These two names alone set up familiar reverberations within me. Madame Arcati was a pivotal film character in Noel Coward's *Blithe Spirit*, portrayed brilliantly by the actress Margaret Rutherford.

I had met her at the Stage Door of a St Martin's Lane theatre, where I queued for her autograph without seeing the play she was in. My pocket money wouldn't stretch to it. I was 12 years of age at that time, in my Grammar School uniform, although it was Saturday afternoon; I had no other clothes besides my Sunday best for attending our Welsh Chapel in Chelsea's Radnor Walk.

She had just performed the matinee, and might have been popping out for tea before the evening performance. Her appearance was positively breathtaking. It was early autumn and she had chosen the autumnal hues to match the season.

When I am asked, as I often am, where my sartorial influence originated the reaction is always astonishment when I claim it to be Margaret Rutherford. Hers was the most seriously inventive, the most artistic, and original. Her outfit consisted of a floor-length shimmering bronze velvet cloak, beneath which was revealed a cashmere garment of burnt orange enhanced by several knee length ropes of varying amber beads, some opaque, others transparent shades of chrysanthemums.

On her head was a swathe of pleated jersey turban, matching the amber jewellery. But her smile outshone anything she wore. She was radiant. She smiled at me, signed my shabby little autograph book, then came the hug. I never wanted to vacate that perfumed embrace.

Withdrawing eventually, I released my grasp. The smile was still there. She whispered one word in her gloriously actressy voice. 'Darling,' she said.

Perhaps she saw something of how she once was in me. Me, unformed clay, vulnerable with optimism. Yearning to reach where she was already.

I rode back home to the deeply depressing suburb of Willesden, shutting my eyes as I always did along Willesden High Road to blot out the suicidal-inducing visuals. I may have been there on the top of the bus but I was borne aloft on angel wings. Having toyed around with my school hat, trying to bend the resistant felt and shape it into that of Margaret Rutherford's turban, secure in the knowledge of how I would be in the future. A goddess of distinction, with amber and cashmere and cloaks of velvet. Drawers tumbling with turbans. And calling everyone in a charm-laden voice, 'Darling,' whether I'd only just met them, or not.

So, all these decades later, now clad as my idol, my heart leapt to read a message from Madame Arcati. Just the words brought a thrill. I responded immediately telling him my Margaret Rutherford experience.

And when he told me his actual name, Victor Olliver, though the spelling was different, the name sounds the same as the famed violinist, Victor Oliver. A name from my past. My father having heard of the fondness the star harboured towards young girls during his marriage to our Prime Minister's daughter, Sarah Churchill. That ended in divorce, rare then.

My father forced me forward at another stage door, I believe the big Hippodrome in the centre of London. But a scandal had just broken involving a minor and the press were hungry for quotes from the star. Head bent, he hurried past my father's offering, leaving us behind on the pavement. Yet in his passing chauffeur'd car I caught a glimpse of him eyeing me up and down, from my long fringe and my sweet cotton socks. His lewd wink remains with me still. I didn't gratify my father by divulging this.

So I didn't come to my fiancé with an entirely clean slate.

But at the Green Carnation, he asked me to dance and it felt utterly right to be in his arms. We laughed a lot, and danced some more. Then said goodnight with a chaste kiss. We were not unaware of each other, far from it. But with Victor I have learned what patience is all about. Allowing the blossom to unfurl gently, instead of speeding proceedings.

Having said that, he posted on Madame Arcati, that he had fallen in love with the turbaned beauty, Molly Parkin and was planning to ask me to marry him.

I declined. But he has persisted, and refers to me as his 'fiancé'. Now I refer to him in the same terms. He resides in the South Coast, not in London any more. And family commitments mean that we rarely meet, just for now. It will not always be thus. We may still marry. Who can ever tell for certain what lies ahead? We make each other happy.

We spent a glorious holiday together in Croatia last August, when he and my family became cordially acquainted. Some view the relationship with a certain reserve, not to say a pinch of salt, observing the age gap between us.

These are individuals who have never experienced the precious chapters throughout my youth I cherished with men and with women, 20, 30, 40 years older. There exist no age barriers between kindred spirits.

Those who question the closeness between Victor and myself neither receive nor send the sparkling emails we exchange on a daily basis. Nor do they overhear the combined laughter during our lengthy telephone calls. Or share in our mutual declarations of devotion.

I have been told that this relationship will prove to be the most profound of all those I have had with the opposite sex. Which gives hope to all. The universe keeps secret treats tucked up her sleeve, to expend on her terms, not ours. We both regard each other as heaven-sent. An act of God.

We genuinely share these beliefs.

Sex disappeared when I ditched the booze. But it delighted me in the long run, late in my life, to discover that friendships, straightforward and loyal, deep-rooted and discreet, drenched in devotion, purified by spiritual bonds, side-stepping sex altogether, actually do make for an immensely rewarding existence. When all along I had considered sex as the strongest form of communication. The only sure way of getting to know strangers, male, being to first allow physical entry. Both bodily responses, theirs and mine, preferably conditioned and heightened by alcohol to speed things along with a swing.

Yet that was not how it was with the legendary Black Soul and Blues singer, Bo Diddley. The most brilliant of all my highly valued One Night Stands, in Olympic athletic terms, in achievements of physical stamina. Sexual activity, spliced with affectionate exchange, lasting non-stop from midnight through dawn. The tongue as powerful an organ as the penis, used to blowing through horns, unabashedly exploring every orifice.

Not a drop of alcohol, no smidgeon of drugs. The sex being the sole stimulant. And the laughter. And the marvellous music that had gone before.

Our eyes had met as soon as Bo Diddley had sauntered onstage, to tumultuous reception from this vast, young, mixed-race audience at Brixton's Academy.

I had been persuaded to meet up with some youngsters, girls in their 20s, one Elaine, an artist who kept herself going by waitressing at the Chelsea Arts Club, where I was living at that time. She was the one who had talked me into going to see Bo Diddley perform, claiming black lovers to be the best in the world in her experience. Especially black musicians.

But I had already been booked for that evening, being interviewed on television about my travelling One Woman Show, now on a national tour. I agreed to meet up with them there, going straight from my own TV appearance.

So I was more than inappropriately garbed, top-to-toe, in gold lamé, with giant hoop earrings and jangling gold chains. Plus the crowning glory of my David Shilling theatrical gold pillar-box chapeau perched on my piled-up black hair, with eye-lashes from the television studio make-up department, halfway down to my cheekbones. And lips the shade of black cherries. All show-off stuff. Fine for television audiences watching at home, but wildly misjudged and out of place midst a sea of blue jeans and t-shirts, the age range from 16 to 25. As in an audience at a music festival such as Glastonbury.

But I was blessed by the limo, organised by the television team to pick me up and take me home, so I arranged instead for the limo to take me to the concert.

I consulted the hip young, black driver of the limo as to whether I may appear over-dressed in my gold outfit.

He grinned and told me to wait and see how Bo Diddley would appear onstage: 'Man, he's a superstar and wears groovy threads!' Adding encouragement, 'You'll fit in fine!'

His words hadn't prepared me for the first glimpse of Bo Diddley. Top to toe in gold lamé, just like me! Gold chains, real gold I discovered later, when he presented me with one. And an ivory and gold deep crowned hat, based on a western Stetson.

He was built on impressive lines, like an athlete, a wrestler. A huge guy, with a massive presence, strumming and crashing huge chords on the gold and white instrument strapped over his shoulders, reaching down to his crotch. I couldn't bring my eyes on what may be nestling there.

Elaine whispered to me, 'Glad that you came now, Moll?'

I beamed in her direction, unwilling to tear my eyes away from the superstar. That's when he caught my eyes. I felt a hot flush coming on. I was clearly verging on the menopausal stage of my life. Though this was the first time I'd been aware of it. From then on I never once looked away, angled as I was at the side of the stage, right there at his feet.

By the end of the concert, some three hours long, he was on his knees to me, serenading each number.

Elaine, sidling past, as flabbergasted as myself, hissing in my ear, 'Fuck me, Moll, you've pulled! I can't believe it!'

Nor could I.

But when Bo accepted the hysteria of the final applause, he turned towards me, winked and inclined his head to the exit for the artistes back stage. And before I knew it I was being escorted by his minions up to his dressing room. Hustled into his limo and rushed off through the traffic up to his hotel suite.

Anybody reading this would be excused for thinking it couldn't possibly have been as easy as that. After all I was hardly groupie material. But it was that uncomplicated. And for that one single night of my life I did behave like a groupie.

He said that what had attracted him to me was the way I was

dressed. He appreciated the sophistication and in the States, the female audience vied with each other to attract his attention, but he hadn't found that to be the case in England.

I explained I was Welsh, with Romany blood.

He'd chuckled. 'You dress like a gorgeous black woman, I love your style. And your company, and your conversation. Neither of us are kids anymore.'

Then he said he'd like to get down to business, give me the number of his tour manager to contact, as to where and when in the world we could get together again.

I explained that I was onstage myself with a string of planned venues. 'Cancel them all. I'll get my people to sort out legalities. I'm not letting you go now I've found you. I'll look after everything in your life for you from now on.' And he rolled me over and fucked me again with his huge erection, which never appeared to subside, even when so-called limp. It made me pleased that I had given birth, twice, and widened the passage, otherwise I would have been ripped asunder.

I staggered out when the light broke outside the window. He was astonished. But I simply couldn't have taken any more.

As it was I seemed to have lost control of my limbs. Weak at the knees, I pocketed all the numbers he gave me and promised faithfully to ring. I broke the promise.

But my Colony crowd adored the tale. I am an old woman now, and here I am still squeezing every drop out of it.

Adventures of that nature don't only happen to the young. I was over the age of 50 when it happened to me and he was older. But we appreciated what each had learned and could offer from experience. When I heard of that huge man's death, I actually shed tears for that magical time we spent together. He had died at home in his bed, surrounded by his loving relatives of all generations. The sad news was covered by global media. Various friends rang to make certain I had heard the news.

It felt like the passing of a giant.

I have led an exalted existence,

blessed not least by the warmth of profound friendships.

But the longer you live, the more frequent the funerals, the spaces left in my own life by the departure of loved ones, apart from parents.

One winter, whilst in India, I returned to London to be told of the unexpected deaths of as many as fourteen of my close acquaintances. A mixture of friends and former lovers. The loss was mind-numbing.

Yet Nature abhors a vacuum and the spaces filled up again with fresh blood and new faces. Whilst the departed returned, from time to time, on their own terms, in abstract form, yet none the less vital despite that.

My friend, the painter, poet, performer Jeff Nuttall was the first to pay me such a visit, soon after his untimely death, which occurred not long after he and I had spent an afternoon together on a film-set down in Pontycymmer, my birthplace in the Welsh mining Garw Valley.

It was drizzling rain as usual and we had sat in the front of his car between takes, at the bottom of the mountain behind the Ffaldau Square, where my grandfather had been the engine-winder in the Ffaldau Colliery.

We were reminiscing over old times. Giving each other answers over why this and that had happened to such and such a person in our closely linked artistic circle. He, telling me filthier and filthier jokes in his own inimitable chuckling style. Me, coaxing yet more. We were always each other's most appreciative audience.

Until he could hold out no longer and went off to assuage his pressing thirst in the nearest pub. I didn't accompanying him, though in the previous years we had sank pint upon pint together, neck and neck, non stop, to the point of collapse. Up in London at the Chelsea Arts Club. Or in Soho, at the Colony with Francis Bacon and other friends.

But I had relinquished my drinking habit before it obliterated me altogether, so I didn't accompany Jeff to the pub. And he didn't press the issue. Embracing me instead, as a bear embraces a cub.

It would be the very last time we saw each other. In the flesh.

I wrote this prose-poem down after his wake as soon as I got home, still moved, so that I can read and re-read the words from time to time, reliving the enormity of the experience. They never fail to move me to the same tears.

The generous imprint of Jeff's final embrace lasted the afternoon and is with me still and shall be always. I saw it then as I see it now as the profound embodiment of everything that he and I had ever felt for each other.

We loved each other but were never lovers, we by-passed the exchange of bodily fluids, of saliva-strung kisses and passionate marathons. Strange to explain, but there seemed no need for all that. We were linked more powerfully, we sprang from the same soil and the recognition of that was there from the very start.

To have made love to each other would have seemed uncannily incestuous.

But only we two fully understood the sublime pleasure we shared in each other's company every time we met. We quite literally fell upon each other, the reunion of twin-souls. Wherever it took place, in Soho or the Chelsea Arts Club, or down in my Welsh valley, the place of my birth. The joy was as pure and unadulterated as it had been the first time we ever met.

That first time

My heart leapt
My cheeks burned

My mouth dried
My throat closed

My knees buckled
My eyes sparkled

My lips smiled
My spirit soared

We burst into laughter
Which never stopped

When me and Jeff
Met that first time

I always took such relish from the look of him. Those rumpled curls and the roly-poly belly, reminders of Swansea's son, Dylan.

The eyes of the artist. The gait of the jazzman. The tongue of the poet. The voice of the preacher. The chuckle of a cherub. All the elements were in place to create the captivating essence of the inimitable man/child.

I didn't fully comprehend when they told me Jeff had died. The blood drained out of my very bones. There was a sudden space in the world and I was feeling the draught. I didn't want to attend his Service in the church, I would have preferred to grieve the sense of loss on my own. But I did go and was re-united with Jeff, all over again. Nobody had said that he would be there. He has been with me ever since and my life is immeasurably enhanced because of it.

'MOLL! Get off your fucking arse!' That's what he said to me there in the hallowed confines of the church, even whilst everyone was singing his praises. 'Where are the WORDS? Write the BOOKS. Paint the PICTURES. Dance the DANCE. Listen to the JAZZ, girl!'

Yes, the imprint of Jeff's final embrace is still with me, all right. But the grasp and the grip of him is stronger than ever. I went to Mexico for the first time, a place we had spoken of together. And whilst I was there, in Mexico City, I wrote my first book in a decade and completed it in six weeks. Since my return, the paintings of Mexico have been pouring out of me. I renewed my membership at Ronnie Scott's, and every week I go to Paul Pace's basement jazz club at the Spice of Life in Soho.

My gratitude knows no limits. The bond is deeper than it ever was. I now await further directions from the ether. The trust in my twin-soul has always been unwavering.

My life is putty in your hands. I'll always love you, Jeff. But you know that, don't you, boyo?

Looking back on my life, my worst quarrels have taken place with the opposite sex. I cannot remain seriously angry with my own. I was blessed—and I choose to see it that way now—with wonderful women in my upbringing. And so it has continued in my adult years.

My grandmother was something from a storybook. Wise and warm, with the ability to restore calm to troubled waters. Sometimes I would sit beside her looking into the fireplace, me on a low stool barely up to her knees, leaning against her. The strength of her lean body, the power of her spiritual faith, her certainty of self would flood through me. And it seemed to me that I would arise, a different child. Like a bible story about Jesus. Or a tale of King Arthur and the Knights of the Round Table.

She would glance at me, sensing a growth and I would gaze back, unblinking. Nothing needed to be said. Thus are things so important that they have no name, passed from the ancients to the young. The oak tree giving the meaning of life to the acorn.

My mother passed on her madness, without the insanity, or the desire to self-destruct utterly, the fascination with perpetual ill-health, the need to sabotage any happiness presented to her.

An American friend, who happened to be an eminent psychiatrist in his own country, and was over in ours working with the also eminent R.D.Laing, explained that my mother's psychic burden must have been intolerable. She was the only child to survive from twelve; the others all died in infancy. Two perished within one month alone.

I agreed.

But on looking back at my grandmother, who lost all these children and chose the way of faith, accepting God's will, she now seems an even more extraordinary human being. She was regarded as a saint in our valley, the old timers who were still alive then had told me.

But my grandfather, her husband, so tall (for Wales), so distinguished in bearing, he was no less extraordinary. He possessed all the qualities of mercy and kindness that my own father lacked. And a disposition so sunny that it wouldn't matter what the weather was, and in the valley it was invariably raining for the height of the mountains and the lowering clouds bump into them at the top. That's how he explained it to me.

'That'll be God coughing,' was his explanation for the thunder. 'Now he's lighting the candles.' As the lightening ripped the skies.

When I was ill with my periodic bilious attacks, he would sweeten my pillow with Lily of the Valley perfume in a tiny, tiny bottle bought from the doll shop, to be placed in their dolls' house. And arrange cut rose blooms from his garden in a tall crystal vase, so that the vase would catch the light from the window and scatter rainbows around the room.

When I was eight years old I was caught in our outside lavatory, knitting a little warm cardigan for my teddy, singing to myself on a Sunday, which was blasphemy in itself unless the tune was a chapel hymn.

This one wasn't. It was my school-cleaning auntie's favourite one of the moment, a wartime ditty to raise the morale of the nation. They used to sing it whilst mopping the schoolroom floors and they had taught it to me:

Run rabbit, run rabbit, run, run, run,
Before you get caught by a hun, hun, hun.
We'll get by without our rabbit-pie,
So run rabbit, run rabbit, run.

My granny sent me to bed without my tea and left me alone at home, whilst they attended the evening service in the chapel. I didn't like any of this.

When my granny returned, I heard her wearily climb the stairs. She had brought me a glass of fresh farm milk and two Digestive Biscuits, both my least favourite things. I was missing my Sunday tea of fish-paste sandwiches with the crusts removed, followed by redcurrant tart and farm cream. The best treat.

'Have you had time to repent, dear child?' Her tone of voice was as soft as the skin on her cheeks, as deeply comforting as the brush of her lips in a kiss.

But repent? I was as far from repentance as it was possible to be. And I didn't know where my knitting was. I was full to the brim with blind fury.

She soothed my fevered brow. It wasn't good enough. I turned to face her, green eyes gleaming and narrowed like one of Auntie Lizzie's cats.

'God is waiting to forgive you, little one.' She spoke gently, as she always did.

I hissed in her face, almost spitting. 'I don't care. When I grow up I won't want God and I won't want you. I shall drink and I shall smoke and I shall wear red dresses and, and, I shall dance with men every night.'

I regretted the profane words as soon as they had leapt beyond my lips.

To my pain and horror I watched my beloved Granny's eyes fill with tears. She allowed them to spill from her eyes and roll down her soft cheeks. Words of anger were never spoken in this house.

'And will that make you happy, child?' Her voice quavered, her chin trembled.

'Yes, it will. I shall be very, very, happy.' I burst into tears.

'Leave the bed and join me here on our knees. Let us both pray for God's forgiveness now.'

I scrambled out of the feather-bed. I couldn't wait to join her, to say sorry, sorry, sorry, I didn't mean any of it. I bowed my head in prayer and then we kneeled there in silence, allowing the power of God's forgiveness to soothe our troubled souls. I felt the calm returning. It was as if I were being blessed.

I turned to my Granny and clung to her tightly whispering my apologies. I helped her to her feet. She was smiling again, though the tears had returned. She tucked me up in bed and turned out the light, leaving the door to the top landing ajar so that it wasn't completely dark in my bedroom, knowing that total and pitch blackness unnerved me.

My grandfather joined her on the landing going towards their bedroom. I heard my grandmother breathe a deep sigh, before saying to him.

'I fear for the child. I really fear for the little one. I believe that the very devil has entered her innocent soul.'

The two of them, my grandfather and grandmother, taught me all about love. They didn't even have to mention the word. They proved that there was such a quality in existence. Only to be in the same room as both of them, to sit at the same table quietly eating our home-made meal, was to savour contentment.

I doubt that I would ever have survived the life that I later chose to lead, but for them, the light at the end of my tunnel. Though they had both passed away by then. Their presence remains and has never left me. They have always been my saving grace.

From my father I experienced childhood corruption, wrath, violence, and eventual resentment and jealousy. All were means of venting his own frustration and sense of failure. I wish it wasn't the case, but it was whilst he was alive.

In death, however, his redeeming quality has saved my life. This has been the ability to stir pity, compassion and eventual forgiveness.

The karmic experience finally resolved itself.

I was reared by beautiful women.

It gave me a taste for them, an appreciation of the aura of beauty, which remains in the life of a beauty, long after the radiance and buoyancy of youth are but a memory. As with a rose when the petals have begun to droop. The perfume lingers on.

So, when I saw Barbara Hulanicki for the first time, I was put in mind of my favourite great aunt, a sister of my grandmother, who was as exquisite even in her later years as any silent screen star. A combination of personal style, perfect features, a graceful build and in my aunt's case a mouth to equal that of Ingrid Bergman.

Barbara had, still has, the bones. From top to bottom, like a greyhound, or a racehorse. Imbued with breeding. The closest renowned being which the sight of her summoned up was, still is, Greta Garbo.

She was in her 20s when we met then and married to a man as visually stunning as herself, Stephen Fitz-Simmons. They must have been the handsomest couple in London then in the early '60s. And effortlessly the most stylish, setting an enviably high standard for everyone else when they opened their very first BIBA boutique selling clothes designed by Barbara and going on to sweep the world of fashion with their next three BIBA emporiums, centred in and around the select, and up until the BIBA phenomenon, the particularly staid Kensington High Street.

I supplied the hats for the very first BIBA, a tiny corner shop, previously a chemists in Abingdon Road, on a side road off Kensington High Street. I sauntered past it not long ago, finding myself in the area, though I seldom frequent any other part of London these days other than Chelsea, where I live and Soho, where I come to life.

No sooner had I passed the locked, empty premises, shabby and unrecognisable now, I retraced my steps, feeling myself drawn back into the past, by the blare of Beatles and Stones music through the welcoming doors of the boutique, the very first BIBA, as was. And by the stunning physicality of those leggy London 'sixties 'dollybirds', as they came to be described.

Their skirts barely grazing their pert buttocks, their bra-less nipples clearly visible beneath the gossamer frills of their BIBA frocks.

I stood there on the pavement and closed my eyes, with my arms apart, sensing the presence of them all over again. Me, delivering my cargo of hats, which would be sold out by the weekend. Parking my canary-yellow 1932 Vintage Rolls Royce, a gift from a besotted aristo, who had combed the country for this vehicle created in the same year as my birth.

In the Rolls with me would be a gaggle of small girls, my two daughters, Sarah and Sophie, with school pals. All licking ice-cream cones. I would let them loose inside BIBA, knowing this was the only way to extract the cash in payment due to me for the hats.

At the start of our transactions, darling Fitz would escape through the back window in retreat for the pub, to get out of paying me. Not after my first visit with my sticky-fingered gang. From thence forth, he greeted me charmingly at the door, cash in hand. Through the following decades when both Barbara and Fitz and by then their scrumptious little son, Vitold, would come over to play badmington in the tournaments we set up, my second husband and I, in our badmington court behind our mansion in Notting Hill.

By then their fame as BIBA was global, as well known as Dior and Yves St Laurent. Even more popular, certainly more influential. They dictated a sophisticated inner-city life-style after taking over what had been the department store Derry and Toms, selling furniture and food, high fashion and cosmetics. And developing the roof garden into an extension of the night club, from the ritzy restaurant inside, which served chic afternoon teas, and cocktails from the Hollywood-style cocktails bar. There had never been anywhere in the world such as that final BIBA. It was a mecca, a must, for visitors all over the planet. The most extraordinary aspect being that their prices were the cheapest in the capital. And that in this husband and wife emporium, Barbara had designed every single item on sale and in use. Down to the tiniest teaspoon. Such was her genius, and perfectionism, and application.

I suppose Barbara and I saw each other every day in those years. We share this enthusiasm for hard work, and for hurling ourselves into our passions. And despite living in various far-flung corners of the globe throughout the decades we have still maintained our close friendship, spanning close on 50 years.

And we have much in common.

We had both been students at Brighton Art School. I studied painting on the five-year degree course, and became an art teacher in London. Barbara studied Fashion Illustration, left college within her first year and became immediately successful in the world of fashion illustration in London and Paris. As BIBA took the world of fashion by storm, I was similarly, throughout the '60s and into the '70s, becoming influential as Fashion Editor of *Nova*, *Harpers* and the *Sunday Times*. Neither of us took our successes as solemnly as perhaps was expected of us. It just seemed to maintain this sense of equal footing.

Since then Barbara has become one of the most internationally esteemed designers of interiors and exteriors, following her revolutionary approach in the resuscitation of Miami's South Beach, when approached first by the Rolling Stone, Ronnie Wood, to design his nightclub, *Woody's*, in Miami. Then she was offered Chris Blackwell's fleet of dilapidated '30s hotels. Where the roaring blend of clashing colours on the exteriors alone brought the Manhattan fashion crews bombarding the area for fashion magazine spreads. Her reputation was relaunched.

But tragedy struck. Barbara's beloved husband, Fitz, died. Her loved ones gathered with sympathy. But I knew, I trusted in her resilience, she would make life work for her again, even after this devastating blow. And Fitz would be immeasurably proud of how she has done so.

Recently she has been travelling the world with her autobiographical documentary film, *Beyond Biba*. My daughter Sophie and I are both in it, gossiping with Barbara in my eye-watering Schaparelli pink studio apartment. Laughing, as usual. Relaxed, as ever.

As Barbara has slid from one career effortlessly to another, I have done the same. Following my decade as Fashion Editor, I spent the next ten years writing comic-erotic novels, one for each year. For the following two years I toured with my One Woman Show, as a stand-up comic, and did masses of telly work, appearing wherever and whenever invited, becoming a prize Media

Whore, I think that's the term. Becoming a fully-fledged alcoholic along the way, too. Then gratefully I put the glass down and returned to painting.

But now, here I am back at the laptop completing this book, which I had begun in Mexico City several years ago.

Neither of us are living in the land of our birth. Barbara left Poland. I left South Wales. We both still regard ourselves somewhat as refugees amongst the English.

We are both Cineastes. Avid film-fans throughout childhood.

We have never exchanged a cross word, ever. We share the same sense of the ridiculous. We are equally loyal and generous with each other and always available when needed.

Wherever we are in the world, we manage to pop over and pay a visit. Barbara visited me to dip into the ancient grandeur and spiritual quotient in India. I share the visual splendours of modernity in Miami.

The last time we saw each other was earlier this year in our Alma Mater, Brighton College of Art. Our still hectic lives and careers flowing as creatively as ever. We both fielded questions from the packed audience, following the showing of Barbara's film. Now we have already published both our autobiographies, and had films based on our lives.

We are each other's Muse and Mentor. But we just regard ourselves as Best Friends.

I met my other great mate, Zandra Rhodes, when she was still a student at the Royal College of Art, adjacent to the Albert Hall. I tell everyone, I always have, that she was a teenager, which is what she still appears to be. Magenta hair, atop turqoise lids above shocking pink mouth. And whoever can guess what rig-out beneath all that. She is a visual riot, I have never seen her off-duty.

She takes my approach to life and her appearance, that we actually dress to please ourselves. To rise in the morning and lighten our load by tossing on what's nearest, just as long as it clashes, as long as it turns heads spinning, our own first of all. To quicken the blood and just make ourselves feel bloody marvellous, ready to face the day and take on the world. On our terms.

Our first meeting took place at a party on Eel Pie Island. And that felt appropriate too at the time. Something so faintly ridiculous and off-centre about the name, Eel Pie Island.

Each time I meet up with Zandra I want to squeeze the life out of her. She has this childlike, cuddlesome quality. And she is a great, great giggler. I wondered once if she ever, ever got depressed. If so she never shows it. And I am like that, too.

Though actually, with Zandra, I honestly believe that what you get is what you see. That she is transparent enough and so utterly and honestly herself that we would know if she were ever down.

I think that, like me, she is one of life's happy individuals. That she lives by the Hoagy Carmichael lyrics in one of the very best songs ever penned and recorded:

Accentuate the positive
Eliminate the negative
Latch on to the affirmative
And don't mess with Mr In-Between.

I speak as myself in teenage years, 13 years of age, who actually met Hoagy Carmichael and got his autograph outside the stage-door of the London Palladium, where he was performing in the 1940s.

And knew what it was to thrill to a pair of twinkling eyes with an American accent, and fall into immediate full-blown infatuation with a male stranger. And still to feel this way now, 65 years later. They never hinted at anything of this in my Welsh Chapel when they preached of Heavenly Love.

One of the things I really approve of in Zandra is her choice of close male companions. The legendary Divine of poodle-shit gobbling fame, directed by superb film director John Waters. Divine adored Zandra to pieces. When he came to London they were inseperable, he stayed at her abodes, they travelled together constantly. And she travelled the globe with one of my other closest pals, Andrew Logan. They are joined at the hip, those two.

It was following his first trip to Indian with Zandra, that Andrew began nagging me to go there myself. Knowing, sensing that this would advance my outlook beyond measure. And it did, of course it did. Andrew knows me better than I know myself, even.

We were all together in the Cannes Film Festival, for the film showing of *Andrew Logan's Alternative Miss World* in the late '70s. Divine, and Zandra, Andrew and his partner Michael (who always designs and decorates Zandra's extraordinary homes), my daughter Sarah, who played Monroe in the film and captured the adoration of the paparazzi by posing topless in the sea at Cannes, causing traffic jams on the Esplanade. And myself done up as some kind of insect. I had supplied the running commentary in the film's soundtrack.

This last *Alternative Miss World* before Christmas, which took place in the Roundhouse in Camden Town, Zandra and I sat next to each other as Judges, alongside Celia Birtwell, Ken Russell, Bruce Lacey, and Richard O'Brien of *Rocky Horror* fame. Most of us have been judges throughout the long years. My own companion, Madame Arcati, aka my fiancé Victor Olliver, was most impressed to be introduced by me to Julian Clary, who is still astonishingly pretty in the flesh.

Zandra designs and makes Andrew's superlative metro-sexual costumes as compere to the whole show, split down the middle, half female, half male. I love Zandra's clothes so much and yet I have never owned anything of hers through our lengthy friendship. Perhaps because they are so utterly Zandra. She does look miles better in them than anyone else. Rather like Vivienne Westwood in hers.

And for that matter Barbara Hulanicki wearing BIBA.

When I was sent as Fashion Editor for *Nova* to my very first Chanel fashion show at the time of the couture season in Paris in the '60s, I had to admit that Chanel, herself who must have been nearing 80 if a day, (but I may be wrong!) and scarily skeletal, still looked stunning in her minimal tweed two-piece, and fringed wig and crimson mouth. Not one of the global fashionistas in the hallowed front row, who must have forked out a fortune on their very own Chanels, came even close to Madame Chanel's effortless and elusive throw-away chic. As if she had stepped straight from an Avedon fashion page in *Vogue*. In comparison, her own models drifted the catwalk like suburban secretaries out window shopping in hand-me-downs.

Glamour is in-built. It can't be glossed on.

Edith Head, the famed Hollywood Costume designer through the '40s and '50s, claimed there was no point at all in slaving over luxury outfits for Elizabeth Taylor. She looked just as sensationally sultry and seductive in a binliner, with a bit of string around the middle.

As judges of *Alternative Miss World*, Zandra and I do have fun comparing notes on who should win. Our conclusions are always the same as each other's. They never vary. But why should that be any surprise? We are just a mirror image of each other, utterly and totally. The minute we get together we begin giggling with glee. And I mustn't neglect to mention Ms Rhode's legendary homemade Apple Crumble and Custard. Mouth-wateringly magnifico! What more would one want from a life-long buddy?

I have just polished off my sixth family-size tub of Haagen-Daz ice-cream, Pralines and Cream flavour. I am sitting in the cinema, in my usual central seat, second row from the front. I'm on my final film, my third of the day. But I have no memory of the players, the plot, or even the titles. I'm as confused as an ancient, as an inmate of those homes for the bewildered, though I am still merely in my fifties.

It is the view of the majority, including myself, that I look stunning, sophisticated, every time I am on display. And this morning is no different, despite the early hour, I am in cocktail-hour silver and black and sporting full maquillage.

My green eyes are outlined with smoky hues and fringed with sooty black mascara. My lips, pencilled in dark carmine, glow with the latest Parisian femme-fatale Magenta. This startling colour is echoed by my suede shoulder bag and shoes. My complexion is matte, subtle irridescent rouge lifts the cheeks and as it edges up to the eyes it seems to brighten the entire face. The eyes themselves sparkle from the addition of blue eye drops.

My entire appearance is reinvigorated by my recent face-lift. At fifty six, I am so delighted with the results, now the bruising and swelling and numbness have faded away. It's taken absolute years off me, people claim. And it's true I do look much younger than my age. But what I'm most relieved about is that I no longer appear exhausted and dejected and dissolute, even depraved.

Those decades at the bottle truly played vicious havoc with my beauty. The portrait up in the attic from *The Story of Dorian Gray* was resting between my shoulders in my case. The frightening end-result of too many cocktail parties and bars, and night clubs and juggling lovers. And frantic delusions, of a nightmarish nature, in the dank hour before dawn. They all took their sour toll.

'You are a prematurely aged woman.' That's how the cosmetic surgeon in Harley Street had briskly described me. 'But we'll soon see to that,' he'd added with that comforting smile of his. 'No problem.'

The make-up is completed to perfection on an immaculate canvas now, my mask is in place, now nobody can see the real me. I glide in a positive thundercloud of perfume, keeping the masses at bay. This is how I have chosen to present myself to the world since I was a girl.

I have always been blessed with a beautiful body, all the women in my line have had that. My silhouette is slender, and still shapely, without the aid of cosmetic surgery such as liposuction.

One of my friends has dabbled in that one to disastrous effect. The fat cells once removed, so she told me in tears, leave the rest, well, lonely, and they immediately reinvent themselves at an alarmingly rapid rate.

It is quite surreal. She is now piling the pounds back on, at least they are piling themselves, with no apparent help from her. She has only to sit in front of the *Six O'Clock News*, or digital reruns of *Sex and the City* and our favourite, the spellbinding *Biography*

Channel and can rise, an eighth of a stone heavier, without a morsel passing her lips.

Today, feeling I needed to get out of the house and could do with the exercise, I walked all the way and had begun my cinema viewing extra early at 11.45am (cinemas mercifully open much earlier than in my youth). As usual, I purchased a small tub of vanilla ice-cream. Normal size for a normal person, which I am not of course. Unfortunately, I had absentmindedly opened the tub the moment I was seated. I was the sole occupant of the stalls at that point, just as I like it. It gives the sensation of owning one's personal screen. If you feel like it you can kick off your Manolo Blahniks and perch your ankles on the back of the seat in front, lowering your entire body into a slouch-back position. The sprawling sloppily is unusually liberating.

Lately, I have been given to bringing my own Indian Hindu prayer pillow to make my ankles more comfortable, also one for the small of my back. I carry these in a light plastic holdall, black to go with most of my clothes. But I mislaid that this morning and had to opt for a patterned turquoise, more suitable for the beach, which didn't go with anything in my autumn/winter wardrobe.

'What the hell!' That's what I said out loud. After all, who is actually on the Fulham Road at that time of day. They are all too busy coffee-ing it in Harrods. Or strolling to Fortnums from the Royal Academy. Or, fortunate buggers, getting the first of the day down their graceful necks in the Chelsea Arts Club.

Let's face it, I am the only one in the pictures. I do so prefer that name, pictures to cinema, like wireless instead of radio. That tells my age.

Having opened my small tub of vanilla, a safe flavour which has never enthralled me, of course I had to finish it. I only choose vanilla because it never tempts me to a second, or third or fourth and so on. That's the way I am. One is never enough.

My astonished husbands, watching me imbibe—champagne mostly—used to ask, both of them in the different marriages and quite early on, too.

'Doesn't the word "enough" ever occur to you?'

I was interested, nobody had mentioned the word before in my presence.

'When does this word "enough" actually occur? And how will I recognise it?'

'It's more of a feeling than a word. The sense of being full up, of not having room for another. It starts in the stomach, but the brain signals the, well, the word…' both husbands would flounder then.

'The word "enough", you mean?' I genuinely wanted to be helpful, to improve myself for them.

'That's the one, now you've got the message.'

But bound by chapel-honesty, I'd have to shake my head. 'I haven't really got it. Sorry. The only words that I've ever heard are "more" and "much more".'

They both gave up then.

With an empty vanilla tub in my hands before the trailers for next week's films had barely begun, I peered at my '30s diamante watch, a present from my darling daughters. Very decorative, very 'me' as they'd said on presentation. Yes, but utterly hopeless to read the time without a powerful magnifying glass, the sort used by botanists to enlarge microbes.

Placing my jewelled tri-focals on my nose I could see that there was still time to hop downstairs for another tub, so at least I'd have oral satisfaction as well as visual by the time the feature film started.

Instead of at the cinema kiosk choosing yet another oh, so small tub of boring vanilla, I found myself at the vast supermarket food store along the road. The selection of ice-cream flavours there is stupendous. I made a swift decison. One family tub of Pralines and Cream would hit the spot.

'Bootiful li'l gan'chilrun comin 'roun', today?' My favourite Asian assistant smiled, eyes shining, ringing up the family tub.

The perfect excuse! 'Just a moment.' I ran like a dervish and feverishly emerged from the refrigerated cabinet, two more tubs of the same flavour in my hands.

'They are greedy little tykes,' I laughed, adding to make it less accusatory because Asians love children, 'like their grandmother.' I patted my stomach.

'Lubly Glanny,' he said admiringly. 'Here, speshal offer with h'ice cleam.' He gave me a shining table spoon, all the better to shovel the stuff down in the merciful darkness of the auditorium.

Interesting how eating in the dark, like drinking out of doors, or on a train, and certainly whilst flying through the air, doesn't seem to...count, somehow. Not like a sit-down meal, which you know will show on the bathroom scales.

So, let's face it, I am basically here in the darkened cinema on my own, in the middle of the Fulham Road, Chelsea, I am here to guzzle, to split my sides, to stuff my face. And why? Because it makes me feel so miraculously marvellous to just, I don't know, to just let go. I mean, who actually cares when push comes to shove, what I thrust down my gullet? I haven't got any husbands now, with their 'steady on, old girl' or 'have you thought about Weight Watchers?' Or a mother, a look of horror on her face after I'd given birth to my first-born, declaiming like something out of *Hamlet*, pinching my midriff, 'Is that a spare tyre that I see before me!'

The absolute truth is I've stopped boozing and getting into all sorts of romantic tangles. I have the least need in the world to hook myself a man. As to having a husband, really ever again, thank you very much, but no. I'm sick of being slender. I have tired of being the object of desire. I am intrigued by the idea of adopting a different persona. I'd like to give a shot to being fat and frowsy and frumpy, see how that works out. Elizabeth Taylor is doing it, after all, and I've always used her as my guideline. She looks contented enough on it, so now I want to look as plump as a peach, as happy as a sandboy.

I will always remember that glorious British blonde bombshell, Diana Dors, telling me how marvellous it felt to throw the diets out of the window. We were at a get-together thrown by our mutual publishers. It was a stand-up buffet, meaning you were expected to talk to the assembled company, sales teams and executives, whilst forking down chicken salad.

Diana's plate was piled to overflowing. I'd never seen anyone eat so much in public, and with such obvious enjoyment. When she'd polished it all off, she hailed one of the hovering waiters.

'Darling, would you mind terribly.' She handed him her plate. 'Same again, please.' And this was before she duplicated her sherry trifle, with ice-cream and double cream. I was speechless with admiration. No skulking in cinemas for her.

But I want to be left all alone with my favourite food, ice-cream. I am like Elvis Presley at the end, he was the same about ice-cream. I quite simply cannot get enough of the stuff, and I don't need any distraction. I may be in the cinema but there's little left over in the way of concentration on the actual film. I feel about it as I felt about alcohol and sex, when I discovered them. And since ice-cream is considered to be just about top of the list of most fattening foods in the globe, it fulfills all my current needs.

Nobody knows I am here though the cinema is marginally

filling up, certainly this scattered audience is unaware of my presence. The homeless row at the back is snoring. The illicit couples are snogging. The truant schoolkids are sniggering over a porno mag in the front row, running back and forth to the gents to relieve themselves of the excitement. Well, calling a spade a spade, to indulge in a juvenile wank.

And I am here minding my own business with the huge tablespoon from the supermarket and a fluffy towel, which I also bought there on my way out, the better to get this creamy, sticky, oozing confection more speedily down my eager throat. The towel is spread from my chin downwards to catch any drips. By the time I get round to the third tub it is possible to drink it down, just like a malted milk shake. So that when I sneak out for replenishments, for I don't in any way feel finished and there are still two more films to see, I purchase another three family tubs. I can dump any I don't consume after all. That's how I justify it to myself. But I polish off the lot, no problem.

It goes without saying that I have given up sex. Why bother, when the replacement is so much more enjoyable and with such a superior after-taste? A pop star in the 'seventies once claimed that he'd rather have a cup of tea than sex, any day. He quite obviously hadn't tasted what I'm tasting.

There was a time in my life when this behaviour would have seemed to me to be utter madness. And madness it is for when I emerge from this cinema, I stand reeling on the pavement outside. There on the Fulham Road, the corner of Drayton Gardens, where I lived when I met my first husband.

I don't live there now, fifty years later, of that I'm certain. The point is though, where do I live? I am totally and utterly disorientated. And so dizzy I have to cling to the wall.

Passing pedestrians glance at me and look away, obviously

presuming that I am drunk, for it is early evening now. Nobody is concerned enough to extend a helping hand. I was later told that I urgently needed the helping hand of a stranger, preferably one who turned out to be a doctor. The sugar rush to the system had been sufficient to send me into a coma. Seriously dangerous.

I have always had this compulsion

to gobble down as much sugar as I could get hold of in as short a space of time as possible.

During the wartime, sweets were on ration. We were all given a card with coupons in to be spent on a monthly basis. The first day of a new month my sister and I would queue up in the nearest sweetshop.

She would buy Callard and Bowsers Toffee Brazils, the big ones which gave her about six sweets to a quarter of a pound. Me, I would spend the entire month's supply of sweet coupons, one whole pound of sweets, in that first day on what were known as Hundreds and Thousands. They were literally that. Hundreds and thousands of boiled sweet chippings the size of a sparrow's fart, so gritty in texture that they tore tramlines down my tongue. But they came in every colour of the rainbow, which for me was everything a sweet should be.

I was ecstatic about the fact that they were shovelled into and sold to me in a brown paper carrier bag. There were so many of them, they were referred to as a bulk-buy. When I plunged my small arm into the bottom of the bag it came up to my elbow. I had lost my whole hand in sweets.

'Here comes the bulk-buyer! Make way!' the shopkeeper would tease every first of the month as I'd hand over my coupon book.

All the way home I would cram my mouth full of the sweets then tilt the bag to my open mouth and pour the sweets in, crunching greedily until that mouthful had gone, then repeat the deliriously sticky process.

By the time I reached home the bag would be empty. I'd be feeling sick, with a pain in the belly that lasted all through the day and into the night. I told nobody, in case they curtailed my confection the following month and thereafter.

I very much enjoyed the whole procedure, even the after-pain of over-indulgence. Later in my life I took a curious pleasure in the agony of hangovers. It was logical, as a chapel-girl, to be forced to endure pain after pleasure. But once the pain was passed, even throughout it, there was something to look forward to. Pleasure would be there awaiting you again.

I liked rubbing my acheing bellyful of Hundreds and Thousands knowing they were inside churning around. I'd examine my shit to see just what proportion were still intact, which colours had retained their intensity. The reds and purples always won, with blue a close runner. It all seemed to prolong the pleasure of the purchase.

I'd watch in awe, like watching an alien, as my older sister cut her six big toffees into tiny squares. They were a very ordinary brown in colour and barely worth having, I thought. She would arrange them carefully in a special tin kept under her pillow. Then each evening one was placed to melt on the tongue ever so slowly. Until the following week when she'd buy more of the same. Extraordinary! It did lead me to wonder if we shared the same father.

One month, there was a dreadful family drama, the very worst. As a change of habit, and this was curious for my sister was not one noted for change, she decided not to cut up her toffees any more. Nor would she keep them in a tin underneath her pillow, but in their white paper bag on the shelf next door to the dolls house. She would eat them in their entirety, one a week. This made four out of the six. The two extra she would keep until the very end of the month. Then she would give herself the treat of savouring one toffee a day for two consecutive days.

The final toffee was stolen.

It totally disapeared.

The crumpled white paper bag which had contained it was still in place on the shelf near the dolls house. But now it was empty. My sister, not noted for tears, was absolutely inconsolable. And this was as appallingly shocking a concept as the stealing of the toffee in a chapel-attending household. That this sweet-natured and placid child should be robbed was unthinkable.

Naturally everybody looked straight at me with accusing fingers when anything went wrong in our household. And more often than not with good cause. But, and here I was saved by my own nature, they knew in their hearts that it couldn't be me.

When had I ever been drawn to anything *brown*? I refused to eat brown meat, or brown sausages, or brown bread, or wear brown clothing. The colour brown depressed me. I hated my Clarke's brown sandals, but they didn't come in other colours.

I painted my own two small daughters' Clarke's brown sandals an emerald green for the summer months. Only recently one of them confided in me how much she hated that green. She longed for brown sandals, the same as all her friends. Later in life I became obsessed with brown butterscotch, but that was more of a golden brown. And I developed a passion for Toblerone chocolate bars, but that was milky and pale, besides which it was dotted with white nuts.

I would never have stolen my sister's brown toffee.

Apart from the stolen sweet being brown, the act of thieving was simply not in my nature. I was more of a giver than a taker. The Bible had tales in the Old Testament of thieves having their hands chopped off for stealing. How would I paint with no hands? My teddy-bear, who was male, would confront the world naked if I had no hands left to knit his wardrobe.

The mystery continues to this day. We never discovered the thief, nobody owned up. The question was raised at least once every year, usually at Christmas when we all said that it was alright to confess because we were in an atmosphere and spirit of forgiveness.

Nobody confessed. But I knew who had done it, I always knew. Which one of us was not a chapel-goer? Who had kept the biggest secret in the family besides me? He avoided my stare as each of us swore our innocence. It was him alright, no question of it. Yes, it was my father.

Now he had betrayed both his young and innocent daughters in my eyes.

I was labelled a very greedy child. But I was so thin as to be invisible, as if I had a tape worm gnawing away, growing plump and juicy inside. That's the theory my mother put about. But the sugar was the only stuff I was admittedly greedy about. Any 'proper food' and I wasn't interested.

The year that the Second World War started in 1939, I was rushed to hospital. I was, at the age of seven, diagnosed as suffering from chronic malnutrition. My mother fell into a fury and scolded me by my hospital bed, for 'showing her up' in front of the medical staff.

Weak tears filled my eyes, I would never in a hundred years have wanted to show my mother up in front of important people like doctors. I understood how very important that kind of thing was to her, how appearances were everything.

I tried to mouth the word, 'sorry'. But the movements weren't there, the muscles were too weak. Within an hour I was placed in intensive care. It didn't look as if I would make it through the night. The mastoid infection had spread to both ears now, they would have to cut away the bone, behind the right ear. The gaping hole is still there to this day. And the total deafness.

I could dimly see my mother's anguished face now, bent close and mouthing words in the way that I had tried to do earlier. 'Hang on…hang on…'

My eyelids fluttered, then closed. But there was a whisper in my own brain which seemed to need to be listened to. 'Let go, child,' is what it was saying.

When I returned from convalescence after six months of chronic illness and recuperation I was sent down to live with my grandparents. Oh, the joy. And, oh, the food. There is something very extra special about food cooked on an open fire. And this was fresh food straight from the garden. New potatoes and carrots and broad beans, and goosegogs, and rhubarb and redcurrants, to make jams and succulent tarts. And fresher than fresh eggs which I could take from the hen, still warm, at my aunties further down the road. They kept chickens at the bottom of that garden in a beautiful big playpen, made of twisted wire.

They had to keep the chickens in there to protect them from the big red cockerel, the bugger, so they said. He'd be backing up to them all day and all night, every single one of them, banging his big old thing into them, just as if there were no tomorrow.

They shouted all this diatribe, shaking their female fists at him.

The cockerel would strut past, taking no notice. I swerved away speedily when he was anywhere about. I didn't want him backing up to me at any time. By his 'big old thing', I thought they must mean the huge red frill on the top of his head, waving at full mast. Was that what gave the chickens their warm eggs? I dared not ask, I was afraid of the answer. I preferred knitting little garments for my new teddy, that seemed far more interesting to me in those days.

I returned to London before the war ended, the enemy doodle bug bombs were the big scare then. They would cut out, before they landed on their objective. The droning would simply stop and we would be crouched under the stairs, holding our breath, fingers crossed, praying hard that the bomb would pass us and kill the neighbours instead. Nobody actually put that into words, but those were the facts. It was a case of saving your own skin.

But you could carry the guilt to this day, if you didn't have a wise and wonderful grandfather living with you like me, to explain how God works things out.

My grandmother was dead now. I'd cried so much, sobbing through that first night when I'd been sent back to London because she'd become so frail before she died, that my father came in and thrashed me, saying that here was something to really cry about now. He said my sobs were upsetting my mother, in the bedroom next door and how selfish a child was I.

Now my grandmother was dead, but she came to visit me often, to see me through these worst bits of my life. The doodle-bug bombs being one of them.

Sweets were still on ration then, we had small books with coupons in them. Though mine were always used up, the full supply, on the first day of the month.

One of my favourite aunts, she was actually a great aunt, sister of my granny, she had a sweetshop just outside London, in a place called Watford. When family came up to stay with us from Wales, we'd all take a trip to visit this aunt.

My cousin Barbara came up to stay as the doodle bugs eased off and the end of the war was in sight. She was the same age group as my sister and myself, but just a few years older. We were very close, particularly because I was the one kicking people on the shins, hard with my tough boots, when they turned round to stare, to snigger and point at Barbara because she had no neck.

Her head just grew straight out of her shoulders. Small boys were the worst, they would pull the collars of their jackets to the top of their heads, whole gangs of them in the street, and chase after us when they spotted Barbara, shouting, 'Hunchback of Notre Dame! Hunchback of Notre Dame!'

This was the title of a Charles Laughton popular horror film. I wasn't allowed to see it at the time and I wouldn't have wanted to anyway, because cruel things happen to the hunchback and that would have upset me, thinking of Barbara. Though wicked things never happened to her, the really bad thing had happened at her birth with the deformity. I worked it out. So events after that would have to be good. Everything evens out in the end and in Barbara's life they did.

She became an art student like me. She met and married the most talented fellow student, another painter. They adopted two lovely daughters. But then she died one winter when there was the worst flu epidemic, her chest was always the most vulnerable part of her physique.

I still mourn her passing, all those who knew her do. She was an example to everyone of how to overcome a disability. The radiance and joy she spread wherever she went would put discontented people, with all their faculties, to shame.

Anyway, she came up to stay with us in London, which she often did after the bombing ceased. She was really much more a sister than a cousin, in our family. We were preparing to set off for Watford, my sister, Barbara and myself. We were all three of us looking forward to it hugely, because we always had such fun travelling, making up rude rhymes and concocting stories.

It felt pretty heady not to have the restraining influence of an adult with us, to tell the truth. Barbara and I particularly, never took kindly to any form of authority. We liked to think of ourselves above all that. I suppose, if we had had the phrase then, we would have described ourselves as 'free spirits'.

Before our departure, my mother was checking that we all had enough sweet coupons in our ration books to give our aunt, for sweets that we had money to buy. I knew that my book had no coupons left although we were only three days into the new month. I hid it in my pocket, thinking quite reasonably that my auntie could cut out my coupons from the following month. There were plenty still there for then.

But my mother had other ideas. She snatched the book from my bulging pocket and sent me to my room in disgrace. My trip was off. The other two, in tears, had to leave without me. This was yet another example of my inordinate greed, so my mother was ranting, as if I was trying to cheat, hoping that my auntie would let me have sweets anyway without giving any coupons. This would have been illegal at that time. If that had been the case I wouldn't have bothered taking my book at all. Other members of my immediate family always had difficulty understanding my motives, it seemed to me.

But, locked in my bedroom, I began drawing and painting and soon the disappointment about the cancelled trip was forgotten. I was in my own, favourite world. I always preferred the drawing and painting to any other pastime, even eating sweets, though oddly enough the two gave me the same exhalted feeling, like flying. And writing school essays could have that effect, too.

Suddenly there was a bang on the door. My mother came in bearing the most enormous portion of ice-cream in all three flavours. Chocolate, strawberry and vanilla, added to which was what must have been the whole contents of a small tin of mixed fruit salad.

The feast was enough for six at one sitting. I looked at it in amazement. What did it mean? This certainly must have taken up the entire month's supply of her own sweet coupons, for ice-cream was on ration in those days too, on the rare occasions that the shops could get hold of it.

My mother's expression was grim, her mouth ran in a straight line in the centre of her otherwise beautiful face. I'd never really seen her this angry before. My father had the priority on rage in this household.

'This is to cure you of your greed once and for all.' She put a desert spoon in my hand. 'All to be eaten by the time I come back for the dish. I give you half an hour.' She locked the door behind her. There was no tipping half of this down the lavatory, she knew her daughter well enough to know that I would wriggle out of this situation some way or other.

I was one of those children with an inordinately small appetite. Once my stomach was full I couldn't put another morsel in it. I usually pecked at everything like a bird, even stuff such as ice-cream that I thought I could eat forever. I was well known for bilious attacks which could go on for days, retching up nothing. Even the doctor despaired. So I felt bilious before I was anything like halfway through the pile before me. By the time my jailer returned, I was ready to throw up.

'I'm going to be sick.' I turned a stricken face towards my mother. I was positively green.

'Be sick.' She was implacable. I vomited over the melting ice-cream, all over it and my nearby painting, and the brushes beside it. 'All the more for you to eat up. You are as greedy as a pig, and must eat everything in sight, like a pig.'

We remained together in the room, long after my sister and cousin had returned from Watford. Each time I managed to swallow the vomit and congealed ice-cream, my body rejected it. It came hurling back up again, and again. The process repeated itself, smelling more and more vile until I fainted dead away. I slithered to the floor and lay there, covered in the putrid stuff.

As I was shaken back to consciousness by my furious mother, the vomiting began in earnest all over her skirt and shoes now. The bilious attack continued, with the complication of diarrhoea, for the remainder of the day and into the night. Until they had to call the doctor. His diagnosis was that I had been poisoned.

I would have been grateful to be cleared up with the rest of the mess and thrown in the outside dustbin, due for refuse collection the following day.

The experience didn't put me off sugar, certainly not off ice-cream. Quite the reverse. Only now I eat it at my own pace, in the cinema, on my own, in the dark.

I like anyone who eats out a lot.

So that my preference for linking up with pals is to meet over a bowl of soup, or a seafood salad, or succulant scallops. Rather than a teatime or coffee break.

I have always favoured bon viveurs. The sort with distended bellies and avaricious appetites, which denote a love of living.

Both John Mortimer and George Melly fell into my favourite category.

Though press reportage would have me down in print as the mistress of both these lovers, I never did fit into that category in my own estimation.

For a start, are not mistresses usually expected to reside in apartments or discreet housing in the St Johns Wood area of London? I have never been offered these. Although to be truthful, I was never the kind of creature any lover might expect to be ready and waiting on their way home to the wife and kiddies in the home counties.

I just am not mistress material.

I met John Mortimer when both of our first marriages were behind us, with divorces firmly in place. We were single and curious to find out at this stage in our emotional and sexual journeys, just what was on offer. Looking back, I would say that we were equally hell-bent on collecting scalps. Mutual fidelity was simply not on the agenda.

I had been faithful throughout my marriage, but was already making up for that following my divorce. I more than suspect it was the same for John. So there was this unspoken sense of glorious freedom from the very start. And I warmed to John immensely for that. There was no jealousy, no heightened sense of propriety, no cumbersome possessiveness on either side.

Though, whilst out together, there was no flirting with other people. We were too preoccupied in conversation with each other, even in parties, with music and dancing, and all hell let loose going on. There was a mutual fascination, as much mental as physical.

He was a very touchy-feely man. He liked holding hands in the cinema, or the theatre. I liked that, because there was no on-rush of desire involved, no having to leave the film or play halfway through, overtaken by mutual lust and the urgent need to consummate there on the spot.

Dining at the latest 'in' restaurants, and we spent hours in those, he would stretch forward and hold hands for all to see, and blow kisses to me across the table. He was ever theatrical, and relished an audience.

And required as a companion the sort of female who would draw attention. As our affair continued, during which time I had given up painting and was now Fashion Editor on *Nova*, with the appropriate wardrobe and appearing increasingly on television programmes in talk shows, eyes would be drawn to us as a couple. He was already an exalted literary and legal figure, with an impressive reputation, so attention always would have been showered his way.

But he wanted more. He required a public response.

We never made spontaneous love in the back (or front) of a car. Or on a deserted beach, or at the top of a wind-swept mountain. Nothing romantic like that.

Much of the time it felt like an innocently adolescent affair.

Like being out on a date with the cleverest school swat, with a dash of the young Woody Allen, and the look of an Edwardian dandy. He had the perfect companion in me, beneath the stylish exterior, still vestiges of the repressed Welsh chapel upbringing rooted in puritanical response. Penelope, his first wife, with whom I became friendly later on, found we had much in common. She was the daughter of a vicar.

John and I both enjoyed 'talking dirty', exchanging filthy jokes. He had millions at the ready, reeled off with added exaggerations at the drop of a hat, to fit any topic, or current news item. He was particularly hot on insider, royalty and political gossip. His indiscretion was boundless. And he knew, as only a practiced womaniser would know, how to continually interest, excite, and entertain me. We went out a lot and when we stayed indoors it was to entertain. He approved highly of my personal style and actively encouraged sartorial excess. He would take me to places where the two of us could make an entrance. He a dandy and me his trophy girl.

We were not in love with each other. My heart didn't leap when I heard his voice at the other end of the phone. But I felt a warm glow, a surge of fondness, anticipation over meeting up with him. It was the same for him, I am sure. Perhaps it was because the sexual side of things was not actually in place.

He enjoyed being spanked on his bare buttocks. A wearying activity, and not one which raised my sexual temperature. I was in my early '30s, just emerging from a decade of domestic harmony and disharmony. I was the mother of two small children who needed to be taken to school every morning. I needed my right arm for painting. Further down the line, when sexual experience fuelled my fires, I would have been more able to indulge this lover, and even learn to enjoy whacking the shit out of him. But at that stage I could only equate good sex with tenderness, and murmured declarations of devotion.

Decades later, when I was organising New York orgies in the Chelsea Hotel, I would stand on a chair yelling directions, a la Cecil B DeMille. I think I even waved a whip in hand, or was it just a furled brolly? I remember bashing a few writhing botties with something, swilling down Champers at the same time. And maybe it was the champagne, always at the ready with John, or the far from serene buttock-display at such close quarters, but it put me in mind of John. And I had a twinge of regret that he wasn't there to be part of this.

He and I never went in for group activity. Surprisingly few of my present friends actually have. Those who have are now dead. Snatched from us by Aids.

We had got to know each other slowly, just by being in the same place, the same party, the current favourite bistro, the theatre, swanky restaurants. We were always with other people. Then I bumped into him on the Kings Road, my stamping ground. I lived in Old Church Street, four doors down from the Chelsea Arts Club, just off the Kings Road. We laughed, it was obvious that he would ask for my phone number. Later that evening he invited me to dine with him, at a small gathering in his new apartment at Holland Park, the following week. It started from there.

We went our different ways when other, more urgent love

affairs stole our attention from each other. Then we both married other people. But the fondness remained.

George Melly and I were soul mates, different sides of the same coin. We got involved later in our lives, when I was 48 years of age already and divorced from my second husband. We were both public figures by then, meaning to say that we appeared on the same television chat shows, bantering, sparring genially, generally showing off, dressed up and over the top. Usually promoting either my latest book or his. We made for immensely popular viewing, so much so that when we crossed major London train stations on journeys to and from our shared professional appearances, there would be a stampede from fellow passengers to sign their autograph books or to scribble our names on their t-shirts or the peaks of their caps. There was no stress from either of us around this. We both enjoyed meeting new people and the public was nothing less than friendly in their familiarity.

Having resided in the Chelsea Hotel in New York for a year, right up to the demise of my second marriage and resulting divorce, I was now living in the Rolling Stones' mansion on Cheyne Walk, overlooking the River Thames in Chelsea Embankment. My friend in New York, the mother of Keith Richards' children, Anita Pallenberg, had arranged this.

It was where Mick Jagger had lived, first with Marianne Faithful, when she attempted her first suicide bid in the four poster I would be sleeping in, and then again, with his second wife, Bianca Jagger.

Both beauties shuddered when I told them that I was now in residence there. Refusing to drop in and take tea with me. Nothing could induce them to step over the threshold.

On my very first visit, standing on the front step awaiting entry to be given the keys by the Rolling Stones' staff member who I had arranged to meet up with there on the premises, I inexplicably shivered. Goose pimples broke out all over my body. It was a sunny day, very hot. Yet here I was absolutely freezing. When I entered, I felt worse.

The house had been uninhabited for some time. It was clearly haunted. I moved in with Sarah and Sophie, together again to our mutual delight. But something had to be done to change the oppressive atmosphere in the house.

George came up with the answer. To give weekend parties.

I was famed for my legendary get-togethers, now I was bent on bringing life and laughter, once more, to this grand mansion. And it worked.

We chased the malevolent spirits away and welcomed back the benign forces. The whole house brimmed with happiness once again.

The complication was that in the course of this, George and I had become lovers.

Sex was never exactly high on the list in our relationship, it wasn't of paramount importance. We rollocked into bed when we were so inebriated and missing focus that it just seemed at that point to be the jolly thing to do. A bit of a laugh between pals. He was more partial to youth. And I already had my own posse of regular bed-mates.

But George was married, even though he and his wife had regarded it as an open marriage for years, each forming separate relationships elsewhere. The situation became difficult. Too difficult to continue.

George and I agreed not to see each other, until we were in our dotage, we enthused. Then we could sit side by side in our wheelchairs, whiling pleasant hours away in convivial conversation.

'Will we remember each other in our dotage, though Georgie?' That had been my whimsical query.

He, charming as ever, replied that he would always remember me. How could either of us forget the other?

And that is more or less how it turned out to be. When we became reunited some 25 years later along our journey, George was in a wheelchair and near to death, in 2007, when he asked a mutual friend, the artist Michael Wood, to arrange a meeting with me.

We came face to face at the private view of Michael's exhibition in Holborn. I was shocked by his frailty, astonished that he was out, not in his bed at home. I would not have recognised him.

'How slender you are, my darling.' Those were my first words. He had been so robust, such a bon viveur, a liver of life.

His response banished my concern and solemnity.

'Yes,' he beamed. 'It's the *cancer*, Moll.'

And we both laughed at that. We were back together again, relaxed and happy. Then he caught hold of my hand.

'I couldn't leave this earth without seeing my Moll again.'

The BBC was there filming our reunion. But we were oblivious to any cameras, so thrilled to be with each other again.

He begged me to visit him at home, assuring me that he had talked about it with his wife and received her consent.

So I went to pay him a visit on his deathbed, and the BBC cameras were there again, filming me being greeted cordially by his wife. Then they left us alone in his bedroom to bid each other fond farewells. George lay there smiling so sweetly at me, so instead of sinking into a subdued silence, smiling as sweetly back, I found myself asking how his cock was these days, and whether or not it resembled a wrinkled walnut now.

We had always had a lot of fun with this kind of talk. And he perked up considerably, pushing back the sheets inviting me into the bed to come and have a look.

'Moll, let's have a last cuddle, at least, to re-live the old times!'

I resisted, though drawn, pointing out that we had the BBC and his wife the other side of the door. And he accused me of being a spoilsport, not being myself at all.

And he was right, of course. Because now I do regret betraying the spontanaeity we had always supported between us. It was a dying man's wish and I had denied him the pleasure. But, being Georgie, he did forgive me on the spot and we held each other close and cuddled without words until it felt time for me to leave. I was saving my tears until later.

I turned to wave to him one last time, when I reached the bedroom door. He gave me a radiant, satisfied smile and said that it felt as if we'd just had a jolly good session in bed anyway, now. So both of our hearts had been lifted.

And George will always remain in my life.

My craving for ice-cream, Haagen-Daz, Pralines and Cream, and Ben and Jerry, any flavour really, came to an unexpected end in my seventy-second year. It had lasted from the age of seven, and had lasted on and off for about sixty-five years or so. It had even survived the bile-scalding culinary experience of the force-feeding by my well-intentioned mother. She was only attempting to help kick my sugar habit in the teeth. It is an act of nature, a medical miracle that I have never succumbed to diabetes, all the symtoms are there and all the behaviour.

But no longer now they have disappeared.

Of course the march of time has something to do with this. The excuse to have a refrigerated deep-freeze full of ice-cream for the grandchildren could no longer cut any ice.

There comes a time, in the development of the adolescent girl/child when the child part gets cancelled out and the girl/woman makes itself apparent. This happens normally between the ages of thirteen and fifteen. Something physical happens as well of course.

The delicate bud is unfolding to become the most delicious,

the most ravishing, quite intoxicating blossom. Overnight so it would seem, some gravitational force has pulled the tresses on top of the head in one direction, and at the other in the opposite direction, the toes. The end result is breathtaking.

Songs are sung about it, poems are written, an entire film industry survives on the promotion of youthful beauty. The fashion industry, if not controlled, would have us gazing at child-nymphets in barely-there creations along the catwalk, the younger the better.

For the most sublime shape does emerge between that one stage and the next. Long and narrow waistlines, coltish limbs, graceful necks, tip-tilted breasts, taut barely-there buttocks. And sweetly soft faces with sharp cheek and jaw-bones, dominated by wide eyes and beautiful, bee-stung lips. With fine-pored facial complexions, and smooth seamless bodily skins stretched to fit everywhere, just so.

Nowhere is there any room for ice-cream, not any more.

'No, thank you very much, Granny.' They gracefully decline, a delicate blush barely at bay. Where are those torn tee-shirted, tangle-haired, scabby-knee'd tomboys of yesteryear?

I do truly adore them, these glorious creatures, on the unimaginably exciting, yet-to-be-revealed, dreams-to-be-realised brink of their adult lives.

I ate all their favourite flavours in just the one single sitting as I recall. But I didn't replenish those tubs. That particular shelf is empty now. The end of a glutinous era.

What came next was that I began writing a book, this book. And in that very month met my agent, to lend the venture that extra impetus. I hadn't written a book in the past ten years, I had been primarily involved in my painting in the last decade, the two always go hand in hand with me and always will. For one evening the writing bug decided to return, as it always does when the Muse decides and when the timing is right.

And the timing was right. There was a space in my life.

The television viewing simply wasn't the same without the ice-cream. And I didn't want to return to pound slabs of fruit and nut, or Giant Toblerones by the dozen, or even sample their latest, Milky Way. I did however, get hooked on Werther's Butterscotch, for a while, to the exclusion of all else.

That had started quite innocuously on one overnight visit to my sister, taking in the sea breezes and ozone-laden air down by the shore in Barry. As a change of scenery the next morning we tootled further along the coast.

We didn't want to break our journey with a motorway coffee break, but both felt dry in the throat, which bottled water didn't seem to quench. I was needing a sugar-blast, no doubt, for I was still caught in the grip then. So my sister produced the neatest little sweetie-jar from the glove compartment, one she had concocted herself.

I was impressed, it contained something to suit everyone, since she has eleven grandchildren, from a family of four offspring. The choice was indeed catholic, as varied as could be. Peppermints, toffees, chocolate toffees (but dark chocolate because that's what my sister likes—'better for you'), minty toffees, hard boiled sweets in every fruity flavour, fruit gums, fruit pastilles, wrapped Turkish Delight and the most delicious butterscotch lumps which stayed forever on the tongue.

I was captivated, and sampled everything. She herself just had the one. Like a normal person, she said. She wasn't exactly disapproving, that isn't in her nature. But my enthusiasm had all but emptied the small jar.

'We'll stop on the way back,' she said, relaxed as anything, 'for replenishments.' I was all for it. Secretly worried that there wouldn't be enough for the rest of this outgoing journey, never mind the way back. I polished off what was already there and we refilled at our destination. But immediately, and on arrival.

This was at my request, high as a kite, and exhausting with it. I was 'jabbering', as my weary mother would have put it, 'seventeen to the dozen' and 'would you kindly cease and give us all a well-deserved rest'. My very first request was for the butterscotch lumps. They had completely sold out, they didn't have them in stock, though they had everything else, and there was a fresh delivery in tomorrow. I was seething.

'Thank you very much,' my nice sister smiled to the boy behind the till. I paid for everything, after all I had consumed the whole jar. My sister thanked me, consoling.

'Never mind about the butterscotch, we'll probably get some back home tomorrow.'

'Tomorrow!?' I was outraged. Twenty-four hours ahead! I wanted more of them NOW! 'Surely there's another shop selling them here,' I said, a broken woman and hoarse now with frustration. 'What kind of uncivilised hell-hole are we visiting here anyway?'

'This is a famous beauty spot, look at the horizon.'

My sister is pleasantness personified. They should bottle her up and sell her in shops. Probably be more easily available than the butterscotch, which I was determined to buy right away and no messing about. Or else. My brain was teaming, just as if it was heroin I was after. I only needed my fix, goddamitt. Was it too much to ask?

'Let's jump in the car and drive off back to your hometown, where you know it is stocked. And let's get a move on. Yes. Very nice horizon. Let's go now, right away, before your shops shut.'

'It's early closing. They'll be shut already. Wednesday is half-day.' Calm and unflurried, she didn't mean to send me absolutely stark, staring, raving mad like our mother. But I did have the same blood. Better be careful, sister, before I strike out.

We managed to track them down in a motorway stop. Werther's Butterscotch. That was the brand. I bought two dozen, their entire stock, just to be certain. I didn't want a repeat of today's performance. I gave one packet, they came wrapped in tubes, to the communal sweetie-jar. Then kept the other eleven for myself. A towering addiction had taken root.

The tubes of butterscotch accompanied me everywhere. To the post office, the cinema, the hairdresser, the shops. I bought three at a time at first, that crept up to four, then jumped to half-a-dozen, finally to twice that.

They became my constant companions. Certainly to my tongue, which was now permanently brown, as if I'd been licking arse, a habit I had deplored in others. I was reminded of the colour of my sister's chosen Callard and Bowsers rationed toffees of wartime. How I had decried the colour brown of those, when my own Hundreds and Thousands were so rainbow-hued.

I didn't care, these little brown butterscotches had become my most favourite thing in the entire universe.

The two components were there in the one rare combination. Firstly butter, especially salted. It had come like that from the farm at the top of the mountain, where my grandparents used to take me on what felt like utterly magical walks.

I can still feel the warmth of the reception from these old family friends, going back generations. The farm dogs, which they used for herding the sheep, would signal our imminent arrival even from when we'd approach the steep gradient right at the bottom of the mountain. They would race back and forth, barking at us up to the first gate then the second. Until finally we would reach the fifth and the final, remembering always to put the clasp back firmly in place. Horror tales had scaled my memory of an entire flock of sheep, accompanied by the new-born lambs, streaming out of an unsecured gate escaping to what they though to be new-found freedom, only to crash into the cars and lorries beneath on the main road out of our valley.

Once there we would settle in; my grandparents with the elders of their generation over tea by the roaring fire, which was there even on the hottest days of high summer, as it was in my granny's house, always.

I'd be taken around by shy farm children to barns full of seductive smelling hay, a cloying aroma which caught in your throat. One or two of the boys would try to steal a kiss, to be pulled away by a disapproving sister. They would pretend to tussle, as if seriously fighting. It was just showing off in front of me, the visitor.

I'd be encouraged to hold my fingers out towards the animals, the horses, the dogs, the pigs, the chickens, the cats, the sheep and the lambs. It seemed another world, and preferable by far to the ones that I had always known. If only I could have remained there, with my grandfather and grandmother, and never left. I should imagine that my life would have been heaven on earth. But God had other ideas for me.

Then came the hugest treat, which went on for hours, almost to sunset. The extra long oak table, cut up from a mountain tree and carved lovingly to this shape by the male members of the farm family, ran down the entire length of the farmhouse. It had played host over the years to as many as sixty revellers, thirty each side, at celebrations such as family weddings and christenings. And such sad occasions, though still celebratory in spirit when loved ones passed on and their lives were to be remembered and toasted with home-made elderberry wine.

Every time we went there, the family meals felt like those feasts. But my favourite of all the offerings was the butter. I still track down Welsh butter wherever I can find it. Harrods still stock it. And so did Sainsburys, though strangely enough not in Wales! Not the Bridgend branch when I recently asked for it. Maybe it was coming in fresh the following day. For Welsh butter, strong in colour, almost the same shade as marigolds, and salty as a seaman's vocabularly, this is a culinary experience.

So the butterscotch was half that. The other half being the scotch. Not that the sweet contains alcohol, as far as I understand. It's just that scotch, the alcoholic drink, was my favourite tipple right from the very start of my drinking career. I think the reason was that it got me drunk far faster than anything else, more especially when drunk through a straw.

I used to pretend that I drank through a straw, like smoking with a cigarette holder, because I wished to protect my lipstick being smeared on the cigarette or on the sides of the glass. Ugly to look at, waste of good lipstick. The cigarette holder enabled the smoke to get to the lungs faster, somehow. The first cough came sooner anyhow. And the straw certainly worked alcoholically.

I loved boarding the oblivion express. Whenever I was out for the evening, I wanted to make it a memorable occasion in every possible sense of the word, without having to remember any of it the next morning. I wasn't one for self-recrimination. I don't enjoy living in the past, regarding misdeeds.

I have only seen that hurling oneself to the elements in the totally hedonistic sense, in Celtic countries. Compared to the Celts, other nations are amateurs in the art of enjoyment, it seems to me. When we talk about getting drunk, we actually do mean, completely out of it. Comatose, but still standing. In actual and very real alcoholic blackout.

Before I'd reached that vulnerable, quite poetic stage, a pushover for men lacking scruples, being drunk had given me an edge, cutting, coarse and very, very rude, in language and attitude. You can get away with all that when you are young and beautiful. It also made me feel incredibly, we used the word, 'horny', in those days. But the true feeling was actually one of immense love for the entire human race. And I wanted urgently to express that overwhelming emotion.

I'd embrace everybody, anybody. I'd put my arms around their neck and wait for the kisses, with my lips actually pursed up and pouting. That ready. A few more drinks and my mouth would be open, tongue lolling, like a dog. Complete with the panting. That's why I loved the stuff and couldn't get enough. It released an abandoned behaviour which wasn't there when I was sober. So just the word, 'scotch', fills me with fondness for all the fun and adventures it secured for me in the past.

I had come to love the humility of butterscotch, like the brown hen of a peacock. Who needs flash and glamour? My own appearance matched the sweet now. I found myself dressing in shades of brown, that very shade which I had always loathed. My magenta lips were a thing of the past. It would have been difficult to judge, had I been positioned against a brown wooden fence, where I began and ended. My dimensions had soared. Even the outsize departments couldn't accommodate my size. But I was happy as a sandboy and felt as free as a bird. Strangely enough, I began to be asked out on dates again. I couldn't work it out. Were these men flesh perverts, or what?

I accepted luncheon dates, then dinner ones too. I'd eat with gusto and obvious enjoyment, secure in the knowlege that there was a complete and unopened packet of butterscotch in my handbag for the way home. And once I got home, a drawer crammed with them. Who needed puddings? Well, me. Old habits didn't die that easily. I did, chocolate mousse being top of the list. Absolutely anything and everything with double cream, runny of course, not that whisked stuff and certainly not slimming crème fraîche. I would laugh and make light-hearted conversation all through the meal. I must have been positively irresistible.

'I haven't laughed this much in years. What a delightful dining companion you are. Same time next week?' The dates were piling up. I was reared to believe by my anorexic mother that men didn't like flesh, that it was only Rubens and me who found it lush and beautiful.

'Absolutely, next week and the week after that!' I'd dimple up, flesh wobbling like a jelly. What a joy, indeed, I must have been as a dining companion. The days of picking through food with a fork were well and truly in the past. But so, from choice, was the sex.

'Any chance of sex?' The men would ask the big question in their very sweet and different ways. Boldly. Tentatively. Nervously. Seductively. Coarsely. But the basic need was there.

Any female, whatever age, who is gagging for a bit and is not getting it and that is crudely put, but to the point, should consider that maybe they are…well, too thin. That they could do with a spot more healthy weight. Think of Monroe and Elizabeth Taylor, consider the proportions of the sex goddesses and just why so many girls fork out for super-dimensional breasts.

I know that the Duchess of Windsor and Mary Quant both stated that you have to make a clear choice between food and clothes. They didn't mention sex. The fashion plates, believe me, are not necessarily the ones with the greatest love-lives.

'I'm a grandmother.' I'd draw my estimable bosom up proudly in response to requests, as if to state that I expected respect for that venerable status.

'That wasn't the question,' one cheeky suitor replied with a twinkle. 'I asked do you still do sex?'

'Sex? Whatever is that? My memory fails me. It happens at my age.'

'Don't worry, Gran. I can take you through it slowly, step by step. You'll soon pick it up. It will all come back, you'll see.'

'You dirty little rascal. I don't know who you think you're talking to.'

I was loving all this, even pondering on whether to purchase a king-size bed again. A normal double bed barely fitted me by myself, let alone the body of a virile lover alongside.

I reached for my butterscotch, one in each cheek, to drift off to sleep that night. That was my custom by that time, the comfort was unbelievable. When I awoke in the morning, especially if in the night when I evacuated my bladder, I sneaked an extra one on my tongue, the taste was still with me. Total bliss.

But was it my imagination or had it actually become more uncomfortable than it used to be, accommodating my bulk? Just turning in the bed, the heaving of the belly and bum, felt like a major construction job, worthy of a hefty pulley. I needed a pair of strong, young masculine arms to roll me over.

The image of reclining sows rose before my eyes, prodded and poked by a farmer's boy, to prevent straw-sores festering beneath the weight of them. A deeply unpleasant thought with very little to do with me, of course. I heaved myself to a sitting position and waddled out to the kitchen drawer. I needed reinforcements, my under-pillow supply of butterscotch was running low. It wouldn't do to be caught short in the middle of the night.

Then as suddenly as the butterscotch came into my life, it went out.

I'd started writing again, words came rushing into my head. They were single words at first. Emotive words, such as compliance, eliminate, prophecy, skittish, transubstantiate, flagrant, exaltation, corrugation, yarn, archaic, zeal. I can't imagine what a psychiatrist would make of that in terms of associative word-link.

For no reason at all I bought a small spiral-bound notebook to write them down when they came to me, and I carried the notebook with me at all times. Then sentences flooded my brain, obliterating other thought, just for that second. I wrote them down, too. And with them came paragraphs. It was as simple and ludicrously pointless as that, for none of it made any sense to me, not then.

I went, though unwillingly, to the Memorial Service of Jeff Nuttall, a close friend for decades, the poet, jazzman, writer, painter and philosopher I spoke of earlier. An intellectual giant who had made an immense contribution to the progress of that particular world where he'd carved his niche up until his death.

I say that I went unwillingly, in fact I very much wanted to go, but up until then I had not been showing my face at all the many memorial services held for my friends who had died in the past several years. I would have found it too emotional and made my farewells in a more private way. But for this time, for Jeff, I went with my youngest daughter.

We were both asked to give an address, to say a few words, like many others present. It was a riotous send off, just as he would have wished. It took place in the Poets Church at Waterloo. My daughter whispered to me:

'This is the sort of send-off we'll be giving you, Mother.' And she squeezed my arm.

'Thank you, darling.' I was quite moved. It made me feel good. I squeezed her back.

There I met many old friends and aquaintances that I hadn't seen for years, not since giving up on the booze. To them I must have appeared to lead a reclusive existence. But now, meeting them again, I suddenly could see what I had been missing all this time. I had been denying myself this quality of conversation, the warmth, the wisdom and the wit. It beat spots off television with butterscotch, let alone ice-cream. Empty companions in the end.

It was as if Jeff, who understood me so well—there had been such similarities there in his super-high energy and creative output in the past—was giving me a shake-up call.

'For Christ's sake get on with it, girl! Stop pissing around. Where's the writing, what about *the words*, missus. Pull that fucking finger out!' I heard his voice bellowing, loud and clear.

I went to the doctor's clinic around the corner, simply for something to cure a long-running cough. My usual doctor wasn't present that day. There was a female locum instead. As I followed her into her office, I noted with interest how extremely slender, yet shapely she was from the rear. The front, when she turned to face me was just as pleasing, with high and perfect breasts. I couldn't help myself, I had to compliment her, adding that it reminded me of how I used to be.

'And can be again,' she smiled. I was astonished.

'Really?'

'Absolutely.'

I asked her if she could help the process by sending me to an

Obesity Clinic, if such a place would see to someone like me. She burst into laughter. I still don't know just how heavy you have to be to be granted that request. She said she'd set up an appointment for me to see a nutritionist, either that or a dietician.

'The next time I see you, you will be an entirely different shape.' That's what she said, shaking my hand as I left.

From that day, vowing to listen to Jeff and get off my fucking arse and produce a book within the year, I made a study of everything that went into my mouth. Writing, more than painting, had always demanded the utmost energy from me. And this was my main objective now. I would only eat that which gave energy to me, rather than stole (like sugar) energy from me.

I started studying what I put into my mouth the first thing in the morning. I liked eating porridge oats. They keep you regular, as my mother would say.

'Have you "been"? Have you opened those lazy bowels yet?'

Porridge oats produce excellent and regular evacuation of immaculate stools the consistency of firm chocolate mousse, not to put too fine an edge on it. But they also release slow energy throughout the morning and can take you all the way to 2pm, without a single hunger pang. Excellent.

The only drawback to this was that I was finding that within the hour of eating them, I was exhausted enough to want to go back to bed for a little lie-down and I'd already had my full quota of eight hours sleep in the night, and awoken refreshed. The culprits were what I was adding to the porridge. Cow's milk, full cream. Honey, a full teaspoon. And a pinch of seasalt. These three had to go. I replaced the dairy milk, with soya milk. I replaced the honey and salt with a sliced banana. And I saw a difference almost immediately, no more weariness. Better.

Since then I have replaced the soya milk with still mineral

water. Even better.

I cut out all dairy products, having already dumped the milk. Then avoided all other dairy products, every single one of them. All the things which, inexplicably when I ate, seemed to slow me down. Butter, my beloved butter went. Mashed potatoes have not tasted the same since, nor baked potatoes in their jacket, which I used to drown in the golden goo. Cheese had to go, too. We'd had an especial bond for years and years. From student shared cheese on toast days, to the glorious excesses of the finest Port and Stilton end of grand banquets, up in the Highlands of Scotland.

But cheese on the scale that I over-consumed certainly clogged the arteries. So, out, begone! No big deal, though I did miss Welsh Rarebit. Cream had to go. And certainly ice-cream, but I'd knocked that on the head already anyway. Eggs went, no problem. When I was Fashion Editor on the *Sunday Times*, the health correspondence wrote an article suggesting for health reasons that only the white of an egg should be consumed by humans. When asked what they should do with the yolk he suggested feeding it to the cat. There was a national outcry. From animal rights groups.

Bread, the gluten in it, so it was suggested to me, could be the cause of my distended belly. And I'd thought that it was all the other stuff. But apparently, if you are allergic to gluten, the nitrogenous part of the flour of wheat insoluble in water, and many people are without knowing it, the gluten in wheat can blow up your gut and cause swelling. I didn't need heaviness in any part of me anymore. Weight, the carrying of so much superfluous poundage, can prove utterly exhausting. So I dropped bread. It had never been a great favourite of mine, except as something to spread butter on, or rather lather butter on. I did especially enjoy hot buttered toast—now that I do sometimes recall wistfully.

Then came the final test, expelling all sugar from my new regime and here I did experience a struggle. Sugar lifts you as high as the sky, then drops you down in the deepest ditch, wretchedly worn out. That had to go. No messing, seriously.

To my surprise, it wasn't the milk fruit and nut chocolate, the Kit Kats, the Bounties, the Ferrero Rochers, the Toblerones, the Magnum ice-creams, no. It was the innocuous brown things, the Werther's Butterscotch, that wrenched my heart out. The yearning was like being in love, then losing the lover. I had to try to imagine that one. Not a familiar situation for me, of course. Since I was always the one to scarper first, sensing that if I didn't take control of the situation then I would probably end up being dumped myself. Maybe, maybe not.

But this little brown sweetie had got me by the balls. I had to avoid all supermarkets, all food emporiums with boxes of the stuff near the check-outs. That's a mean, low down trick, that one, placing small items, easy to pick up last minute, just by the till.

I knew, understanding about impulse buying, that was the thing to do in our own sweetshops and tobacconists. And it never failed. Just as my mother had ears like gimlets as a customer was on the way out.

'Is that loose change jingling in your trouser pocket?' she would say to the men. 'Well, I think we can relieve you of the weight of it,' waving anything other than what they really wanted, until they gave in and parted with the odd coins.

It took two weeks of intense withdrawals, actual stomach cramps and it seemed a permanent state of awakening depressed, feeling there was something important, no, vital missing from life.

That's what leaving butterscotch sugar behind did for me. I can say in retrospect that it was as bad, if not even worse than the withdrawals from dumping alcohol and nicotine which I did on the same day, so it was a double set of withdrawal then.

But I did it and I've done it all. I have lost well over three stone up to date. Superlatively fine effort, old woman! My life has never felt better. By the time my appointment with the nutritionist came around she couldn't believe my weight loss. The second time I went, she claimed me to be unrecognisable even from the person who had lost that initial weight.

The energy had returned, so she claimed. It was as if a light had been switched on, where before there was shadow. She doesn't need to tell me, I am free of all the garbage at last. The yearnings have gone. By that I mean the cravings. The need, the compulsion, to pour or stuff anything, preferably sweet in my case, anything down the gullet to make oneself feel better.

As for the body, I don't know when and I have no idea if the medical locum is due again in my doctor's clinic. But I would very much like her to see me. I would enjoy the expression on her face. She's the one who started me off, though the whole process from the grandchildrens' ice-cream and the dropping of that to recognition of just what a stranglehold the small brown sweet had on me, to the writing again, so needing the energy, they were all part of the process. Every small piece has a meaning, that's what I love about it all.

We are all completing our own individual jigsaws as we go along. Our completed lives are simply the end product of just that.

When Lord Rothermere was introduced to legendary, world-reknowned artist, Francis Bacon, at an anniversary party for the *Daily Mail* in 1990, he asked:

'And what do you do?'

'I'm an old poof,' answered Francis.

It had slipped the good Lord's memory, but Francis had already distinguished himself as the only guest in living knowlege to have booed, hissed and jeered Royalty offstage, namely Princess Margaret warbling Cole Porter, hopelessly off-key, in Lord and Lady Rothermere's very own ballroom.

The posher the occasion, the more outrageously Francis would behave. This was one aspect of his irresistible personality. That and his ability to slide down and skip well away from his own pedestal.

In this he was neck-and-neck, in tandem, alongside Muriel Belcher, his closest female friend, each choosing as partners those of their own sex. But responding to each other with the strongest link of profound love from the moment they met.

United in this bond of bad behaviour.

Both I regarded as mentors.

Before Muriel died in 1979, she was transferred to the Middlesex Hospital from a private nursing home (financed probably by Francis) following complaints that her behaviour was obscene and uncomfortable.

Jeffrey Bernard and Dan Farson were asked to give an address at her memorial service in St Paul's church, Covent Garden, on the 29th of November. Dan began by saying:

'I cannot imagine a finer opportunity than a service like this to give thanks as we do now for our great good luck in knowing Muriel Belcher, who turned life into a marvellous party.'

Afterwards, Francis left on his own, more ashen and distressed than anybody had ever seen him before.

I was asked to write about my friendship with Francis Bacon by *Time Out*. Now, on re-reading, I find the piece curiously stilted. Whatever I write, nothing could ever recapture the essence of the times we shared. There are no labels for exhilaration.

I met Francis Bacon in the early '70s in The Colony in Soho, shortly after his lover George Dyer had committed suicide. I went to The Colony when I first came to London. The club was owned by Muriel Belcher, a pivotal character in the capital at that time. Muriel attracted free spirits. She was a free spirit herself—a handsome, gay Jewish woman.

She and Francis became instant friends the minute they met in 1948, when she opened that club and he wandered in. She gave him £10 a week and free champagne just to bring in like souls— you know, mirror images of himself.

Lots of people say Francis couldn't draw but I've taught enough people to know drawing doesn't matter. It's the juxtaposition of a colour, a shape, that then induces a response in whoever looks at it. He compared painting to the act of making love—you're there and yet you're not there, and unexpected things happen along the way.

Meeting Francis, I saw immediately a kindred spirit. He was the most charismatic man I had ever met. I have chosen to move among charismatic men—people like George Melly, John Mortimer and Bo Diddley—and I learned about jazz in the arms of Satchmo, for goodness' sake! I would like to have been kissed by Francis Bacon, who was equally attractive to women as he was to men.

I found him to be a fun drinker. Everyone looked up to Francis. He was like a young emperor. He said that if he hadn't been a painter, he would have been a criminal. He would have liked that.

Others have said he would have made a splendid drag queen on stage, a performer, because he did like to get into the fishnet stockings—his father found him at the age of 14 dressed like that. That's when he kicked him out!

Francis did have a sensitive air and a kindness to him, and there was definitely an aura of fun. He always had a sense that in a moment something totally marvellous was going to happen. He never could give a toss what anybody ever thought about him. He was no respecter of rank.

I couldn't wait to get up in the morning to get over to the Colony to be with Francis. It was like lifeblood to me (before I gave up drinking altogether 21 years ago). This was a divine way to spend a day as far as I was concerned. Francis would go from pub to pub, and then from gambling place to gambling place. One evening we were out in Soho at the Golden Lion, which was a gay rent-boy pub, like a gin palace and very wonderful to go into. Francis loved those boys. I loved those delicious boys, too. We walked onto the street, he linked his arm in mine and said to me, 'You'd like to come gambling with me, wouldn't you, Molly?' Well, gambling was for me a totally forbidden area because my great-great grandfather had gambled away our castle in Wales, and the surrounding mountains! I said 'No', and he was astonished.

I didn't go to Soho again, I didn't see Francis again. I left him on the pavement and I went.

It was Muriel Belcher who introduced me to Francis, after she had made me a life member on the spot the first time I visited the Colony.

'You two fucking reprobates should meet each other.' She gave that affectionate, all-encompassing grin. 'A right pair of cunts, the both of you.'

It felt like a blessing, the way she had voiced it.

And we had more in common than the blessing, for Dan Farson and I shared the same literary agent, the blue-stocking, intellectual, Irene Josephy.

Dan adored Francis, with a dog-like devotion, which Francis never ceased to abuse, whilst cherishing the nature of their abiding friendship and being reliant on Dan's loyalty. But this was beneath his dismissive attitude.

On social occasions in the Colony and elsewhere he took delight in humiliating him, bringing Dan to the brink of tears. I saw this often enough, so did Irene. Unafraid, I would fly to the defence of Dan, risking my own cordial relationship with Francis in doing so. We would all be drunk. It was dangerous territory. But then Francis, mercurial to a fault, would change the situation in a flash, with an act of kindness or generosity, which could take your breath away.

He was a bully, there is no glossing over that. With a laser-wit, and an infectious laugh that carried the whole room in its wake.

He would tease and provoke pomposity, charming his way out, wrangling himself free, from social embarassment. He was sure footed socially, in command of every situation.

A masochist in the bedroom, he was certainly sadistic, the other side of the coin, in company, in social situations.

I was there when he aimed his drunken arrow at Jeffery Bernard. This was when Jeffery had been barred from the Colony and was swilling it down daily and by the hour in the Coach and Horses, with Norman, the landlord, writing his exploits up there every week in a column for the *Spectator.* That and Arthur Marshall was everyone's weekly favourite read then.

His pal, Keith Waterhouse, subsequently translated Jeffery's column, *Low Life,* into the hugely successful stage show, *Jeffery Bernard Is Unwell*, the phrase pasted in his space when as we all knew, those pals in the know, that much of the time Jeff missed his deadline, just too pissed to put pen to paper.

Peter O'Toole, emaciated, still handsome, acting on the edge of intoxicated collapse as the role demanded, gave a charismatic and brilliant performance. The play put cash in Jeffery's pockets, but it never sweetened his sour disposition.

I had always given him a wide berth, he could be cutting and cruel and I didn't wish to be on the receiving end. Nor would I put up with his constant hectoring to go to bed with him. Despite his general demeanour and shambling drunkenness he had great success with ladies, which I could never understand. Apparently, in his heyday, he had been a hell of a handsome rake and a formidable lover. Though many of his past conquests had already passed on.

'The drink and Jeffery did them in,' was the phrase.

Jeff cornered me, after I had been filmed in the Coach and

Horses, standing at the bar, reviewing the play, with Jeffery behind me at the bar, uncomfortably within earshot. The filming went without a hitch.

Then Jeffery lunged into me.

'However pleasant I have appeared to be through the decades, I have always resented you even being on this planet. I actually hold you personally responsible for all the very worst aspects of the fucking Sixties. Before you stampeded onto the public arena, stealing the limelight from gentle, feminine, refined role models, women knew their place and how to behave with decorum and dignity. They existed to support men, accepting and respecting them as the superior race, then came you and the other ambitious nightmares like that Aussie cunt Germaine Greer, upsetting the balance, demanding their place in the sun for themselves and their bloody so-called sisters.

'And overnight, or so it seemed, men lost their role and have been floundering ever since. Small wonder that male homosexuality has gained a global hold. Poor sods have taken refuge in their own gender to protect themselves from brilliant, and beautiful ball-breaking heartbreakers such as you, Molly Parkin.

'I've always despised you and everything you stand for!'

The tirade lasted for a full fifteen minutes, maybe more, He had me pinned to the wall. Shouting.

The television camera and crew had left by then and the rest of the pub regulars were astonished at first, then thinking it was a joke between the two of us, turned away. I made my getaway from the malevolent attack. Was scooped up by pals and ended up in the Colony, of course. Usual thing.

News travels fast around the Soho circles. I was greeted warmly by Ian, now enthroned on Muriel's high stool our side of the bar, with his young student friend, Michael Wojas, behind the bar.

They were scandalised by the incident. Francis, my friend and protector, was incandescent with rage. It was always love/hate between Jeffery Bernard and himself.

But he got his own back, when the opportunity arose.

'Tell me, Duckie,' he said loudly, 'what do you plan to do with yourself, now that you've completely lost all of your looks?'

But Jeff came back with his own vicious riposte to the insult.

'Well, I won't be resorting to a face-lift, darling.'

There were plenty present who were unaware that Francis had even had one. It was certainly never dicussed in my presence, but explained his astonishingly youthful appearance given his age and hectic way of life.

I was single again by this time, following my second divorce. And living back in Chelsea, my usual choice of abode.

I was free to spend as much time as I wished in the company of my Colony cronies. Francis was not the same person now, as when we were first introduced all those years ago, after the suicide of his partner, George Dyer.

His mood was lighter, he had met the love of his life, the sweet-dispositioned, street-wise, handsome young East-Ender, John Edwardes.

I liked him immensely, he was such a happy soul. Unhampered by his own inability to either read or write. But his illiteracy made no difference to Francis, who had David Sylvester the art critic on the *Sunday Times*, when I had been fashion editor there, so that we bumped into each other in the corridors. He had him and others for intellectual conversation.

John was in his life to lift his heart. He reminded me of the South London schoolgirls I had taught in Elephant and Castle. So many in the age of secondary modern schooling, still unable to read and write. Heading to the flower-making factory where their mums and grans worked up the Walworth Road. This was when the area was populated by small houses huddled in narrow streets, rank with the detritus of poverty. But brimming with the life and vigour of the underdog. Before being replaced by the hideously isolating nature of tower block building and the mass transportation of families over to Essex.

The end of my drinking days were closing in, taking its toll on my mind and my body. What I admired most amongst other qualities, about Francis, was his dedication to his art and his disciplined working schedule. Up at dawn, straight onto the canvas. All afternoon drinking, every evening gambling, but leaving the Casino when he reached losses of £2,000. More often than not he came away with winnings, sometimes vast, which he would distribute freely to his friends.

Meanwhile the booze was making tragic in-roads into my own creativity, the flame diminishing by the day.

I had an acute and classic case of 'Soho-itis'. Standing at bars, joining the throng talking about the next novel, never writing it. Or the planned exhibition of paintings, which never happened. Me, who had prided myself on my artistic achievements. Soon I would lose the very will to live.

But in the meantime, I had the Colony. I had Dan and Ian Board, and most importantly, I had Francis Bacon, who implanted by example in those crucial years of my own development, the passion of the artist, whether using words or pigment, which though dormant then would resurface and flourish again in my later years.

My loveliest memory of Francis, was to be my last. He had taken my arm and led me down the stairs of the Colony along Dean Street to the hurly-burly interior of the Golden Lion.

'A change of décor, darling,' he'd beamed, as if offering a precious gift. Which it was, for our entry into the crowded pub was greeted with a deluge of eager boys, the prettiest of Soho's gay rent boys. This is where they congregated, where Francis showered them with cash, helping to keep them afloat. They made a beeline for this pub, from every small village and town, from all over the country.

They reminded me of the black-haired and handsome boys from my own valley back home in Wales, with the looks and swagger of youthful Richard Burtons and Tom Jones, and the raw vulnerability of Tony Hopkins. And they pestered me to know if any of my female friends would like to be 'rogered' and could I put any clients their way. They pleasured both sexes, they claimed, if the price was right.

I took their numbers. I knew plenty of women and girls, single, married, divorced or widowed, who would give their veneered eye-teeth to entertain these beauties between their Habitat sheets. But I lost all their numbers on my subsequent drinking binge, to my shame and self-disgust.

Then, when Francis suggested we go gambling, I withdrew. We had gamblers in our family. I had promised myself that I would never allow myself to be drawn in this direction, the final bastion, that and heroin.

I said that I would head back home, Though I was aiming for the Chelsea Arts Club, to continue drinking. It would be the start of my final binge pattern.

Francis, kind and courteous as ever, guided me across the street, hailed my taxi and paid the attractive cabbie in advance, flirtatiously instructing him to take good care of me, then waved me off down Shaftsbury Avenue towards Piccadilly, blowing kisses as he walked away.

We never saw each other again. Within the year—this was 1987—I was in self-help Recovery. And couldn't trust myself to go to Soho for the next 18 years. The lure of the Colony and Francis and Ian Board and Dan Farson, let alone Ronnie Scott's and all those hot jazz giants was too beguiling, like sirens in the night. My self-enforced sobriety, encompassing celibacy, would never have stood a chance.

At 73, my widowed sister took her first lover. She regarded him as her toyboy, since he was 10 years her junior. But she balked at marrying him.

'I don't want to be tied down at my age. Sorry.'

My late brother-in-law had been the only other man in my sister's life. She'd married at 22, a case of love at first sight and a mutual physical attraction which continued until his untimely end. They were together for 46 years. He left her free from financial restraints, with 4 children, 11 grandchildren, a lovely house by the sea, and a comfortable car in the garage. She just doesn't want to be a domestic goddess again. When the lover sought a wife elsewhere, she burst out laughing.

To celebrate her freedom from what could be viewed as a narrow escape, the two of us tootled off to Memphis and New Orleans. We went for a spot of get-right-on-down, kick-your-heels-in-the-air, Cajun dancing. We are Welsh women, mad about music, and head-turning dervishes on any dance floor. We always have been.

I was hardly a domestic goddess. I have never baked a cake, a batch of biscuits, or a serving of scones straight from the oven. I was never a slave to the Sunday Roast, like my grandmother, mother and sister. I'd seen what it did to the female equilibrium, juggling Brussels sprouts, cauliflower, carrots, garden peas, gravy, Yorkshire pudding, mashed potato, roast potatoes, lorded over by a lump of sizzling animal flesh. The sheer stress of producing all these quotients at exactly the same temperature on the table, at precisely 1pm every Sunday, would have been a very real factor in my mother's sojourns at insane asylums. And in my own subsequent vegetarianism.

My pious grandmother approached the procedure as a gentle ritual, a sacrificial offering of nourishment from God. Through her, to those she held dear. Sunday being the Lord's Day of Rest, the actual preparation of the meal would have taken place the day before. All that remained was the lowering of pots and pans onto the luminous castle of coals in the fireplace, flanked each side by cast-iron ovens for the roasting meat and baked rice pudding. Dirty dishes were simply stacked for washing-up the following morning.

Then it was Sunday School in the afternoon, a return to our Tabernacle Welsh Chapel at the bottom of the street where we'd already spent Morning Service and where we would also re-return for Evening Service.

Though I envied the heathens (my Granny's word) bouncing balls, playing hopscotch, running races, squealing excitedly just as if it was a weekday, as I accompanied my serene grandmother in my Sunday best clothes, I wouldn't have changed places, not for a minute.

I loved going to chapel. I could get as close to God there as I could up the very top of our mountain, or down by the river which seperated our mining valley from the mountains opposite, or on my own, deep in the forest where my friends wouldn't go. The heathen friends who didn't have a God to guide them and show them that there's nothing ever to be afraid of. Those friends that my granny didn't know I played with. She believed that like should stick with like, believers with believers. Though I was only seven at this time, when my parents sent me down to escape the London Blitz, I preferred living with my grandparents in the place of my birth. I listened carefully when she spoke gravely of such puzzling things as keeping bad company. Perhaps she did know about me playing with the heathens after all.

Was it really as serious as that?

My sister appeared to take all dometic duties in her stride, even including Sunday roast, but no two siblings could have been more opposite. She, the elder sister by three years, the paragon of virtue. Me, as mischievous as a bag of monkeys, always in trouble. Her school reports read 'pleasant and friendly'. Mine, 'a disruptive influence'. We were both clever girls, with an enviable work ethic. But my sister was a reliable all-rounder. Whilst I excelled with distinction in subjects requiring imagination, I came effortlessly bottom in mathematics. My progress in geography was even more distinguished.

It was suggested that I drop this subject altogether at my grammar school. The staff-member explained to my parents that it was a painful and pointless process all round, for a pupil who had no grasp on reality whatsoever. There was a chronic inability to assimilate fact as fact.

As a seasoned traveller, a veritable globe-trotter, dropped by geography at the age of 12, I can state that it's made not a jot of difference. The plane, the train, the coach, the bus, the taxi, the chauffeur, takes me wherever I want to go in the world. All I have to do is choose the destination. I don't have to know the way.

I wasn't my usual agile self with my sister on the dancefloors of the Deep South. I was weighed down by a womb-tumour the size of a small grapefruit. I had actually taken this trip to Memphis and New Orleans in defiance of the Chelsea and Westminster Hospital consultant.

'Nobody will-cums can-ssah into the hise.' The Prince Charles enunciation had distracted from the solemnity of the sentence. But the glacial scrutiny of the consultant had cauterised symptoms of my sniggery, and the averted glance of the nurse had fuelled the impact of his following words.

'How evagh, it would ap-pare that the dratted scoundrel has effected a stealthy entry here. The safe dimensions for the lining of a mature womb is 4cm. Your uterine scan reveals 18cm. We have an emergency on our hands and must operate promptly. Then we shell just have to craws fingers that the blighter hasn't strolled further, shun't we?'

The effect was of a silent fall of snow flakes in the outer regions of my heart. Cold. So cold. The rest of me, numb.

'I won't be here for any operation this week, not after Thursday, I'm afraid.' It was my own voice surprising me that, though in shock, I still remained capable of speech.

'Yes, I'm off to Memphis and New Orleans with my sister. It's a trip of a lifetime and been booked for ages. Several of my friends have not survived operations in this hospital, splendid though it may be. But the dreaded superbug is still roaming these corridors. I couldn't bear to be greeted at the Pearly Gates, never having experienced the Deep South. I'll be at your disposal on my return.'

I tried a smile, but I wasn't up to it.

The consultant's eyebrows had reached his hairline. The nurse was frowning and shaking her head. Negative reaction.

'I am only away for a fortnight,' I added, sounding like a

schoolgirl in the headmaster's study.

This man detested me. 'Re-schedule, Nuss! A condition this dire is not going to be affected by a fortnight's delaya.'

Two of my sister's children are consultants. The kindest kids on the block, always. Same job, different accent. Sour bastard!

An arctic blink, a nod of dismissal, and I was granted permission to leave.

As I descended in the escalator with a bandaged young woman in a wheelchair, accompanied by a male nurse, my blood began pumping again. The drained sensation gave way to a rising energy as if I was embarking on an adventure, a challenge. I could have climbed my own mountain back in my Welsh valley. I could have run at high speed right to the top and yelled up to God.

'Here I am! See to me, please!'

By the time I'd touched base, outside the hospital on the pavements of Chelsea, my stamping ground for the past 50 spectacular years, that same blood was boiling. Bubbles were bursting in my brain. I could hardly contain myself.

'Bollocks to bastard cancer!' I screamed out loud, really loud, on the busy street, not meaning to at all. These were not tears, were they, streaming down my cheeks.

A startled cyclist struck the pavement. An open sports car sped the pedestrian crossing. Apprehensive shoppers scattered. The Fulham Road shuddered to an infinitessimal standstill as a compassionate crowd gathered.

But where the fuck was the nearest off-licence?

Fifteen years of hard-won sobriety hung in the balance as I pondered which bumper-size bottle to buy. Scotch or champagne? Glenfydich or Bollinger? The answer came clear, unswerving from the depths of my hedonist soul. Buy both. Of course. Why not?

Cash in hand and on my way, doing what I always claimed I'd do if death came close, reclaim my former lifestyle, speed up the process with a smile on my chops and a glass in hand. I was swallowing the first gulp before I'd even reached the store.

But now other images swarmed in my mind. Small faces and trusting fingers of devoted grandchildren who had never seen me ruined, drunk. Daughters reunited with a mother in bonds so profound that it made me emotional to even think of them. A sister restored to resume the carefree fun of childhood times. Nieces and nephews and stalwart friends, and fresh aquaintances. A life free from the stranglehold of conscience. Serene awakenings unsullied by vile after-effects. All the result of putting down the bottle.

The alcohol could never again be an option. Why would I choose to live that chapter of my life all over again, repeating past mistakes?

I side-swerved into Luigi's Delicatessan instead, bought a roasted chicken and bore it home to my vegetarian kitchen, which hadn't seen edible flesh, ever. Then I dumped it unopened into the communal rubbish bins outside.

All I'd been seeking was an act of defiance to delay facing an unfamiliar fear. Fear of danger, fear of death? Surely not that, not after the recent decade spent in India where I had learned that death was to be celebrated. I had joined in enough funerals, following corpses displayed in open coffins through my village, the simple wooden box held high on the shoulders, often simply balanced on bicycle handlebars. The eyes kept closed with the fragile weight of orange marigolds on the lids.

And the joyous chorus of chanting amongst the cheering relatives and laughing children dancing alongside. Helping the ascendancy of the spirit, embracing the radiance of the departed soul from this mortal coil to arrive resplendent in Nirvana.

Where there is faith, there is no fear.

I had started bleeding on my last visit to India. As I was crossing the bedroom in my nightdress, I collapsed to the rush matting on the floor, caught in a spasm of the fiercest pain I had experienced other than childbirth.

I awoke to discover that I had been bleeding all night long, right through the mattress. It had to be burnt. The bleeding continued for the next seven days. I assumed that at 70, I was menstruating again. In fact I made a joke of it to my family on my return to London.

They didn't laugh, insisting that I visit my doctor. She examined me and sent me to the Chelsea and Westminster Hospital for a scan the same morning, resulting in my appointment with the consultant.

I had cancer. Everybody told me that's what it was, the symptoms could not be ignored. But on the trip to America I met enough women, my age and some a lot younger who had been through the same experience and reassured me that it needn't be fatal, not at all.

I had a week before the scheduled operation. On my return to London the letter was waiting for me. I recalled the sect of holy monks whose belief in the healing power of laughter led them to devote an hour each morning on awakening to laughing out loud, non-stop. So, for that week I hired five videos a day, all comedies. I couldn't wait to get up each day.

I began with all the British films that I'd grown up with, beginning with *Whisky Galore* and the Ealing Studio classics. Ending with Woody Allen, Preston Sturges and my favourite film, Hal Ashby's *Harold and Maude*, the love story between an 80-year-old woman and a 17-year-old boy.

My surgeon, a beautiful Asian woman, came to reassure me before and visited me afterwards, eyes glowing. Lying on my back, woozy with the after-effects of anaesthetic, in her long white operating gown, with a white cap on her head, I mistook her for an angel. Had I arrived in Heaven?

'I believe that this tumour is not malignant. You've had it a long time, over 12 years. It was extremely large, like a small grapefruit and the weight had torn the wall of the womb. This was why you bled so heavily in India. But it came away cleanly as I removed it, so I think it's benign. Laboratory tests of the tissue will return in three weeks. Then I think we'll have very good news for you.'

And she did. All benign. No cancer at all.

When I asked her if my laughter regime might have influenced the outcome, she beamed.

'I set great store by the healing power of laughter.'

Now I had other matters on my mind, rather crucial ones. Finances and imminent homelessness. When we returned from New Orleans, there was a pile of post. I waved three of the letters at my sister. Notifications of changes in my senior citizen state pension. Hospital details of my operation. And a charming missive from my editor informing me that my 12-year-old Agony Aunt column was no longer required. They were changing the editorial format of the magazine.

'Old, ill and now unemployed!' I announced. A body-blow to the pride!

I opened a fourth envelope regarding the renewal, with increased rental, of the already astronomical lease on my Chelsea Harbour houseboat.

'Shit! Fuck me, homeless too! Full set!'

The warm width of my sister's grin wipes every slate clean.

'Nice one, well done!' We collapsed into each other's arms, hanging on tight, helpless in the grip of gut-wrenching giggles. Bad news has always had that effect on us.

I never meant to be this vulnerably disorganised in my later years. I had been reared to understand that the most important thing in life is the roof over your head. Always be certain that you have your rent ready, however threadbare and hungry you may be.

But on my first trip to India, I rode a camel called Daisy over the deserts of Rajastan. Falling asleep on the sand under stars so close you could touch them, so brilliant they'd burn your fingertips, I awoke to a sky-roof as pale as pearls.

Afloat in the Arctic, perilously negotiating fluorescent-blue icebergs, the skies were transparent as tapwater. The sensation was of gliding through outer space.

In Egypt, the tangerine sunsets altered the Nile green to ochre. A Grand Canyon dawn ignites the spirit until the soul and the soil become one.

This is as much roof as anyone would wish for.

My gypsy blood could relate to the concept. This blood comes from the maternal grandfather who taught me how to embrace the spirit of mountains before I'd ever begun to paint them. But I also come from a family saturated in poverty-thinking where owning property was all.

My maternal grandmother's crew had bankruptcy as a Karmic companion, alighting like a vulture through the generations. One ancestor had even managed to lose our family castle (a 14th century roof) and miles of mountain, as far as the eye could see. That was more than careless, that was certifiable.

My own bankruptcy, now years ago, only lost me my beloved

mountain cottage back in my own birthplace. But the pain of loss was as keen. Then, not now.

Now I shrug it all away. Money. Easy come. Easy go.

I've had over 50 homes in my adult years. I am unable to comprehend the concept of 'settling down'. I am a bird of passage, I embrace migration. I am as happy on one perch as another, that's all they mean to me now, properties.

In just a few weeks, at the end of October, my sister and I will be on our Autumn Caribbean Jazz Cruise. The ports of call include Georgetown (Grand Cayman), Roaran (Bay Island), Belize City (Belize), and Cozumel (Mexico).

We are delirious at the prospect of Mexico, which I have always saved for the pudding-stage. Mexico represents the ideal dessert if you regard life as a meal. But Mexico combined with floating on oceans, jazz dawn to dawn, can only be a holiday conceived in heaven.

Especially when, at the end of it, we will be met off the liner in the Port of Miami by my soul-sister, Barbara Hulanicki. We'll be staying with her in her plush, swim-pool, South Beach apartment.

And how lucky am I?

My sister is treating me to this trip, she's picking up the tabs. She's the wealthiest of the two of us now. It's taken a huge gulp of humility to accept this generosity. My entire family, including her, accuse me of pride, and it is pride, false pride. They say I should practice graceful acceptance, pointing out that they have done just that over many years in the past when I flung my money in all directions.

'I don't like feeling the poor relation,' I whine.

The countence of self pity is not a beguiling sight.

Nevertheless, I am the poor relation, only in comparison to my sister however. Everything is relative, as I discovered last year when I went to Scotland to paint on the Isle of Skye. What mists and mellowness. What mythic mysteries. The Isle of Skye should be made compulsory for all as a glimpse of unearthly earthly beauty.

I stayed in a tiny waterside hamlet known as Plockton. That is where I was fated to meet the first of two young singers, 18 and 19. The refugee sisters from Azerbaijan (between Russia and Turkey, I'm informed). The ones who are coming around to sing to me this afternoon.

I live in Sheltered Accommodation on a Council Estate, in Chelsea's Kings Road. It is called The World's End Estate. My American son-in-law claims that this address wouldn't be allowed in the States, being too down-beat. But he said that in the aftermath of 9/11.

When I visit the Post Office to collect my weekly income support, proof of penury, I scuttle round a back way to avoid the King's Road if I'm in a rush. I have a history in The Borough of Kensington and Chelsea. Everybody knows me even if I don't recognise all of them.

Male strangers approach with a particular twinkle, ripe to remind me of whatever.

'Were we intimate?' I cut to the jugular. There is a theory that if you can remember anything of the Sixties, it's proof positive that you were never there.

It can take an hour to buy bread, waylaid by friends and old acquaintances. Just like village life back home in Wales. But this end of the King's Road remains the village that the whole of Chelsea used to be.

Small community businesses still flourish. The fish and chip shop. The bicycle outlet. The antique treasure trove. The florist. The butchers. The bakery. The corner pub. The nursery school. The doctor and dental surgeries. The second-hand bookshop. The Mona Lisa Café, providing scrumptious nourishment far into the night, from dawn. A truly democratic haven with a mixed clientele from long-distance lorry drivers, Chelsea Football Club supporters, to the sons, daughters and parents of the privileged classes, battling addictions in nearby Recovery Groups.

There's also Vivienne Westwood's first boutique at the corner of World's End. And Keith at Smile, the sixties hairdresser, where the famous still have their hair done. Marianne Faithful, Michael Parkinson, Marc Almond, Me, to mention a few.

But the conglomerates have captured from Sloane Square to our end and stamped out the character. The kiss of death, that renders uniformity to every High Street in the country. Marks and Spencer. Sainsburys food. Gap clothes. Russell and Bromley shoes. Habitat furniture. Building Societies. Banks. Boots the Chemist. Orange Mobile Phones.

My youngest daughter battled bureaucracy when I went to hospital. She established income support immediately, with no difficulty.

'What do you mean, your mother has suddenly become unemployed? She shouldn't be working at her age, anyway. At 70 she was lucky to have been in any job at all!'

Where does such dismissive scorn come from, such contemptuous undervaluation of upper age groups?

Frank Lloyd Wright started to design the Guggenheim Museum at 88, and lived to see it completed when he was 90.

A South Korean performed over 600 full pull-ups, at 69.

Sir George Sholti conducted Beethoven's Choral Symphony in 1996, at 85.

Bertrand Russell wrote *Human Society in Ethics and Politics* at 82.

A golfer recently shot a hole in one at 87.

One in five of 65 year olds and over are learning computer skills. The next most popular subjects are business and administration.

There are 20 million people in the European Union over 50, which is one in three of the population and two out of five voters.

Though the income support proved simple, the housing was more complicated. I was commanded to present myself to the Homeless Desk at Kensington and Chelsea Town Hall. The experience knocked any lingering grandiosity on the head. My old geography teacher would have chuckled. Here, once and for all time I was face to face with reality, forced to accept fact as fact. It was the ultimate lesson in humility.

Mine was the only white face in the hall, apart from the clerks behind the desks. This was not a new experience for me, many times on my travels in market places and teeming thoroughways I would be the sole representative of my race, and welcomed as such. But these were refugees in urgent need of shelter, aliens, scared, alone in this country. Small families with children huddled around their knees. The silent air was thick with misery.

Now I was humbled, now I felt out of place. What the hell was I doing here? How had this happened? Mine had been a life of rackety splendour, raffish in the extreme. Was this my punishment, issued with a ticket, queuing, cap in hand to officialdom? Taking a space from those who needed it more than me? My grandmother's warning flashed through my mind.

Could my choice of dubious company have brought me to my knees? Would it all have been better if I had stuck with the Believers?

Then another thought followed. It reminded me that I had chosen the path of Bohemia from the very start. I'd moved amongst artists, painters, writers, poets, actors, actresses all my life. As a clever woman I could have been top of the corporate ladder by now. Chair-person of I.C.A., as long as it didn't involve mathematics. A Speaker in the House of Commons, I have the gift of the gab. Senior in the Civil Service, with all the bollocks of an O.B.E., except that I didn't want to move amongst such a boring set of conventional cunts.

Homelessness. Penury. These come with the territory in the exhalted province of High Bohemia, where Art is for Art's sake. True paucity means lack of imagination, the inabilty to create, to communicate ideas, to spread the word, to maintain the balance and fan the flame.

Now I could accept that I had as much right to be here as everyone else. With a relaxed mind I was free to investigate this situation, to take a hard look around.

When had these fellow humans around me last seen a friendly face? Not in this country by the look of them, not in these intimidating surroundings. I turned to my right and tickled that baby under the chin, smiling at the other children and the parents. I did the same on the other side of me, then in front, and behind. Then introduced all to each other, as best I could, within the restriction of language.

This was the gift that I had learned in my chapel. When I left I blew kisses in every direction, they waved me out. I was glad that I was wearing scarlet and crimson, top to toe that morning. I'd revived the life-blood of a room, dumb with despair. I had been brought to the place for a reason.

I left however, seething inside. I was so unsettled by my own treatment at the hands of the clerks that I could have been run over just crossing the road. I looked neither to the left nor the right of Kensington High Street. I saluted both former sites of the famed BIBA emporiums, created by Barbara Hulanicki, my soul-sister.

I'd been passed from one inscrutable official to another, male to male, then to female. They all addressed me in the same way. It was as if I'd committed a crime. I suppose that dealing with human dross on a daily basis must finally get up a person's nose. Theirs were held high in the air as they looked at me. Constant exposure to suffering can create an immunity.

Had I ever cared how many hearts I had broken, how many marriages I'd wrecked? Did I even cast another glance over my retreating shoulder as another discarded victim lay slain, sobbing in the boudoir?

The cruelty was coming my way now. Granny approved of the morality of my bedtime book, *The Water Babies*, by Charles Kingsley. Do as you would be done by.

My spirits lowered as I looked at and listened to the female clerk. The face of authority has always made me queasy. My clothes were too colourful for her. I was wearing lipstick. My Elizabeth Taylor-as-Cleopatra general appearance was grossly inappropriate to the occasion. A travesty in fact. She'd got me by the ghoolies.

'We are placing our homeless either in King's Cross or the East End of London.' She said it without raising her eyes from my notes.

'Your colleague has just told me that I should be in Sheltered Accommodation.'

'So you should at your age. But there is none available. You'll be going to a Bed and Breakfast until there is.'

She studied a list, then looked straight at me. I wished she hadn't. This woman could do with a shag. I could see no likelihood of her gettting one in the foreseeable future. 'From this list it looks like you'll be in King's Cross.'

My seething had started. 'And if one should come up in Chelsea—a Sheltered Accommodation? I've always lived in Chelsea,' I added, lamely. Shit, how pathetic did that sound!

'Well, you obviously wouldn't be eligible for that. In King's Cross, you would no longer be our concern. You'll be in a different borough.'

'Thank you very much. You've been so, so helpful.' I was gushing now, the bile was biting my throat.

But on the bus home I had time to put everything in its perspective. King's bloody Cross need not be that bad. My head said to turn it all around.

King's Cross was almost Bloomsbury, that was Virginia Woolf and Vita, and all that lot. They must have left something in the ether.

King's Cross was within spitting distance of the best Art Suppliers in this country, Cornellisson, despite Green and Stone on the King's Road being my favourite. And I had never fully explored the British Museum. That could be utterly enthralling, something to keep me going until the end of my life, certainly well into my 90s.

Friends and family were ringing already when I got back to see how I had got on. Enough of these had offered me homes, but the response of the first one I talked to made me see that I didn't have to necessarily even stay put in London, let alone Chelsea. He offered me a cottage on his property back in Wales. On the glorious Gower Coast, an unfamiliar landscape for me, so used to my valley.

I promised that I'd consider it seriously, but that I'd let him know soon, very soon. Nothing would happen immediately, they'd said at the Town Hall. I decided to clear my head, accept the offer of a trip to Cornwall, to my niece's caravan on a Cornish cliff.

The first of my miracles was about to happen for me, but not before I had embarked on another miracle for someone else.

It has been my experience that we are all linked, all part of each other, that in saving other people we are saving ourselves. Few would allow another person to drown in front of their eyes, for instance. Our natural human instinct is rescue, and protection of our own species. Unless it all collapses and then we are at war.

We are truly blessed when there are people within our own family who are in every way on our own wavelength. I have been thus gifted with my sister's eldest child. She is my god-daughter, the name alone is sacred to me and strengthens the profound link between us, for I have given natural birth to beloved daughters of my own. But the link with the Welsh for Wisdom, is on another plane.

Her caravan is sky blue. At certain angles, viewed against the sky, the two merge as one. And the sky here above the beach is always blue on this stretch of the Cornish coast. Blue on arrival and blue on departure.

The sensation of running down the sandy track and straight into the ocean, before the sun has even shown its face, is otherworldly. I stand, not shivering at all in the cold light of dawn.

My swimsuit is already on, matching my towelling robe, several shades darker only than the caravan-blue. There is nobody about, not even early dog-walkers, and this is just the way I like to swim. All alone in a deserted sea-scape.

I step over the frills of spume and seaweed, until I am out of my depth, then dive straight into the approaching wave. There is no hesitation. I've always done that whatever the temperature, whatever the time of year. I organised the daily swim every day throughout the calendar when I lived near Land's End with my children and one of my husbands.

I have never dithered at the edge of anything in my entire life. I like to jump into the deep end, whatever the consequences. It's more than spontaneity. It's the knowing that everything always turns out for the best in the end, so why not just get on with it while you can, while the opportunity is there.

In recovery lingo, it's listed as Acceptance.

Since it is high tide now and there is a dramatic drop in the sloping sand here, I take care not to swim too far out from the shore. These are unfamiliar waters for me and if the tide is on the turn, I can get caught in treacherous currents. There is nobody around at this hour to hear cries for help.

But this will not happen, of course. I'm too cautious. I have too much respect for the sea. Many summer visitors drown, ignoring red flags around the Cornish coastline. The death-toll where we used to live was especially high on precisely the beach, the surfers' beach, where I led the swimming club. We ourselves took the precaution to be linked by ropes to each other in the howling gales of winter, when the wind factor was so intense that it was warmer under the water than above.

'You'se mad, you am.'

'Bloody lunatics an' tha's gorra be a sure fact!'

'In the water, all weathers, with snow on the groun' an' all! Where's the point innit, for gawd's sake?'

The locals had their say.

Impossible to explain, no point in even attempting to fathom the lure of the ocean. Ask a sailor why he goes to sea.

Treading water, surveying the slope of the opposite shore, I await the arrival of the sun. Embarking on sunrises in whatever medium, watercolour, oils, acrylic, pastels, inks, I give a wash over the entire surface first. The first the merest hint of tint, then a swift build-up. Rose Madder. Naples Yellow. Chrome Orange. Cadmium Red. Crimson Lake and Vermilion. You don't have to be an artist to be transported by colour. The tiniest tot picks the brightest toy in the box.

When the sun's rim appears over the horizon, I am transfixed, submerged to my chin in seawater. Tears blind my eyes as the entire orb arises, my heart is about to burst in exhaltation. The setting sun sets off the same rapture. Each signal the start and end of another cycle. The sunrise filled with promise and hope. The sunset sealing the conclusion of disappointment or despair.

All we have to do is to adapt ourselves to the rhythm.

On my return to London, I sat listening to the many messages on my telephone, sorting the post as I did so. One official leaflet informed me that as a senior citizen, placed now on the homeless list for Chelsea, I qualified to apply for a Sheltered Accommodation apartment on the World's End Estate in Chelsea, which had suddenly become vacant. The application list would be closed at midnight on the very day I was reading this.

What timing! Maybe it was meant to be.

I rang the office, nobody answered. But a recorded voice told me that I could leave my details if I was applying for the Sheltered

Accommodation. I did precisely that, and promptly put it out of mind, certain that I hadn't a cat-in-hell's chance of hearing anything further. Such is my faith in bureaucracy these days.

Instead I occupied myself by organising a complete clearance of my studio by getting rid of practically all my belongings before taking the train down to the Gower Coast, accepting the offer of the cottage from my painter friend.

But actually getting rid of the unnecessary, this proved more difficult than I had begun to imagine. The easy part came first. I invited family first to take their pick, and then friends. Daughters, four grandchildren, great friends staggered away, black plastic bags crammed with the skimmed detritus from a life spent in high fashion.

And still there was a mountain left behind. None of it would fit in with the remote ocean-bound artist's life I imagined for myself now. Where would I be going to wear all this exquisite stuff anyway? I'd long since relegated television appearances to a past existence, I had no interest in night clubs and parties anymore.

Manolo Blahnik stillettos, David Shilling millinery, Andrew Logan jewellery, BIBA specials exclusively designed as stage wear for me by Barbara Hulanicki. All gifts over the decades from these very dearest of pals. Art Deco bangles and brooches and dangling earrings, delights from Butler and Wilson, when the two of them were still together back in the 'sixties and 'seventies. Silk counterpanes from India, pottery from Cornwall, masses of my own paintings dating back to the 'fifties. Hand-crafted leather boots from Venice. Fine lawn embroidered blouses from Switzerland. Carvings from Iceland. Kaftans from Egypt. Straw sunhats from Spain. Tibetan cloaks from Portobello Road. Wigs, long, short, curly, straight, blonde, black, chestnut. All from Selfridges' spectacular Wig Bar, some from Shepherd's Bush

Market. Hosiery, sheer, fishnet, and opaque in every colour imaginable from Harvey Nichols. Brassieres from Rigby and Peller (Corsetieres by Royal Commission) reflecting fluctuating weight loss and gain throughout the decades. Swimwear from Harrods. Cashmere cableknit cardigans, and cobweb shawls from Liberty's. Stout walking brogues and open-toed sandals from The Natural Shoe Store.

And drawers full of make up, reflecting a singular lack of brand loyalty. Lancôme. Revlon. Mac. Helena Rubenstein. Elizabeth Arden. Molton Brown. Nars. Yardley. Chanel.

Lipsticks. Gloss Wands. Lip Pencils. Lip Colour Gel. Lip Conditioners. Eye Shadow. Eye Liner. Eye Black. Eye Lash Mascara. Eye Drops. Under Eye Shadow Concealer. Eyebrow Plucker. Eyebrow Brush. Skin Night Cream. Skin Day Cream. Skin Moisturizer. Skin Cleanser. Skin Tinted Foundation. Skin Powder, Transluscent. Skin Powder, Matt. Skin Powder, Irridiscent. Cheek Rouge Powder. Cheek Rouge Cream. Cheek Rouge Gel.

And all the Perfumes from Arabia, so it would seem. Enough to keep the Sultans of over a dozen harems in a permanent swoon.

What the hell had I ever needed this much junk for anyway? And why on earth had I hung onto it all for as long as this?

Then, when I thought hard, it hadn't been that long. I'd had regular and necessary clear-outs on a regular basis over the years, moving from one to the other of my adult 52 homes. But I'd been in this Chelsea studio for over 12 years now. Can one single person accumulate this much dross in just this time? Yes! Well it all had to go. I was on the start of a different life now where none of this had any purpose.

I left a message with the automated answer phones for both Oxfam and also the Salavation Army Charity lines, expecting to hear back, at least within the week. No response from either ever came.

I took the suggestion of a friend and leafed through the Yellow Pages and dialled several House Clearance numbers. Two arrived hot on the other's heels. One said he'd charge £500 to clear the lot immediately, darlin'. The other said, £400 in a fortnight, missus.

I exploded, 'Fuck that for a lark!' to both of them, and sent them packing.

Emerging from the Post Office on the King's Road, having cashed my weekly old age pension, and pondering whether I could afford a coffee and cake in the Starbucks opposite and deciding I couldn't, I let my feet take me where they wanted to go. I do that quite often these days. My brains have a way of ending up in my heels.

They turned left and I found myself in the Cancer Research Charity shop. I felt an affinity there as soon as I stepped inside. My recent escape from cancer should be rewarded in any way possible, I thought. This was the right place for all my stuff. So I approached the counter.

'I'd like to donate many things,' then I stressed, 'many things. At least one lorry load, but it needs collection.'

A really beautiful human being with shiny, black, shoulder-length curls and burning brown eyes stepped forward.

'I'm the manager,' he introduced himself, with a Christ-like smile. 'And where are these donations?'

I explained that they were around the corner, one street away and that I planned to leave London for Wales within the week, so the clearance needed doing right away. Within moments we were walking towards the studio. He told me that he knew who I was, that he recognised me and had wanted to thank me for the many years of vast enjoyment that my comic-erotic novels had given his girlfriend and himself during their youthful sex life.

'How very kind,' I'd replied. 'I'm glad to have been of service.' It felt a good omen.

Everything had gone by the next evening, my studio was empty and ready to hand over. Now I could relax, spending time with my family before my departure. The two youngest grandchildren were taking it hard. Tears in the eye stuff, but putting on brave faces. They clung tightly, saying goodbyes. Even the older teenagers spoke with gruff voices.

Other grandparents always know what I mean when I speak of the strange hold grandchildren have on the heart. It's a more powerful bond than one would ever expect, the bountiful bonus of life's later years.

I had one last clear day left in London before moving away the following morning on the train to Wales. I was looking forward to it now everything had gone. Others on the spiritual path have related their own tales of relinquishing all, that at one time they had considered the essentials to happiness. The heady sense of freedom and yes, of strength and relief in walking away from all the material possessions and importance of ownership. The houses, cars, boats, planes, and high-flying careers. Less emotional to ease away from these than from loving relationships, especially those with children.

I was sitting in the garden, pondering on this very situation regarding me and my next of kin, when the telephone rang. It stopped before I could reach it. I played the message that had been left for me. It informed me that I was on the shortlist of three for the Sheltered Accommodation on the World's End Estate, Chelsea.

I rang back immediately. The line was engaged. I replaced the telephone and timing it, rang ten minutes later, having put in a prayer. 'God be with me, thy will not mine.'

A cosy Welsh voice answered. She told me that, yes, I was one of the final three chosen for the advertised apartment.

'But what about all the others? There must have been loads of applications for Sheltered Accommodation like that on the Kings Road?' My astonishment was boundless, that I should be in the final three, but I still didn't believe I had a chance of getting this place.

'The others applicants have died, my dear.'

'What, all of them in such a short time?'

'That's how it is for the elderly and infirm, love. And of course, many of these senior citizens can't actually get to the viewing, for being in the grip of chronic weakness and debilitating disease. Or permanently wheelchair-bound, of course. So can we expect to see you there, tomorrow morning around 11am?'

'Well, I'm not so certain about that. I was planning to leave London for good and return to Wales.'

'Why on earth would you do that? You got family in London, haven't you? Grandchildren and all.'

She'd hit on a raw nerve there and she knew it. 'And how are they taking it then, their gran going off and leaving them? They must be experiencing some sense of abandonment, if I know anything about children.'

Now I was positively tearful myself.

'Trust me, it's worth viewing, this flat. You won't regret it, just a peep.'

'Garden?' I asked, cautiously. 'I do like growing things.'

'Beautiful garden, looking onto the communal gardens. But all the Sheltered Accommodations on that ground floor have their own private garden, one for each tenant.'

'Now you've got me really interested. The only thing is that these things go on a point system, I know, it was explained to me when I put my name down. I'm sure that I don't have enough points to qualify and I don't want to put myself through the disappointment of loving the place and not being eligible in the end. I think I'd rather not see it at all, thank you anyway.'

She was not to be put off. 'I'll check to see how many points you have. Hold on a moment.' She returned to the telephone. 'Well, you have more points than the lady from Iran. And more points than the bachelor from Sloane Square. So if you like the flat and want to move in tomorrow I can put the keys in your hands in the morning, and help you sign all the forms so everything is over and done with.'

I couldn't honestly believe that this was actually the flat on offer when I went to see it the next morning. Firstly it was on the stretch of Kings Road which had always been my favourite, which still had the character that had drawn Whistler and Turner and all those other artists to the Thames, just around the corner. Secondly, this period of architecture, the sixties, was one I liked most. Open plan, with glass panels to all the interior doors for greater light throughout.

I had expressed doubts about the white walls. I told her I liked living in colour, Mexican colour at that. She said it was no problem, the flat if I decided on it, was mine to do what I liked with, for life. That's what she said.

'Until you die in it, dear.' Is how delicately she put it, in case I hadn't got the full message. I was surprised how comforted those words made me feel, to tell the truth, after a gypsy lifetime of pillar-to-post. No more worries about a roof over my head any more, then. Whew, more than relief. Fuckin' euphoria! A truly kept woman now. Kept by the State, by entire committees of men, stamping my documents with seals of approval. In place of one possesive man at a time, stamping in petulance. How good was this!

She called me into the kitchen and asked me if I'd decided. I nodded and said I had, that I loved it to pieces and couldn't believe my luck. Then I hugged her, I felt so emotional.

She crushed the keys in my hands and sat down with me and we filled the forms in together. Within twenty minutes it was all over, the flat was mine.

I had some telephoning to do about my change of plan. The first call was to the Cancer Research Charity. That very afternoon they returned the barest essentials like the bed, table and chair, some crockery and cutlery, the kettle and a saucepan. All the luxury stuff went into auction and sold in the shop; they made a small fortune to the delight of the gorgeous manager.

Interviewing me, a journalist had suggested, not getting the point, that the small fortune could have come to me. Why give it all away?

'Easy come, easy go,' I'd shrugged.

I was ecstatic in my new home. The grandchildren rushed over to see me, loving the place, too. Both daughters gave it the seal of approval, most importantly. My sister did too, up on the train from Wales specially.

'Everyone was exceedingly happy,' as they say on the telly in the Mr Kipling cake ads, or words to that effect.

First you have to give away, before you receive. That seemed to be the lesson learned from this exercise. That and the swallowing of pride.

This party is in Belgravia, just about the swankiest spot, if you had to choose, according to the girl who is taking me. She's American and her absent parents used to be very rich and are trying to get rich again in the West Indies. The aunt she's staying with in London has promised them she'll do her bit and is keen for her to meet up with the best people, socially speaking. And the richest, it goes without saying.

I'm not the best people, by no means am I the best, socially speaking. And I'm certainly not rich, quite the opposite. But I am a remarkably beautiful, eighteen-year-old virgin, innocent, yet with a sultry intensity. Virgins do possess an air of suppressed and smouldering passion. Whereas girls who are experiencing sex regularly, lack the aura of heat that we virgins exude.

My English teacher at school told me every bit of that, when he kept me back after school. He said I was to study the Brontës to comprehend his full meaning.

He chuckled and put an avancular arm around my shoulder. 'That's my theory anyway.' Then he tried to stroke my nearest breast in my regulation school uniform. I felt sorry for him. He was an excellent teacher and unhappy at home, with a wife who hadn't given him sex in years, so the girls said. But then he started stroking the other breast, explaining that he simply couldn't keep his hands off me and hoped that I didn't mind too much.

'I don't want you to get into trouble, Sir,' I said, removing his fingers from my gymslip. 'I have too much respect for you as a person.'

I'd seen that in a Jean Simmons film, and already used it more than once. It worked. He covered his face with trembling hands, shamed.

'But I will study the Brontës, Sir.' And I did and could see exactly what he meant. As a chapel girl I'd like to remain a virgin until I meet the right person. I'll recognise him on sight. It's as simple as that, God will guide me. He has up until now.

The American girl and I liked each other immediately, in a setting where the best people actually do go to eat, around St James, a stone's throw from the Royal Family in Buckingham Palace. How much grander than that can you get?

I would like to have been able to tell my mother about this little encounter of mine so far, but that would have been unthinkable. As it was she had been nervous about me leaving them down in Brighton, where we now lived (on shop premises, as per usual).

I was spending the summer months up in London since leaving Goldsmiths' Art College before continuing the same course in Brighton Art School. But part of the curriculum was the study of the Masters; I needed the London Galleries for that.

One of my Goldsmith tutors had shown great interest in my talent, deploring the fact that I was leaving due to my father's negligence in applying for the next year's London County Council scholarship award. This tutor had offered me work as a studio assistant in his own studio. The payment was good. I would live as part of the family.

But now they had all gone over to Brittany, that's where they were at present on a painting trip, the wife being a fellow artist. They had left me in charge; they trusted me and quite rightly, and had paid me in advance, making certain that I wasn't in need. There was plenty of work still to do, sorting and storing canvasses and drawings in dated chronological order. Refiling the library of art books, stacking on the recently constructed new shelves, the biography of artists section. I loved the work so far and hadn't even begun on the tubes of oil paint and re-cleaning and scraping pallettes. The smell alone, made me swoon with pleasurable excitement. One day, I think to myself, I shall have a proper studio like this, just for me to work in on my own, no sharing as most artists have to do, for financial reasons.

I hadn't told my mother that the tutor and his family were away in Brittany, but there was no way that she would find out that I was in London all on my own. Nor had I told her that I'd already been paid in advance. I'd handed over my first week's money already to her.

But now they needed more. It would be my father's petty gambling debts, I guessed that, though my mother hadn't said anything about it. That and the drinking in the Seven Stars every night now, with Cliff, the Welsh owner. They had both taken a real taste for the local cider, Scrumpy, or Merrydown Cider, to give it the proper name.

'It's made from apples, it's not alcohol,' my mother had explained to me. She must think I'm a half-wit. I'd watched enough students in London get out of their heads on the stuff. Apples indeed. Yes, right.

I don't drink. I hate the stuff, the thought of losing control scares me rigid. I am very mature for my age. I have had to grow up quickly, I'm not a normal 18-year-old. I read newspapers and magazines, I devour films and books. I like to be in possession of facts, when it comes to human nature. I intend to move amongst interesting people who will be able to impart more knowlege to me. I want to widen my scope, but absolutely not in the sexual sense. That much must be made clear as soon as I start moving amongst these people. I have a sense that it will be before too long, now.

Since leaving my grammar school and becoming an art student I have been overwhelmed by attention from the opposite sex. My thick black hair is past my shoulders now and I sweep it to the side, instead of wearing the long fringe dangling into my eyes. But it falls over my cheeks, I suppose in a seductive manner. I have a straight back and an extremely small waist but my breasts are as full as ripe melons. I think they are the culprits. If you have curves where they should be you will never be ignored. But my face is the main thing and my cloud of hair, and my cat's eyes. Pale as gooseberries. The Elizabeth Taylor look.

We met in the Ladies, the American girl and I. We were by far the youngest females in the place, certainly the most desirable. We were both dining with gents, elderly ones. She at one side of the room, me at the other. They were not our grandfathers, but they were in that age-bracket. Except hers was a family member, a distant great-uncle wheeled out by her aunt. Mine was a sugar-daddy. At least that was what I was hoping he would turn out to be.

Sugar-daddies are men of a certain age, even of advanced years, like the one I'm dining with tonight. They become interested in young women, the younger the better really, particularly the inexperienced, once they themselves find their sexual powers are on the wane. I've read all this.

They will always have their place in society. It's a fair exchange really. Firstly there's the redistribution of wealth. Sugar-daddies have made their mark in the world. They are established in their professions. They are usually married, with families, even those of the second and third generation, for whom they generously provide. In addition to providing monentary 'treats' for young girls of slender means. Girls like me.

There doesn't necessarily have to be any sexual activity involved, that is the attraction all round. Otherwise that could be construed as a form of prostitution. In my case it would be a tragic waste of my further education. If I was meant to go in that direction I could have left school at fourteen, without staying on and working hard for all my excellent qualifications. Matriculation Distinctions in both English subjects. English Language and English Literature. And of course, Distinction in Art. That goes without saying.

My father would have preferred this of course, me being put on the meat-market at that tender age. Had my mother died from her many ailments, or destroyed herself by taking her own life, as she was to try doing so many times in later years, then I would most certainly have been launched into prostitution by my father. It's not at all unusual for sexually abused children. The logical step in many ways.

The sugar-daddies' wives are normally caught up in works of charity, or they are a part of a circle of women who adore nothing more than getting together at every available opportunity, just as schoolgirls do. They go to the theatre together, the opera, the races, to Ascot and Henley. They like to travel. Some even get the India bug and become spiritual zealots.

There is scant room on the active agenda for sex, unless it takes the form of an extra-marital affair. Then the get-togethers with female friends become more fervent, more frequent. They too, following the lead of the first, may embark on mostly unsuitable couplings. The chauffeur gets lucky. The family solicitor's clerk. That likeable ski instructor. The gorgeous hunk at the golf club. The masseur, the hairdresser, the dressmaker's brother, their own son's best friend, their own husband's business partner, or cousin, or brother. No holes barred.

'It doesn't feel like a betrayal. I still adore my husband to pieces. We are each other's best friend and always will be. There is not even the teeniest chance that I would ever leave him. I mean, all I want is for him to be happy. And, who knows, he may have some nice little mistress tucked out of sight somewhere, may have had her for years. Who am I to complain, as long as it doesn't intrude on our beautiful life together, on me and the family? And as long as I don't know, of course. I'd much rather be kept in the dark. I don't tell him about Pablo, after all. Yes, I'm seeing him now, the new chef from the Mexican restaurant. Didn't I tell you? He's divine! Such stamina.'

I was hoping that I'd struck lucky this evening, that my dining companion would be the sugar-daddy that I could certainly do with, because my parents were in dire financial straits again and had taken me aside on this last visit, this weekend, begging me to 'help out just this last time, promise, we won't turn to you again'. I needed ready cash but had no notion of how to get it, other than standing on a street corner, which I'd promised myself would never be an option. I was too special for that.

But things weren't going the way I'd hoped. This old codger had just confessed over the brandy, that he believed, quite honestly, that he was actually falling in love with me. That he couldn't stop looking at me. That he suspected I would even enter his dreams. Though we'd only just met earlier this evening, alighting from the Brighton train at Victoria Station. He from First Class, me from Third.

'May I offer you a lift, may I drop you somewhere?' He'd lifted his eyebrows and his hat at the same time.

He seemed dazzled, that's the right word, dazzled at the sight of me. I wasn't even wearing my gladrags. But the jumper that my mother had knitted for my birthday, which she insisted I wear up on the journey from Brighton, was a size smaller than it should have been. She'd run short on wool and it showed every inch of me, especially my nipples. They were standing free of me now, like baby's dummys, due to the cold, and my extreme hunger. So I must admit that I did welcome his next words.

'Better still, I say, would you care for a bite to eat? Would you agree to dine with a lonely old fossil, lovely young lady?'

It's never a good sign when men, whatever age, start babbling on about love. Because what comes with love is respect. And that's where the fun ends and everything gets serious. My spirits were sinking, I had the sixth sense inherited from my grandfather, the one with the gypsy blood, that this meal was never going to end up as hard cash.

The American girl at the other side of the restaurant was smiling and beckoning to me to set off for the party in Belgravia. The time had come to see just where this sweet old gent actually stood. I jumped in at the deep end, interrupting his declaration of love at first sight.

'It's not that I don't like you, because I honestly do. I find you very interesting and I could sit here all night hearing all about your experiences. It's a learning experience for me, listening to the elderly. I did it all the time with my grandparents. But that nice girl over there, the one smiling at us, the one with her uncle, she has invited me to a party in Belgravia and I really want to go. It's full of young people, would you mind terribly?'

'I love young people. Shall we leave right away?' He pushed back his chair, all alacrity. I'd never seen such an instant change in anybody. It was as if I'd given him an injection of instant vitality fluid.

And before I could protest and explain that he had got the wrong end of the stick and that he hadn't been invited to the Belgravia party, only me, he was striding over the room between the tables.

I trailed behind. The party would be off now, that was for sure. I'd be boarding the bus back to Chelsea and getting an early-ish night, ready to work at clearing and re-organising the studio in the morning.

Nothing of the kind. Arriving at the table the two old gents took a second look at each other, falling back in amazement.

'I say, Nobby! It can't be!'

'Tadpole, it never is!'

They'd been pals at Harrow together, a hundred years before. So all four of us trooped over to the Belgravia party, arriving in splendour (now this my mother would have adored) in Nobby's Daimler, with liveried chauffeur.

Nobby was the American girl's uncle, I liked him immediately, even before seeing the car which had been waiting outside the restaurant all the time. And he obviously responded to me, and that was no surprise.

The American girl took to my Tadpole, now he couldn't take his eyes off her, doubtless it was she who'd be haunting his dreams that night. Not me. But I didn't mind, not a jot.

Nobby had taken my hand and was rubbing it between his own two, as a pretence of keeping it warm. Now and again he would lift it to his lips. And we'd look at each other, as if we were on the brink of falling in love. We'd smile in the way people do when they know that there are going to be lots and lots of good times ahead.

It was a new and overwhelming sensation for me. It may have been the company, the lighthearted occasion. Or, and I have to be completely honest, it might have been a shamefully venal, and blatantly materialistic reason. I have to be honest with myself, because that's how I always want to be now. I have kept one appalling secret all through my childhood and I have vowed that I will never do that ever again. Be secretive, I mean.

So, being completely honest, it could have been the Daimler, for I certainly had never, ever ridden in a chauffeured limousine before in my life. I'd barely ever even been in a taxi. But it was much, much more than that.

I was fascinated by the ease with which these two old friends spoke to each other, and their genuine affection. Their beautifully modified tones, their cut-glass accents, the elegant way they wore their clothes, their haircuts, the clean, freshly laundered aroma of them. And the gleam of their polished shoes. I responded to the fastidiousness, the belief that it was important to present as pleasurable an image to the rest of the world as it was possible to do.

There were always two older British actors who exemplified relaxed privilege to me, the sort of men that I would have liked to have in my life. And those two reminded me of Nobby and Tadpole. The ridiculous schoolboy jape-names were all part of that.

The actors' names were A.E. Matthews and Alistair Sims. I was immensely drawn to their affable jocularity, and their tweedy style. Their misleading air of absent-mindedness, masking brains and wit as sharp as the keenest minds. These were men who would always see to it that you were all right, who would take care of you for as long as you wanted them to, without being posssesive and jealous and suspicious. They had too much going on in their own lives for that. They had been effortlessly popular since as far back as they could remember.

I decided there and then, as the car rolled so smoothly along Eaton Square, that I would come clean right away. The moment seemed to have presented itself, as it does when things are going as you would wish it to. Pretty soon we would be arriving, according to Nobby.

'Almost there, my beautiful child,' he had just whispered into my hair. Thank goodness I had washed it that very afternoon, was my first thought. Then, I'm not your child, I'd thought fiercely. I am on a mission here tonight. I need funds to relieve me of family financial problems. What suggestions has anyone got?

These were my teeming thoughts. I took courage in both hands. I said it all aloud.

They all burst out laughing, perhaps they were drunk. I was the only one who had not drunk alcohol in the restaurant. I didn't realise then, because I had never met these sort of people before, that men like Nobby and Tadpole actually carry rolls of notes, hard cash, on them at all times. Just in case, I suppose, a situation like this should arise.

Nobby kissed me on the cheek and patted my head. 'Well, we certainly cannot have this spoiling our evening.' He thrust a bundle of notes, what they were I couldn't tell until later, into my hands. 'This should see to any family financial embarrassment, I trust. Now, let's sail ahead and enjoy ourselves. The night is still young, eh what!'

So could life really be as simple as this? Ask and ye shall receive?

Resorting to the lingo from early British films of the Jack Hulbert variety, we all had an absolutely 'spiffing' time, even on the ride over to the party. Nobby and Tadpole had a lot of catching up to do. As it happened they were both friends of the host's father, anyway. There was a good chance that he'd be there. He was, another school chum from Harrow. His name was Billy Boy Brumleigh.

The interior of the Belgravia mansion was like a film set, like a scene from the film *Grand Hotel*, with Garbo and John Barrymore, and Joan Crawford playing the role of a slinky secretary. I'd been taken to a special screening of this at Streatham Library, by a regular customer of ours who ran the Classic Film Society there. It's not the sort of film that you can see in the ordinary cinemas any more. And it had stayed in my mind. The utter luxury, the dramatic lighting which highlighted the silver and gold and rich damson velvets, whilst throwing deep shadows beneath inlaid ebony and across richly patterned carpets.

And now here I was stepping straight into the same shimmering setting. I would never have imagined that people could live like this. But, of course, these were not ordinary people. Their tastes were refined by generations of breeding and an abundance of wealth.

The American girl nudged and winked at me as we were ushered in by a butler, though if her parents had been so rich at one time, she must have become used to this style by now. But Americans don't do it like this, so she explained to me later. And in any case the money had disappeared by the time she would have been old enough to appreciate it.

'I could sure get a taste for it now,' she chuckled. I remained silent. So could I.

'Hey,' she continued, she was quite irrepressible, 'I didn't know, you didn't tell me that your old gent was in fact a Lord.'

A Lord! Good lord! How would I have known? He didn't tell me either. Now that really would have been something to tell my mother, if only I ever could.

I had changed from my too-tight knitted jumper, in the lavatory at Victoria Station, before accepting the dinner invitation to the restaurant. I had felt slightly crumpled and creased but those had smoothed out by now so I didn't look out of place at all. Though my old gent had seemed disappointed, he claimed to have fallen as much in love with my tight jumper as me. Well done, mother!

I was wearing an antique crepe-chiffon dress that I'd found, browsing in amongst all the old antique shops down in The Lanes. It was hanging up between an ancient bugle and a slightly tarnished set of copper saucepans. Much of it was hidden by a ceramic bed warmer on a long oak handle.

You can get real finds in The Lanes. If you were on the look out for interesting people, you could do worse than linger around that area, the collectors come from all over the world. And are as friendly as friendly once they realise you are an actual resident of Brighton. Especially if you are an art student already, and going to be going to the Art School there.

They tell me how very much I look like Elizabeth Taylor, the movie star and give me their cards, men as well as women, with their addresses on and telephone numbers, begging me to get in touch when I happen to be visiting their countries. America. Austria. Venice. Switzerland.

I accept and smile sweetly, not to be thought rude, then I throw all the cards away when I get around the corner, as if I'd ever be able to afford that kind of travel in my lifetime. But now here I am in the most luxurious surrounding I could ever have imagined. Pigs can fly and elephants dance. Why shouldn't I lead the most splendiferous life in the world?

If that is what God has in mind for me.

The dress is a rich peacock blue, with inset swirling panels of deep sea green. It was designed and handmade in the 'thirties and I liked to think that it hadn't seen any more wear than the especial occasion it was made for. But that the person wearing this piece of absolute poetry had a really magical time in it.

I'd bought it this weekend with my own money given to me by the tutor, before he'd left for Brittany. And had hidden it from my mother who would have questioned as to how I could have afforded such a very exquisite thing. Though it wasn't expensive, things aren't in The Lanes, yet. Though in years to come, everything becomes exhorbitant. You'd need to be a millionaire to even enter the impressive emporiums.

It is extraordinary just how many doors youth and sheer beauty can open for a girl. For a boy now, too, I imagine since homosexuality is no longer taboo. That evening will always remain in my brain, in my blood, in my bones, as the beginning of the realisation of my female power. It wasn't simply the exquisite robe and what it did for my green eyes and my pallor. It was as if I so connected with the beauty of my surrounding that I became a natural part of it.

I had absorbed the essence, if that's the appropriate word. I was in the right place, with the right people. I was utterly in my element amongst other human beings in a social situation, for the very first time in my life.

But, by no stretch of the imagination the last.

My poverty-thinking was always with me. The sense that there was never enough. Never enough of anything. Toys to be played with. Books to be read. Children to be friends with. Hours in the day. Sugar for the tea. Material for the frock. Wool for the jumper. Never enough money for the fare, for the cinema, for food, for rent, for clothes, for holidays, for paints, for canvases, for drink. The hole in me could never be filled, there simply wasn't enough of anything and everything, to top up the hole and put a lid on it.

I assumed that everybody felt this way until I became acquainted with the wider world. To my utter astonishment I discovered that far from being the norm, I was meeting many more people, most in truth, who were perfectly content with their lot in life, however small their achievements and reduced their incomes, than the malcontents like me who were never satisfied.

My father's favourite joke was on the back of a box of matches.

First tramp to another. 'Money talks.' Second tramp replies. 'All it's ever said to me is "goodbye".'

He carried the box in the breast pocket of every suit he ever wore and would produce it as a talking point when conversations fell flat. It was a daunting experience to hear the matchbox philosophy reeled out over the years, I wanted to snatch it out of his hands, stamp my shoe on it and shout:

'Get a new matchbox!'

Failure can be contagious. I felt this very strongly indeed. It is as if failure has an abominable odour all of its own. A toxic stench which can damage the lungs and calcify the brain. My father's failure filled me with contempt and more, a loathing for the self-pity that comes with failure. I vowed that it would never happen to me, ever, ever.

I began toiling at the age of nine, earning cash with my mother and sister, as outworkers for a firm making clothing for dolls. I had a greater enthusiasm for this home assembly-line machining than did my sister. She presided as the little lady of the house. I much preferred the chosen role of skivvy. But I liked to regard her as the queen bee and me as the worker, getting things done, putting cash in the communal kitty.

I was the one who made the deliveries and collected more work, riding back and forth to the factory on my bicycle. It wasn't even a full-size bike that one, yet. Sometimes I would be the only one on the road, because the air-raid sirens had sounded and people had vacated their cars and other means of transport and run to the underground shelters as the public were instructed to do. I didn't care.

I was thinking of the money in my coat-pocket and how if I machined through the night whilst my family was asleep, I could go and return with more work and collect more money the following day. I was already the favourite and the speediest outworker at the factory, and by far, far, the youngest.

They made me promise not to tell any of the teachers at school, otherwise they would be penalised for employing child-labour. They all spoke with foreign accents and gave me sweets, which I ate all by myself on the way home and said nothing to anyone.

If the air-raid sirens went again to warn of more bombs on the way, I'd start singing to myself as loud as I could, especially when the bombs began dropping. But they were never near enough to hurl me off my bike and dirty up the merchandise. I made quite sure of that, I could have lost money that way. I was never scared, never. I knew God was keeping an eye open on my behalf. I trusted him with my life. I reasoned that if he had given it to me it was still his to look after, until I reached adulthood.

My next job, and this was a seriously good payer, this one, was at the age of eleven. My first evening paper-round for the busy newsagent at the top of the street. But it was scuppered in the first week by my kindly grandfather who had come to live with us in London after the death of my Granny.

He caught me at it, still delivering at eight in the evening, with more than half the round to go, in the dark. He put his foot down and said he would prefer to give me the money as pocket money, if the family was this hard-up that they had to send their youngest child out to work at the age of eleven. My parents ought to be ashamed of themselves, he said. And that was the end of the matter.

We had him to thank for the roof over our heads. He had a perfect right to express his opinion, according to my mother, and we owed it to him to pay him the respect that he was due and act accordingly. I had to hand in my notice. The first time I'd ever done that, and just about the only time, except when I left my first teaching job to get married.

Every Fashion Editorship job I had along Fleet Street, three to be exact, I'd had the sack from and was foolhardy enough to walk away without compensation from two of them, but not the third. I'd learnt by then. Before that I had preferred to toss my head in a huff, and mince away on my high heels, my nose in the air. Looking very high glamour. Very film-starrish, I chose to believe.

'It is better to have a permanent income than to be fascinating.' Oscar Wilde.

I loved earning money, I could say that I was addicted to it really from the very start. But I never liked being offered it for nothing, from the opposite sex. Because my mother said from the very beginning, as a warning against men, really, her way of saying to be careful what you get yourself into: 'There is nothing for nothing, remember!'

I think that was why I avoided all the wealthy men who were always falling in love with me, trying to force gifts upon me. I wasn't interested in their jewels, their offers of houses, their money. I wanted to earn my own, otherwise there was no challenge, no sense of achievement or self-worth. The chapel teaches you that.

If I had accepted all the benefits that my appearance put my way I would have been merely another beautiful girl making mileage out of her looks. There was much, much, more to me than that. I told those men to look elsewhere, that I was not for sale. One of those men had the audacity to scold me, saying that I was a ridiculous girl, sitting on a goldmine, picking daisies. He was referring to my genitals, I believe. I walked away without comment. I considered it beneath my dignity.

At the time of my bankruptcy, some forty years later, I recalled his blunt words. But by then the gold in the mine was tarnished, the entrance obscured by cobwebs. There weren't even daisies to pick. I laughed. Foolish me, he'd had a point.

I set about earning money and spent that money immediately to show that I was a person with a fine and enviable earning capacity. There was plenty more where that came from. I really did think that the supply of funds was inexhaustible, if you were willing to work for it.

Throughout the passing years until her death my anorexic, poverty-minded mother would telephone me. Her opening lines were always the same.

'How's the weight? How's the money?' Always in that order. If my reaction was laughter, her response was severe.

'These are not laughing matters, these are serious issues. Are you putting on weight, and have you enough money? These are the basics.'

'Both are fine. No, I'm not putting on weight. And no, I'm not short of money.'

And I never was. I was a good earner, I made sure of that. But I was a good spender, too. For me cash was too hot to handle, I couldn't get rid of it fast enough.

I was keen on property from the very start. I couldn't wait to buy my first house. My mother warned to make certain it carried a freehold, a better investment by far. This instinct for owning property I inherited from the females in the family. From my grandmother who ended up owning half of her street and my mother who had a keen eye for businesses with living accommodation, sabotaged inevitably of course by my gambling, gloom-merchant father. I have had fifty-two homes in my adult years. Some I have bought, others I have rented. I like to be on the move, that's the gypsy blood. I have rarely taken an abode which has already been furnished. I like an empty cave, a canvas on which I can stamp my own individual personality.

I lose track of the second-hand outlets, the furniture stores, the design studios, the auctions, the market stalls, that I have scoured picking up tables, chairs, sofas, beds, wardrobes, chest-of-drawers, carpets, rugs, linoleum, cork tiles, rush matting, curtains, window nets, window blinds, kitchen equipment, knives, spoons, forks, frying pans, saucepans, toasters, whisks, tin-openers, garlic-presses, liquidisers, lemon-squeezers, washing machines, Hoovers, gas stoves, electric stoves, electric heaters, blankets, pillows, towels, sheets, cushions, television sets, videos, DVDs, children's bunkbeds, garden equipment, deckchairs, recliners, spades, forks, pruners, secateurs, sundials.

And how many homes did I leave, with the bulk of this detritus in it for the next occupant, because I like to make a fresh start wherever I go?

I am staggered by this list even as I write it. No wonder I went arse over tit, financially speaking. This is evidence of an extravagant lifestyle. It wasn't how I was brought up, when if we made a move we took everything with us, not to have to spend on replacements. And much of our stuff around the place was even handed down from our grandmother's home. My parents didn't even fork out for their own, they couldn't afford it.

And I suppose that is the normal way. But I have never been normal. Perhaps I was a foundling, except I have my father's mouth and my mother's eerie eyes and her colour sense. And his feeling for the Arts.

I made a lot of money, a lot, from selling paintings in the past. And I made as much, maybe more, from my ten novels and my four or five other books. One volume of poetry, another a compilation of journalism, a cookery book. Oh, yes, and my autobiography. I raked it in too, from countless television appearances, and lucrative journalism. And from my magazine Agony Aunt column.

So how did I come adrift and end up a bankrupt? Simply bad management on my behalf. I got greedy, acquisitive. I was like Elizabeth Taylor, I needed more and more. But it was never enough.

It wasn't sufficient to enjoy living in Chelsea in a splendid location, I had to have an artist's studio around the corner as well. Then I thought it would be fun to rent a boat on the Thames, because I'd never lived on water in an actual houseboat. I took trips to India to meditate in the Ashram. I travelled as far and wide as it was possible to travel. Egypt, up the Nile just to see exactly how green it was. The Grand Canyon, and whilst that close, why not pop over to Las Vegas. And whirl off to Memphis, and Nashville to the Grand Ole Oprey. And tootle up, closer to home, to the Highlands of Scotland and take in the Isle of Skye.

And then why not do what I always in my heart wanted to do. Settle back where I was born, back down in my own Welsh Valley as a prize for my old age, since seventy would be my next major birthday celebration. So I bought the first cottage I walked into on my favourite mountain. And a massive king-size bed for my lover to share, if he happened to be passing.

My Granny's house, my own birthplace, was close-as-close for comfort and to trigger the flooding memories. For now that I was sober and capable of holding onto thoughts, and had been sober then for well over a decade.

The immaculate plan was to settle back into writing novels again, and painting Welsh landscapes, to pay for all this and to catch up with and eradicate the pile-up of back-tax. Except that now the Muse had other ideas. I found it impossible to write a word, a sentence, anything. Or to paint. I was as creatively blocked as my father had ever been. My critical view of him began to relent. I could feel the torture he must have undergone, but there were other aspects of life on the mountain on offer now. And I recalled that he had spent all his time up there, when he should have been searching for jobs in the valley. He chose the release that was offered now to me, as well. So we two were more similar than I had ever imagined.

Every morning before dawn, whatever the weather, I seemed to be drawn by the mountain itself with a force that could not be denied. I was up early enough for the sunrise, tears blurring my sight, my heart somersaulting, my throat constricted. The sheer beauty was almost unbearable. I roamed and ran and hurled myself, arms outstretched, absorbing everything. I remained throughout the days, I stayed long enough for the sunsets. The same emotions reproduced a second time. It felt like a healing.

The force pulled me to the very top and tugged me over the slope, down the other side. So I peered into other valleys, pondering all the while on how bloody amazing this mountain was. I never once saw a single soul. The air was so thin it was barely there. The clouds so low you could take a bite. And I got carried away, completely and mindlessly transported. I never wanted to leave.

No experience can compare with the purity of those daily sojourns to the skies from my cottage on the side of my mountain. It was as if generations of Celts were calling to me, communicating through the sheep-shorn soil, responding to my footprints, letting me know that they had been there and that I was one of them. I had made my own imprint, I belonged to my tribe. All was pure. All was poetic.

It was so poetic that I couldn't quite explain it in words to the Official Receiver, at my bankruptcy in Cardiff. I had the feeling as keenly as anything, that he might find it all a load of codswollop. But I truly had meant to write and paint up a storm, and profit accordingly, as I was so used to doing in the past, and effortlessly, too. Instead of which I had chosen to commune with nature.

I was declared bankrupt and lost the cottage anyway. It's impossible to describe, and not how I intended to respond, but it was as if they had presented me with the freedom of the city. The mountain has been there since time immemorial and is still there. It costs nothing, ascension. Ownership is not an essential. That's the lesson I have learnt.

I am a happier and wiser person now. The normal would have phrased that sadder and wiser. But I'm not normal. It took me some time to adapt to my humiliation, to get used to living without credit cards, and a bank account. But it's been ages now, and I haven't had a single debt in that time, nor do I plan to ever again. I live happily within my means, like most of the population. Or maybe they don't, credit cards can fuck a lot of people up, they can lull you into a false sense of security, as I found to my cost.

I have learned my lesson well. My extravagance has evaporated. The thrill of making money, to accumulate for its own sake, has lost its allure. I can walk through a department store, pass a market stall, even a charity shop, and pass on without spending a bean. The shopping bug has ceased to bite.

Once I was fettered by my desire to possess, to own everything, to hug the lot to my chest, thinking, 'this is all mine and nobody can take it away from me'. But since then I have given away to charity more than I could ever own again in my lifetime. I am unfettered and free as a bird on my mountain, I have no attachment to anything of a material nature.

I am a rolling stone now. I gather no moss.

The Elizabethan Age

Born February 3, 1932. Me.
Born February 27, 1932. Elizabeth Taylor.

If my heavily pregnant mother had not skidded on my Auntie Lizzie's scullery lino there was every certainty that Hollywood's Golden Age Goddess and I would have begun life as actual Astral Twins.

Astral Twins are those born on the same day, in the same year, whose lives mirror each other's from thenceforth. Even if they never meet face to face, aspects of their lives are startlingly similar. And their appearances are uncannily alike.

Jolted unexpectedly out of the uterus I arrived a fortnight earlier than expected, due to the chronic incontinence of at least seven of my Auntie's seventeen cats.

The feline excrement demanded regular suds, which weren't quite dry the morning my mother dropped in.

It was the dramatic outcome of this crucial visit which

complicated the future, planned by Fate for myself and Elizabeth Taylor as Astral Twins.

<u>Similarities survived</u>
Both beautiful, high-achieving, talented, foul-mouthed, alcoholic, over-eating, artistic, fag-hag, sex-sirens.
<u>Differences surfaced</u>
I became an Aquarian. She remained a Pisces.
<u>Two 20th Century Icons</u>
Me—National. Elizabeth Taylor—International
Me, a Bankrupt. Elizabeth Taylor, a Billionairess

We were fated never to meet, face to similar face.

I first became aware of my alter-ago in 1944, when we were both twelve. The presentation took place in suitably awesome surroundings, in a palace, a marble edifice based on the Hollywood notion of Babylon.

The gala opening of this, the celebrated State Cinema, on Kilburn High Road in suburban London, was one of the most glamorous public occasions of the last century. Presided over by Royalty, by the Queen Mother Mary herself, roped in pearls and robed in satin, with her trademark towering turban crowning the permanent waves, she could have stepped straight from a Cecil B DeMille extravaganza.

The unemployed masses waiting outside went wild with delight. On the brink of the Second World War, this show of opulence was just what they needed. Escapism was the opiate for their misery. With this in mind, the city architects and municipal town planners were to be congratulated on a cynical success.

Few high streets in the whole of Britain then could compare with the depression-inducing squalor and dinginess of Kilburn.

Even worse than that was Willesden High Road, along which I had to cycle to school, twice daily counting there and back. It could bring me to the brink of suicide, hurling repeated prayers to heaven as I negotiated heavy traffic.

'Please God, don't force me to live in these surroundings for the rest of my life. I promise to be good if you switch the scenery soon.' But at least Kilburn High Road had the marbled emporium, State Cinema. Little did I realise what was about to be further revealed.

The first film in which I saw Elizabeth Taylor fleetingly perform was *Jane Eyre*, adapted from the book of the same name by Charlotte Bronte, which I'd already known at school. The real reason I'd gone was to see my favourite child star, also my age, Peggy Ann Garner, who plays Jane Eyre as a child. She was an extraordinarily sensitive actress with a small pointed face, a tiny mouth and a pair of burning brown eyes, open windows to her soul. It was difficult to see anyone else on the screen when she was there. She had a quality of truth and integrity about her, a shyness and a courage which fitted in well with my own chapel background. If I'd ever thought about becoming a performer she was the kind of actress, intense and honest, that I would have wanted to be.

I'd already seen her in *A Tree Grows in Brooklyn*, about a girl who finds her aim in life early on, like me. She wants to be a writer. I identified with her utterly because I already knew that I would be a writer and also a painter, there was no doubt in my mind from the earliest age.

I could also empathise with the role she played in which she is forced to face the harsh truth about the alcoholic father she had once idolised, and the weary neurosis of the mother who has to run the household on her own. I intended sending a letter to the

Fox Studio in Hollywood to be forwarded to Peggy Ann Garner and maybe ask if we could become pen-pals. I felt that we had that much in common. Until I set eyes upon Elizabeth Taylor.

There is much written about the electrifying effect that a single face can have upon millions; however brief the glimpse, that is all it need be. Faces such as Garbo, Crawford, Deitrich, Bergman, both Hepburns—Katherine and Audrey—Ava Gardner, Grace Kelly, Lana Turner. These are imprinted on screen history.

But my life changed seeing Elizabeth Taylor's face for the first time in dissolve after brief dissolve as Helen Burns, the doomed childhood friend of Jane Eyre on her deathbed.

No film appearance, for she was on for mere moments, has affected me as much before or since. I left the cinema in a daze, spending my first sleepless night summoning her up, then falling into dense dreams in which she played close-up camera shots. The black and white camera work delineated every structure of her brow, her cheekbone, her chin. The lightness of the eyes, the depth of the socket, the darkness of the hair against the pallor of the flawless skin. I was literally spellbound by her beauty.

I didn't want to write to her. I didn't want her as my friend. I didn't even want to watch her in films that I knew without being told were certainly not worthy of her, and there were enough of those after the quality production of Jane Eyre and before her incandescent performance as the tragic heroine of *A Place in the Sun*.

All that I needed to know was that she was in the world. This creation of otherwordly beauty. I hugged the knowledge to myself. It was my secret, my worship at her shrine. The following weeks, months, years even, I was sent in disgrace from so many schoolrooms for lack of concentration. From thinking of her. Had I been male, I would most certainly have married her. Getting there from South Wales, well ahead of Burton, for sure.

In Peggy Ann Garner I felt I had found a friend. In Elizabeth Taylor it felt more like the holy grail. Certainly as pretentious as that. And why? I have never fathomed it out, still can't or don't. I'm free of it now. But at twelve the journey had only just begun. At that time I hadn't really known what love felt like. To be transported out of your own body by worship of somebody else, expecting and asking for nothing in return. A selfless love.

My love of God wasn't like that. I was asking for everything all the time from God. My love for my grandmother and both grandfathers wasn't like that. I was more relaxed and happpier with them down in Wales, than I was anywhere else or with anybody else. Because I felt loved. They asked me to do things for them now they were older and frailer than me, that I did without question.

My mother and father didn't love me and because of that I didn't feel love for them. My father had loved me once, he'd made that perfectly clear with his physical demands. Then the beatings came, with fear and hatred. Now there was complete indifference to me.

My mother would have loved me if she had not been so disturbed. She would have found it difficult, impossible to love anyone when her demons were in residence. My sister, who I hadn't known until she returned to live with us at the age of five, I had yet to grow to love.

But Elizabeth lifted my heart straight out of my body. When she smiled tenderly at Jane Eyre in her dying scene, she seemed to be smiling straight at me. The connection had been made.

It is said that when a person occupies your thoughts to the exclusion of all others, as with people in love, then the person can come eventually to resemble the object of their high regard.

And thus it was with Elizabeth Taylor and myself. It would take a further six years, until I was actually apprehended in the street by strangers shyly asking for the autograph, convinced that I was Elizabeth herself.

I came into this world as a completely bald baby. For the first two years of my life my mother would be complimented on having such a beautiful little boy. I had no hair to speak of, only an imposing dome of a forehead which I choose to cover to this day. The complex is still there.

'Hide that ugly forehead, quick, before anyone sees. You'll never catch a man, never get a husband, with that on display. Men don't want to marry a girl with brains.' A high brow being a sure indication of extra intelligence, according to an old wives' tale. My mother advised wearing hats, or growing a lengthy fringe to conceal it. I took her advice and am seldom seen without either ever since, though I certainly have no need of a husband.

When the hair started growing it didn't stop. The colour was flaxen, a charming combination of top-of-the milk and a field of ripe corn. But by the time I went to primary school and had become interested in having Peggy Ann Garner as a pen-pal, my hair was the same colour as hers. A muted mouse brown.

When I was stopped in the streets of Brighton for Elizabeth Taylor's autograph, by a homely American couple from Denver, I signed it obligingly. It seemed churlish not to. They've probably handed it down in the family as some kind of heirloom, framed and hanging on the wall, with the attention of visitors drawn to it, with pride.

My colouring, by this time, was inexplicably the same as my idol's without any artificial help along the way. Indeed a few years previous to this, visiting my own Welsh valley, a one-time neighbour of my late grandparents had stopped me in the Co-op. 'Why is your mother allowing you to use hair dye? You never were this dark, I've known you from a baby. How old are you now, not yet fifteen?'

At the advent of the autograph hunters, I was nineteen. Global adulation for Elizabeth Taylor was higher than it had ever been, due to the spectacular reviews and box office takings for her latest film, *A Place in the Sun*. Added to which the national newspapers were full of her presence in Britain, and her current romance with the English actor, our top hearthrob, Michael Wilding. The fever was enflamed by the fact that these two were to be married. Which they were, on February 21, 1952, in Caxton Registry Hall, Westminster. There was a twenty-year difference between them. He was 39, she was 19. In six days time it would be her 20th birthday. I had just had mine, being a fortnight ahead of her.

Elizabeth Taylor was by this time the top American film star, with Clark Gable and Errol Flynn the hottest male stars in Hollywood.

She had already been in two films before *Jane Eyre* to fleeting effect. *There's One Born Every Minute*, released by Universal in 1943. And *Lassie Come Home*, released by MGM, also in 1943. After *Jane Eyre*, she played a blink-and-you-miss-her character, listed in the cast as Betsy at age 10, in *White Cliffs of Dover*, released by MGM in 1944.

But the smash hit of her career, catapulting her to immediate stardom, was her next film, *National Velvet*, released by MGM in 1944. Had this been the first film I ever saw of Elizabeth Taylor's I would never have been trapped in my life-long obsession. She would never have enflamed my imagination and caught my artist's eye for beauty as she did in the black and white photography of *Jane Eyre*.

National Velvet is shot in glorious technicolor, of course. The art director was the legendary Cedric Gibbons; the director, the estimable Clarence Brown. Both men served their diminutive leading lady brilliantly.

One setting the violet eyes and raven hair against sumptuous blue skies, emerald fields and the rich interiors of a chestnut stallion against stable hues, worthy of Rembrandt.

The other coaxing a performance so finely honed, so unervingly taut with hope and longing, bordering on barely withheld youthful hysteria, that it reminded you of the finest musician playing a violin concerto.

Audiences were understandably spellbound. I was rooting for the character, Velvet Brown, to win the Grand National; who wouldn't be? But when I emerged from the cinema I wasn't walking on air. The film was over, I was curiously deflated and brought back to earth.

And of course, now I had to share Elizabeth Taylor with the entire world. She wasn't just mine, not any more.

I didn't go to see her next eight films, most pot-boiling nonentities, not worthy of her. In any case most were not even released in Britain. It was obvious that her studio simply didn't know what to do with this incandescent young star. The quality of material was missing in the choices they made for her. But her mother was the ambition behind the girl and she pushed relentlessly.

Glancing down the list, it is truly amazing just how many films she made at such a tender age, one after the other. Nine feature films from 1946 to 1950, that is a hell of a work-load in four years! Child labour of the most intensive kind, an outrageous exploitation. Where was the childhood? Non-existent. I very much doubt if this pressure would be permitted today, not in any civilised country.

Courage of Lassie, released by MGM in 1946. *Life With Father*, released by Warner Brothers in 1947. *Cynthia*, released by MGM in 1947. *A Date With Judy*, released by MGM in 1948. *Julia Misbehaves*, released by MGM in 1948.

I did see *Little Women*, released by MGM in 1949. But I hated what they'd done to Elizabeth in it. All painted up and posing and pouty in a blonde wig. And, for once, she was wiped off the screen by another young actress. June Allyson was a spirited Jo, in the lead. I would have much preferred to have watched what Elizabeth might have done with that feisty part, instead of the self-absorbed Amy.

Conspirator, released by MGM in 1950. *The Big Hangover*, released by MGM in 1950.

Then came *Father of the Bride*, released by MGM in 1950. Hooray! Now we were back in business. This was directed by Vincente Minnelli, one of Judy Garland's husbands and father of Liza Minnelli. He was the director who had made Judy look so beautiful in *Meet Me In St Louis*, and also in *The Pirate*. Thereby earning her eternal gratitude, since she had an erroneous belief that she was so plain, compared to the other beauties in the MGM school room, such as Lana Turner and Elizabeth, of course.

But in *Father of the Bride*, Elizabeth Taylor took a giant leap up and away from the legacy, even millstone, of *National Velvet*. Few thought she could better that film or move forward, but this proved it and placed her firmly as a contemporary girl of her generation. Once again, she was brilliantly enhanced by Cedric Gibbons as her Art Director.

And Minnelli directed her marvellously. The quivering chin, the break in her voice, the humourless intensity, the swooning on the telephone, the yearning in the eyes, all this was the accurate portrayal of an adorable, yet pain-in-the-arse, teenager in the first ecstatic throes of falling in love.

The bewilderment of her family, especially the father, immaculately played by Spencer Tracy, was caught perfectly. He realises with mounting panic that this infatuation may actually be the real thing. That there is a very real probability looming that, as father of the bride, he will be expected to foot a hefty bill he can ill-afford.

The end of the film is ravishing. The audience, including me, leaves with a lump in the throat as father and daughter express their mutual devotion. Then the bride leaves for honeymoon and a new life with another, younger man.

Elizabeth's own father had long since withdrawn from his family and her. His relationship with his daughter was strained and distant. Just like mine with my father. I thought how amazing it must be to have a father like the one in that film. To be able to sit on his lap, ruffle his hair, exchange innocent embraces, have him enter your bedroom and sit on the end of your bed just exchanging pleasantries. Nothing more ominous than that. And more, to bring him any trouble, to share woes and joys.

I was an art student by this time, on a state scholarship. The degree course I had embarked upon would stretch over five years. I would emerge a qualified Artist, with a qualification to teach in schools and colleges of Art. My mother had fought for this right on my behalf. She was the driving force behind me, in the same capacity as Elizabeth Taylor's mother, Sara Sothern Taylor.

They had more than that in common, too. My mother had been and still was a beauty, with talent. Sara Sothern had been an aclaimed actress who had relinquished her career on marriage. My mother was a musician, a fine one, who had been the chapel organist. She also ceased this work when she married my father. Both were slender and loved fine fabrics and fashionable clothes, and appreciated the finer things in life. There was a snobbish element there, a desire for social elevation, which would be possible through their younger child.

Each shared a preoccupation with bodily functions, particularly their own bowels and saw no reason not to include the details of such in polite company. Indeed, at a celebratory dinner for the engagement between Elizabeth Taylor and Nicky Hilton at one of his family's deluxe hotels in Palm Springs, the astonished guests ate in silence as the bride-to-be's mother regaled them with gusto on her problems with alternating diarrhoea and constipation (categorized now as Irritable Bowel Syndrome), apologising to adjacent dining companions for regular explosions of odorous wind.

My own mother would have enjoyed this hugely, adding her own contribution. So would I have enjoyed it too, for that matter. It isn't recorded anywhere that Elizabeth showed any signs of mortification. Later in her life, especially with Mike Todd and certainly with Burton, she revelled in talk of an earthy nature.

I frankly warmed to the mother when I read an account of this behaviour. She must have been far more fun in the flesh than she has been generally portrayed, simply as a pushy stage mother.

My own mother was also adamant that I should be given an opportunity to pursue my talents. She fought tooth and nail, hammer and tong, with my father that I should take up my scholarship and study art. I would hear them quarrelling in the kitchen, listening in my nightgown at the top of the stairs.

'But she's no good, she has no talent,' my father would storm.

'Her art teacher and the headmistress appear to disagree with you.' My mother could put on this calm voice, knowing it would infuriate him further. 'You've wasted your talents and I'll see to it that your daughter doesn't do the same. That's the end of the matter.' And she'd leave him there and make her way up to the bathroom to prepare for uneasy sleep.

I'd run silently along to my own bed and lie down, heart hammering. I'd hear the front door open, then slam hard. My father was off into the night yet again. Destination unknown. He'd return by the dawn, my mother would refuse to speak to him all the following day. Sometimes the sullen silence hung between them for days.

'Please God, don't let me live like this for much longer,' I'd whisper in the dark.

My sister was not living at home with us any more, she had gone off to a residential Domestic Science College in Buckingham Palace Road, Victoria. Though this wouldn't have been her first choice of career. She had wanted to study medicine. My father discouraged her in that. His plan was to open a hotel with my sister in charge of catering. Where the capital was coming from for that, who only knows? It was yet another of his hair-brained, high-flying schemes, which never came to anything.

It would have been a dream come true for me to leave home, as a student like my sister. Instead, each morning I would have to hike up Streatham Hill to catch a train, or board one bus and change to a tram from Kennington to New Cross each day, returning home every evening. Other art students had taken lodgings close to Goldsmith's College, which housed the Art School at the back of the main building. But when I mentioned this at home both parents went berserk. Neither seemed able to let me go. My consoling thought was that Elizabeth Taylor still lived at home, too. And with a mother who barely let her out of her sight. But it was 1949, we were both 17, and our lives were about to really start in earnest.

My first week at Art College was a revelation to me, particularly the student-run Cinema Club. I thought I was already a cineaste, my entire life until then had been divided between chapel and cinema. I could list every Betty Grable musical, these being my favourite films. I knew which movie stars were married to each other. Like Rita Hayworth and Orson Welles, Barbara Stanwyck and Robert Taylor, Jennifer Jones and Robert Walker. I was in possession of little known facts, like Myrna Loy and Jean Simmons having ankles as thick as their knees. And the singing and dancing blonde, June Haver, running off to be a nun, then returning to marry Fred MacMurray, many years her senior, the crinkly-eyes lead in *Double Indemnity*, co-starring Barbara Stanwyck.

And of course, I knew anything and everything about Elizabeth Taylor.

I was apeing as much of it as I could, but there was no way that I could begin to emulate her financial status. Who on earth could match her renegotiated salary, at 16, of 1,000 dollars a week?

But I fared better on relationships. When she chose the football star, Glenn Davis, as a boyfriend, I agreed to accompany the local sporting schoolboy to the cinema on a weekly basis.

He would pick me up from my parents' tobacconist and sweetshop in the suburb of Southfields, where we lived above the premises before moving to a similar set up in Streatham. He would arrive wearing leather gloves and a scarf to protect his throat, explaining that in the wintry weather, as it was then, but other than that throughout the rest of the year, it was most important as a sportsman to take every precaution in protecting his health. That way lay his future as a professional.

To this end, he would purchase a tub of ice-cream each for us and produce silvered spoons from his mother's cutlery drawer, on her advice, in case of germs. I went out with him three times. He was a tall, handsome youth, and all the local girls were after him. He told me that himself, that I was very lucky. But it wasn't enough.

We would walk to and from the cinema, the long way round so that we could converse and get to know each other better. There were lengthy pauses in the conversation, which on his side consisted solely of stuff about sport and his passion for football.

He had already asked me home for tea to meet his mother. He was clearly a mother's boy. But he had sweaty hands. When he tried to hold mine in the cinema our fingers slid off each other's. The last thing I'd do was allow him to kiss me goodnight, there on our shop-front doorstep with customers whistling past, shouting warnings to 'cool it, you never know what you can catch'. I supposed years later that they were addressing him and not me, that his reputation had already spread, as a junior Howard Hughes with an obsession about germs.

I went out with another boy the following week; they were queuing up, I just had to take my pick. But he was a cricketing fan who tried to make me go with him to Lords. And then another, a rugger-bugger, who hoped that my father, being Welsh, could get us tickets for the Grand National match at Wembley.

I was thankful when Elizabeth dumped Glen Davis for William D. Pawley, Jr, the twenty-eight-year-old son of a former ambassador to Brazil. He was a handsome and successful businessman, profoundly conservative and on the social register.

How hard should that be to pin down in Streatham, for we had moved there by now? As it happened not too difficult at all, though the age bracket didn't match the rest of it did.

Handsome, utterly charming, full of the social graces, well born, Conservative, entering his wealthy father's business as a junior partner, driving a bottle green MG sports car. Fitted the picture perfectly. My mother was thrilled.

I didn't meet him in Streatham, it probably goes without saying. Though several of our customers could have qualified on political views, being Conservative, and utterly charming. They would roll in, inebriated, for cigarettes after a session in The Vale, at the bottom of our street on the way up to the park. Though they did sell cigarettes in that pub, these chaps were our regulars. The chat-up line never changed when neither of my parents were about.

'You're such a hell of a looker, getting more gorgeous by the week. Any chance of a swift grope at the back of the counter, eh, girlie?' This would be delivered in a leering, Terry Thomas manner.

'No chance! Correct money, please, I'm all out of change here.'

I'd slam the packet of cigarettes on the counter. And I'd give them the kind of withering gaze from my pale eyes, through my black lashes, which could be mistaken for a kind of come-on passion if you were completely deluded. Or just utterly drunk. It always reduced the men and the boys to jelly.

I'd practiced it from Elizabeth.

I'd met the moneyed young businessman, my own William D. Pawley, Jr, at a party given by a friend from my grammar school. She was a refined girl who would normally have gone away to a boarding school for her education like my mother. Her parents were upper middle class, so my mother was pleased when I was invited to a party at their house. She had met the mother, though not the father at the end of the school year event, when our work as school leavers was on display. The girl's father was an alcoholic.

'Daddy's always drunk, but we all love him to bits. But because of it we've had to adapt to a lower standard of living.' That's how the girl had put it. So obviously he was too drunk to attend this event. My own father didn't bother to turn up either, simply because it was of no interest to him.

The party took place in the summer holidays, immediately before I was to become a full-time art student. The girl who was giving it had already begun a secretarial course. It seemed such a different future ahead for her, compared to the glorious artistic avenues opening up for me.

'You can end up marrying your wealthy boss, when you're a first-class secretary. Then you are made for life, according to Mummy. That's how she met and married Daddy.'

The venue for the party was an extremely gracious home by the river in Richmond which was being loaned to them by absent friends. It was enormous and all the girls were to spend the night there and return home after breakfast. The mother had been on the telephone to my mother explaining this and assuring her that I would be safely chaperoned by the parents, who would be present throughout the evening. My mother had been impressed by her refinement and this was the way she wanted my life to go, moving amongst a 'better class of person' as she put it. So I was allowed to go. Just as Elizabeth's Taylor's mother was impressed at the society circles her daughter was entering, when she met William D. Pawley, Jr.

All the other girls were ravishingly pretty, it wasn't just me. It was as if we'd been handpicked for the occasion. The house was a direct contrast to the last home where I had met the family. That had been in Richmond too, but was a minute caravan then with barely room to turn around. They had been down on their luck at that time. From what I remember now, I believe that the father had once been a solicitor.

'Daddy had just been fired again for being helplessly drunk at the office in front of clients.' That's how the girl had described it at the time. Something about the whole set-up frightened me, made me uneasy. All this up-and-down life. The fearful insecurity, everything dependent on the man and whether or not he could keep his head above penury, dragging his dependants down with him. And all because he couldn't stay away from the drink. But with a wife and daughter always ready to stand by him, because he was such a sweet man and they loved him for that. I loathed the whole scenario.

The boys were handpicked as being a good bet for this ex-grammer school daughter, all ex-public schoolboys, of course. But none who planned to go on to university, which seemed so strange to me. They would all be stepping straight into awaiting vacancies in their family concerns.

Down in my Welsh valley, every child was encouraged then to aim for grammar school and then further education so that, if male, they wouldn't end up underground in the mines ruining their health, filling their lungs with coal-dust like their forebears. Or if they were a girl, rotting their brains out in the local co-op, slicing up cheese and bacon and ringing up tins of tomato soup and sardines all day on the till.

It was as if I'd left school and gone into my 'family business', stuck behind the counter counting out lollipops and sherberts. And constantly re-stocking our nightly best seller after the pubs shut, Trebor Extra Strong Peppermints, sold to camouflage the breath of boozers before facing the rage of the wife.

Unthinkable that anyone should even expect that of me. Where was the progress in that, or the concept of professional ambition, or my mother's personal obsession around social mobility? Though already my father was muttering, outside my mother's earshot, about the gigantic sacrifice my further education would be costing them. Not in actual cash, my scholarship grant would be seeing to that, but in years of deprivation of income, the right that every parent had in expectation of their children's earnings.

He hoped sincerely, he'd heave a laboured sigh as he muttered it, that I was aware of the enormous sacrifice they were making on my behalf. And that I would show my appreciation as soon as I was able, in monetary support, because by then they would be aged and infirm and would certainly need it.

I assured him that I did and that I would. And when the time came I honoured this obligation. But by that time my father had crucified lungs, liver and heart, with his own indulgences. He had sabotaged all that I could have done for him, giving him the life that he'd always dreamed of living which he would have loved. My proud mother benefited instead. She was the one who had battled on my behalf for the opportunities that she must have felt that she, herself, missed.

The ex-public schoolboys in the Richmond party certainly had their pick of beautiful girls. But not a single one of these either were going on to university, college or Art School for five years as I was. I was amazed. Most of them had gone either to boarding school, or private schools in the vicinity. Had these middle class folk no ambitions other than to mate and marry a suitable consort? Was I totally out on a limb here?

My admirer was the most handsome youth of them all. He had been more than particularly intrigued with me right from the very beginning of the evening. My friend's mother made a point of remarking upon it the next morning, over a beautifully prepared breakfast. This was laid strangely enough in a room overlooking the vast gardens, called 'the breakfast room'. It was the first time I'd ever heard of a room named after a meal.

'That gorgeous young man "made a set for you",' was the expression the mother used then. She'd waggled her finger, eyes twinkling roguishly.

'He was actually the one that we'd pinpointed for our little girl.' She winked at her daughter. 'Hadn't we, darling?' My friend, the homeliest girl at the party, but with a beautiful smile and a lovely temperament, blushed with embarassment.

'I'm terribly sorry, I had no idea.' I was genuinely concerned. I had given my phone number when the handsome youth had asked for it. Now I was sorry, I would never knowingly steal anybody from a friend.

'No, no, it's just Mummy's little joke. You two looked so good together. I do hope something lovely comes of it.' Everyone else at the table murmured their assent, teasing me for blushing now, asking if I was going to see him again. Each of them in turn went around the breakfast table, saying which boy they had liked the best. All the way home on the bus, I felt the warm glow of actually belonging and feeling equal, coming away from a party with a date in the offing.

This is what leaving school and being a semi-adult is all about, I thought. Then I allowed my thoughts to linger over the kiss that the boy had given me. It was the very first kiss from the opposite sex that I had actually felt like returning.

I hadn't, so far, met any boy quite like him. And if I am absolutely honest, looking back over the glorious panoply, I never did actually meet another even remotely the same.

He was tall and beautifully built, with the body of an athlete. One of the first things he asked me on our earliest date, was whether or not I played golf. If I didn't, he'd said eagerly, then he looked forward very much to teaching me. It was the most graceful game in the world, he'd waxed lyrical, and it was something he'd like to think of us sharing for the rest of our lives. That's how he talked, with a tremendous love of life in all its forms. It was catching, his more than abundant enthusiasm, it was joyful and good to be around.

Sometimes in the street, or travelling on public transport, you can catch a glimpse of a baby in a pram or in the mother's arms. The baby can be male or female, dressed in traditional blue or pink. But what draws your attention is the expression of beatitude on the baby's face. It is as if this child and the entire life of this child had already been blessed. There would never be any worries, ever.

I got caught up in this aura of sheer well-being at first. He had such plans for me, for us both. I addition to teaching me to play golf, he wanted me to learn how to drive, though I wasn't even eighteen yet and as such could not be eligible for a driving licence. He said none of that mattered. I could practice on his father's estate, miles of room there.

He asked me if I would be his woman. That's how he put it. I didn't know what that meant. Was he wanting to take my virginity, or what? Was it a proposal of marriage? Or did it just mean that he wanted me to become his official girlfriend to the exclusion of all else? I couldn't give him an answer, certainly not the one he was hoping for. This would obviously have been to simply say, yes. But as I explained, in a matter of weeks or so, I would be changing my life around altogether. I wouldn't be the same person any more, so I couldn't possibly commit myself to anything.

I would be embarking on a course of study as an artist that lasted for five years. Two initial years leading to the Intermediate Examination, during which I would study all the rudiments. Anatomy. Life Drawing. Architecture. Textile Design. Pictorial Composition. Clay Modelling. Pottery. Water Colour Painting. Perspective.

Then if I succeeded in passing that I would specialise in whatever field I chose for another two years. I would embark on an intensive study of Painting in all its various aspects. Portraiture. Landscape Painting. Abstract. Abstract Impressionism. Surrealism. Symbolism.

After that, if I got my National Diploma in Design, known as NDD, I would go on for a further pedagogue year for my ATD, Art Teaching Diploma. The whole course if completed was a B.A. qualification. Meaning a degree course, entitling me to letters after my name.

He was confounded and appalled. But why, darling, he wanted to know? What's the point of it all, that hard slog? And taking so long, I mean what about US?

He wanted me to give it all up and take the easy way through life, like him. The job in his family firm was a 'doddle, a cushy number, there for the taking'. He simply couldn't see any possible reason why anybody on earth shouldn't take the easy way out, when it was there on offer. He began to mention getting engaged. All the physical contact we'd had were the passionate goodnight kisses at the end of every date. If he attempted to even allow his hands to wander towards my breasts, I would brush them away firmly until he got the message. He was a well-brought-up boy. As far as he was concerned I was a beautifully brought up girl who had no previous knowlege of sex. He respected that. It made him think more highly of me. That's how it was in the 'fifties.

When he mentioned getting engaged, there and then I held my hand up, and pressed silencing fingers against his lips.

We didn't see each other again. He went off in his car crying. It must have been the only time in his life up until then that this lovely boy had been denied what he wanted. I felt emotional and subdued about it, too.

My mother was furious. She said I could have balanced things out to everyone's satisfaction if I'd only tried a little harder. She really liked him. My father refused to speak to me. He'd had to sit back and watch 'a cushy future for himself' fly out of the window. He would have enjoyed playing golf, hadn't I even thought of that? Or did my selfishness know no bounds?

Sometimes, but very seldom, I have wondered through the years what may have happened to him. But at the time I felt a kind of relief.

Elizabeth Taylor had just ended things with Bill Pawley, Junior for the very same reason that I ended with the lovely moneyed boy. They wanted us to give up our careers for them. We couldn't do that, because the careers were more, much more, than merely that. They were our vocations, our fate, they meant everything to us. Any man in our lives was going to have to accept that.

Elizabeth Taylor went off to play her pivotal role in *A Place in the Sun*, with Montgomery Clift. She fell in love with him. They never became lovers. He was gay.

I went off to Art School, which was the making of me. I immediately got involved with a fellow student, a blond version of Montgomery Clift. He too was talented, brooding, handsome, sensual. But he wasn't gay and despite his determined advances we never did become lovers.

Elizabeth spent every moment she could off the film set, trying to be alone with Clift. But her mother was as ferocious a chaperone as it was possible to be.

I disobeyed mine and went alone to my ardent admirer's living quarters. He tried to rape me. My mother went up to talk to the Principal about what had happened. Her actions, fiercely protecting her young, resulted in him being expelled from the Art

School. My mother had not been the first parent with a complaint. His studies had come to an end.

By the close of the summer term, my parents were preparing to move down to the coast. This was on doctor's orders; my father's lungs required sea air, that was the medical diagnosis. The true fact of the matter was that my father was steadily smoking the profits away in our tobacconist's shop. He was a chain smoker and becoming more and more the victim of congested lungs. His night coughing-bouts kept us all awake.

I would now be plunged into a completely different social set. This was in the fashionable coastal resort of Brighton, known as Doctor Brighton, for the bracing sea air, and raffishly jaunty, theatrical, royal history. But I didn't want to leave London and the Art School where I was already established, as a dedicated and serious student with great promise for the future.

That and a reputation as a romantic heart-breaker and an iron-knicker-clad committed professional virgin.

One of the tutors at my London Art School offered me a job in those summer holidays as his studio assistant. These jobs were like gold-dust for students, if they could find them. They were educational in themselves. This would mean that not only would I be earning money, which would help my parents, but I would be in London, free to study the Masters in London galleries. To my great relief and surprise, my mother agreed. I would live as part of the family with the tutor and his wife.

Then after a week an unexpected offer came from his friends in France and the family flew off to Brittany to paint. I had the place and London all to myself.

My true life was about to begin.

When Elizabeth was almost seventeen and making *Conspirator*, with Robert Taylor, playing a twenty-one-year-old wife, she was filming in London. During that time she met and was enchanted by the man she was destined to marry. Michael Wilding became her second husband, the father of her two sons. He was twenty years her senior, the current idol of the British public, who fell for his suave and humorous style in the light romantic comedies he made for Herbert Wilcox, starring Anna Neagle. (She was Dame Anna Wilcox in real life.)

Around the same time, that summer in London, I met an older man, even older than Michael Wilding who had the wealth and led the sophisticated life-style that Michael Wilding portrayed in his films. My mother would have been delighted, my father more so. But I dare not tell them for fear that they would order me home immediately and spoil all my fun.

We were not having sex, I vehemently wished to remain a virgin, and he respected that. But he was my sugar-daddy in the sweetest sense. He was the age of my grandfather, had he been alive. I never knew whether or not he was actually capable of sex anyway.

I think that when men get older, maybe from their seventies onwards, they regress to the schoolboy stage again, of losing their hearts and putting girls on pedestals. My sugar-daddy was utterly besotted with me to the point of losing the power of speech at times, practically stammering like a schoolboy. My heart did go out to him then, I have always been moved by the frailty of the elderly and infirm. And I did miss my late grandparents so much. He filled a void there.

'There will always be a place in my life for you.' That's what I whispered to him, patting the white-haired head on my shoulder in the back of his Daimler.

Schoolboys, when still inexperienced, dread sex as a ritual

humiliation, unable to control their premature ejaculations. Mature men fear the humiliation of not being to raise an erection, or once raised whether they can maintain it, let alone ejaculate. I think from that viewpoint, females have a much easier time in the sexual arena, whatever their age.

My sugar-daddy may have been besotted with me but my own feelings went deeper than I could have believed possible. Compassion and love and gratitude are powerful ingredients when mixed up altogether. I felt all those but much more. It was as if the very soul of me had been touched.

I know that I was more profoundly involved than I ever could have been with the lovely young businessman. This elderly gentleman, and he was truly a gentle man, was giving me a belief in myself as a human being. He was the balm that life had provided at exactly the right point, for the experiences that I had been through with my father.

It is claimed that nobody is actually given more than they can contend with in the way of difficulties. But the marvel of life is that it recompenses a person who has seemed to have had more than their fair share of pain. I chose to see this man as my gift. He had changed me. I had grown, no longer the silly girl. I refused all his gifts, every offer of money. I had my earnings from my job as studio assistant, my parents could have all that. I had accepted one initial and generous contribution from him, when my parents were desperate for funds at the start of the summer break. But I wasn't with this wealthy man for his wealth. Only for what he could teach me.

I would be leaving him soon, to return to my parents in Brighton. The autumn term was due to start at Brighton Art School. My summer job was over now, the work was completed in my tutor's studio. The family had returned from Brittany and it had been a splendid summer all round.

'Return any time you feel like it, if only for a weekend,' they said to me. The tutor had been more than delighted with the work I'd achieved. He'd claimed it was like returning to a completely new studio and there was a job there anytime I needed to make some extra cash.

It felt good to be appreciated. But as the day of departure loomed closer I knew how bereft my sugar-daddy would be without me. I arranged to spend the final night at his place, sleeping in the same bed, cuddling up together for the first and last time this summer. Who could tell what the future would hold?

I arranged that the chauffeur should pick me up outside Sloane Square Station. I'd told my tutor that I would be spending this final night with a friend, intimating that it was a girl I'd known a long time.

I felt self-conscious but proud clambering into the Daimler in broad daylight. Passers-by stared at the sight. As the driver opened the door of the back seat for me, I heard a familiar voice call my name.

It was my friend from grammar school, who was now doing the secretarial course. I would never have recognised her. She was svelte, sophisticated and sporting a diamond engagement ring. She was shopping in Peter Jones for her trousseau, preparing for her autumn wedding. I asked her who she was marrying.

She blushed and squeezed me tight. She said she had me to thank for her fiancé. If I hadn't finished with the moneyed nice boy, the businessman, she wouldn't be engaged now. She had completed her secretarial course and as luck would have it he was looking for a secretary the same month.

'So, Mummy was right. I have ended up marrying the boss. Thank you, darling, so much!' She was utterly radiant. And he was the one that she had wanted all along. So dreams do come true after all.

I waved until she was out of sight, from the back of the Daimler. Traffic had been hooting from behind, so we were forced to move on.

I told my sugar-daddy the tale, on arrival at his place, which I had not visited before. This was the Belgravia home that he had shared with his wife during their extremely happy marriage, in which he had continued to live on his own since her death from cancer, some ten years before.

They had never been blessed with children, that's probably why I had been sent into his life, as the affectionate grand-daughter he would never have. Our previous meetings had been in plush restaurants and night clubs, or the parties of his friends.

I could barely find the words to tell the tale, in these grandiose surroundings. I would have liked to have felt more relaxed, but I was overcome. I felt myself shrinking into insignificance, I had to let him know that.

He applauded my honesty, laughed at my wonderment, saying I could change whatever I wished of the decor. He said that I was the artist, after all, and that he trusted my judgement. Then he held me close and sat me on his lap.

'Talking of marriages, I know ours is a spring and winter tale—my dearest child, you and I. And I am a hideous and ancient old toad now. But could you find it in your youthful and eager heart to make an old cove a deliriously happy man?'

I placed my fingers over his delicately puckered mouth. And I hugged him very tight, kissing his face all over like an exhuberant puppy. I felt no response between his legs as I sat happily on his lap and that satisfied me the most. It's the way that it should have been between me and my father. He had been sent to me as a surrogate.

If I accepted him as my husband, and stranger things happen all over the world, there was only fifty-five years between us after all, it could be a completely platonic relationship. Nothing wrong with that. Plenty of people married for companionship, based on a profound friendship.

Why shouldn't I?

But I didn't want to be rushed into things. I was expected back in Brighton to enroll in the Art School. Maybe we could keep this friendship going for the next four years, that's all I had left now. I'd done my first year of Intermediate already. Perhaps I'd better ask him if he was prepared to wait that long. Then I could just choose a nice ring and wear it all the time to show I was spoken for.

That could be very good and keep me pure and out of mischief, with my mind just on my studies. I aimed to be top as a scholarship girl, and being awarded all the travelling scholarships to places like Rome to study the ceiling of the Sistine Chapel and view Michelangelo's David in the marbled-flesh. I longed to visit Assisi to see the Giotto frescoes, visit Venice for the architecture. And Paris for the Impressionists. These distinctions were expected of me by my parents and in case, I owed the visual treats to myself.

This was the second time I'd had to forestall a proposal of marriage. It was an extraordinarily enriching experience, quite addictive in fact. It was like being a leading lady, the heroine of my own feature film. Elizabeth Taylor may be playing these roles, as an actress, but I was living the reality and I wasn't even eighteen yet. This was my life. One day I would be able to write a book all about it. And nobody would believe it was the truth.

'I don't ever want to deny you anything,' I buried my face in his wrinkled neck. 'So please, please, don't ever put me in the position of having to say "no".'

Filled with pity immediately afterwards because I'd seen his face fall, his disappointment palpable, I permitted myself to be led into the chandeliered and brocaded boudoir. He lifted me up to lie on top of his Marie Antionette bedspread. Then he joined me within the confines of the ceilinged-four-poster bed, which was elevated on a carpeted platform in the fashion of a shrine.

I had an uncanny, and frankly unnerving, sense of being a lamb led to the slaughter. The ritual was curiously biblical. The Hammer horror films had scenes like this where virgins with low-cut gowns and heaving bosoms were regularly sacrificed.

At his ardent pleading I allowed him to slide his hands over my clothed body, mercifully I was still wearing my overcoat. I'd refused to remove that. I claimed I was cold, though the central heating was turned to high and it was still summer. But the elderly do feel the cold, because their blood has become thinner and circulates more slowly, so he accepted my excuses.

Then the world came crashing down. All my dreams crumbled into thin air.

He drew my hand to his already unbuttoned trousers.

I sat up, my face scarlet. I burst into tears. I was cruelly disappointed and accused him of profane motives. Had he come to the bed, already unbuttoned?

This was tantamount to guilty pre-planned stategy. Just like in a murder case.

He protested his innocence.

But it was apparent to me that I was too much of a temptation, even for one I had presumed impotent. Agreeing to lie on the bed was a clumsy mistake on my part. Events were moving far too fast and certainly not in the right direction. Promising to spend the entire night there was tantamount to insanity.

I'd meant it to be the two of us, sleeping in the same bed having one of our illuminating chats then a brief peck goodnight, after a soothing mug of Horlicks, as I might have done with my grandfather, though admittedly not at the age I was then. This was certainly far from the behaviour of an innocent. What was the chapel girl thinking?

I didn't spend the night. I caught the evening train home.

My parents were most gratified, they hadn't expected me until the next day They could leave me in the shop, serving until midnight to catch the last stragglers from the pubs. They themselves didn't get home until after I'd gone to bed, drinking late, after hours with the Welsh owner, Cliff, at the Seven Stars.

Before drifting off to sleep, I pondered on just what I'd rejected that evening. The full significance struck me of what I had turned down. And why. Was it really worth it, if this dismal reality in the backstreets of Brighton was the alternative? There was no answer to that one, none at all.

I shed a tear for my Sugar-Daddy. He had provided me with a haven. Now I was aching with missing him. More tears ran down my cheeks. I could have left my bedroom and gone to the telephone and rung him to say sorry. I hadn't meant to be moralistic and prudish and shy. My basic instincts would have been to be generous with myself and that meant my body, too.

But I was mixed up emotionally, around anything to do with sex in a normal, man/woman sense. Only I couldn't speak of it, even to him, from whom I thought I'd never have secrets.

I had told him instead that I didn't think that we could see each other any more. That it wouldn't work out and that I knew it was my fault that he desired me, because that's how all men and boys were around me. It must be something bad in me, something I didn't know what to do about. Because what I'd loved so much about him was that it was pure and clean and had nothing to do with sex. So we two had come to the end of the road. Sorry.

He had looked stricken and suddenly ancient, as if I'd robbed him of the will to continue living. And I understood then just how cruel the young can be, witholding or in my case withdrawing the elixir of life itself, whenever they choose to do so. And seemingly so carelessly, without heart.

I didn't telephone that night in the dark. I did go down the stairs in my nightgown to make the call. Then I heard the drunken fumbling of my father's key in the front door of the shop. I ran back upstairs, and hid my face in the pillow to muffle my sobs. I was young, but not without heart, not by any means.

Our lives went in different directions then, Elizabeth's and mine. She had been swept off her feet and went on, at eighteen, to marry Nicky Hilton, the twenty-three-year-old son of the multimillionaire international hotelier, Conrad Hilton. This father, after divorcing his children's mother, went on to marry a blonde film star, scintillating Zsa Zsa Gabor.

But the glamorous pin-up bachelor turned out to be a drunken gambler, and worse, a wife-beater, and the marriage was short-lived. Elizabeth left him and divorce proceedings began. Having departed her parent's home to get married she never returned, to her mother's distress.

She took her own life by the scruff of its neck, and ill and distressed over the failure of her marriage, she turned for comfort and support to Stanley Donen, the director of her latest film. To everyone's concern, especially her studio's, this blossomed into an affair.

She came to London, putting the affair on hold and bumped into Michael Wilding in the studio canteen. She was already smitten by Wilding from a previous encounter. She invited him to dinner and they became inseperable. They were wildly in love. Whilst waiting for her divorce from Nicky Hilton, both celebrated the fact that Michael Wilding's own divorce had become final so that now he was free.

Over dinner that night, Elizabeth Taylor proposed marriage. Wilding accepted. They were married in London on February 21st, 1952. On the 27th of that month she would be twenty years old. On January 6th, 1953, she would undergo an emergency caes-arean delivery of a baby boy, Michael Howard Wilding. At still only twenty years old, Elizabeth Taylor, had experienced two marriages, one divorce, two broken engagements and the marvel of motherhood.

I had done none of those things.

But I had collected a bevy of admirers, three at least became so intense that everyone considered us to be engaged. All dark haired and handsome youths, acceptable except the final one, to my father. He was Jewish, which to my father's anti-Semitic, racist conviction was absolutely the lowest of the low. I think that was maybe why I chose to announce that I was engaged and planning to marry this one. I knew that for my father it would be as a red rag to a bull.

My parents were already in bed, but I'd had the foresight to wear my plimsols, my favourite rubber-soled canvas running shoes. I broke the news, standing just outside their room, the door opening onto the corridor at the top of the stairs. I waited for the roar as loud as the M.G.M. lion, it came from my father's outraged throat.

I began running, down the stairs, through the shop, out onto the pavement and round the block. I returned from my roamings at three in the morning. The shop door was locked. But I'd left the back door to the small yard and the back door to the living premises on the latch. They were both asleep by then.

In the morning I got up before everyone and left the house to have breakfast in the fishermen's café down on the seafront, underneath the Esplanade. I'd rung my fiancé to meet me there and told him the tale of parental disapproval. His news was equally bleak. He'd had a letter from his parents in South Africa to say that his mother was wearing black, the entire family lamenting his plans to marry a Goy. That was me, the word meaning Gentile. The engagement was broken off, the pressure from both families was too great.

I left Art School at the age of twenty-two in 1954, to begin my life in London as a qualified art teacher in Elephant and Castle. I was free as a bird with a wonderful job ahead of me. My excitement knew no bounds, I could barely contain myself. I left home enthralled at the prospect of freedom from parental control. I shared a flat in London with a fellow ex-art student. My heart was not broken about my ex-fiancé, or if there were still cracks, they were about to be mended. The true Love of my Life was about to enter it.

James Robertson Justice was thirty years my senior. A bon viveur. A charismatic force of nature. I gave him my virginity on a gilded plate because he deserved it. And in return he taught me the joys of sex and opened up avenues of pleasure that I had never imagined existed. He was thoughtful and tender, informed, well read, an intellectual. He was charismatic. When he entered a room it was as if the lights had been switched on. He was immense, over six foot. I could lean on him. He was strong as an oxen, he could pick me up and carry me on one shoulder, tossed over like a silk scarf. He made me feel like a Dresden Figurine. He was a gentle giant.

We made each other laugh, so much and all the time, until we ached. Except when we devoured the inner depths in bed, but even in that sensual domain the humour prevailed. And the kindness, and generosity of spirit. I trusted him with my very soul.

But I didn't tell him about my father.

I can see now that I didn't tell him, or indeed anyone, not only because I had made a promise to my father that I never, ever would. And my father was still alive. But because I was afraid that I would have been seen as a sullied object, one to be discarded on grounds of imperfection. And I couldn't bear even the thought of being rejected by this extra-special lover.

I was deeply and utterly ashamed of my childish participation in those 'games' with my father. The guilt and fear that anybody should ever find out lay like an underblanket throughout my teen and adult life.

When I took my first drink of alcohol, it gave me instant relief. It numbed what felt like an inner ache, a distant yet palpable throbbing like a hovering toothache about to become a persistent pain. And it was with me all the time, like words on the tip of a tongue. But these words found no voice, they could not be spoken. The alcohol by the very end became my only solace.

My amorata declared his deepest devotion and asked me for a love-child. I refused then. But a few years later, at twenty four, I was already becoming broody, especially when cradling my sister's small babies. I decided that I would seriously consider having his child, because I was absolutely in love with him and wanted us to spend the rest of our lives together. He was away, filming, but on his return I was about to thrill him with that news, when something happened which would place everything in jeopardy.

My father died.

The reason that I have always provided in the past for breaking both my own heart and James's, by ending our corruscating love affair, was my father's death. And certainly, had my father not died then, we would have pursued our planned happiness.

But I seemed to need, and it was an urgent and terrible need, to exorcise everything to do with my father from my life. I never became involved with older men, old enough to be my father or even my grandfather, following my father's death. I couldn't bear to be intimate with anybody ever again, not whilst I was young and with his corpse fresh in my mind, with that same skin-texture, the veined hands, the wrinkled skin, the slackening jaw-line, the creased lips, the pouched eyes, the authoritative air. They all served as reminders of him.

I was taken unawares by my own emotions. They were contrary to all my expectations. I had thought that when my father died I would be free of him at last, but the very opposite turned out to be true. He was barely in the grave but already he was haunting me.

He had died in hospital, down in Wales. My parents had moved back there when I left home to teach art in London. They felt the need to be near their new grandchildren, my sister's house was close to their own. Even as we travelled back home from the hospital, my father's paltry belongings in a plastic bag, the morning following his death, he was with me.

I took my mother's hand in mine on the back seat of the jolting bus, the same journey back and forth to the hospital that we'd made so many times in the past week. One glance, and I didn't even need to make that glance, told me that the tears were pouring silently down her cheeks. The sight released a flood of my own.

This was for the man who had ruined my life, my childhood anyway. The one who had sexualised me before my time. Whose secret 'games' and violent thrashings dominated those years between infancy and the puberty, which proved my release. But then the mental cruelty had begun, worse even than the fondlings and beatings that had gone on before. So what was I crying about now?

I thought at the time that I was crying in sympathy for my mother, that beautiful, emotionally and mentally frail woman, who would now be left all alone without her partner in life. But the reality was that I was actually suffering a grief of my own for the father who had, so long ago and at the very beginning, been the centre of my small world.

The images crowded in. Me on his shoulders parading the park. The trips to the National Gallery, spending hours in front of Constable landscapes and Turner's tempestuous seas. His Cary Grant mouth and the dimple in his chin. The way he shone his shoes. His undoubted love for my mother. The painstaking manner in which he wrote a letter or sketched an animal, the tip of his tongue protruding from the left-hand corner of his mouth. The tapered fingers of his beautifully shaped hands.

They returned the coffin to the house and before it was sealed, I tiptoed into the front room for the final confrontation. This was the night before the preacher came to give his blessing preceding the burial. Neighbours and family and friends had been visiting all through the day to pay him their final respects. He would have chuckled over that, and fitted together some suitably caustic sentences.

But there were no words from him now. I was able to study the countenance I knew so well, to imprint every detail in my memory for this final and last time. For we would never be face to face like this ever again.

It was a well-proportioned, masculine structure with the flesh distributed to all the right places. He was still a handsome man. The sensual lower lip had retained its shape. The straight nose was the same, and the dimpled chin. But this was only the surface of an ice-cold corpse, whose spirit had departed. It was simply the present shell, the deceased remains, the decaying matter, of a father due soon to be delivered to the bowels of the earth. As such he had lost his power to terrify and subdue, to seduce and diminish, to ridicule and destroy.

'It is over, Daddy.' I said it out loud to him. Then I forced myself to kiss him on the stiff chill of his lips, the final connection. And I thought that it was over but in fact that was far from the truth.

The power of the relentless parent can be stronger from beyond the grave, than it ever was in the flesh and in the blood.

My mother became the child overnight from thence-forward. My sister and I accepted the resonsibility between us and that made our own bond firmer than it had ever been before. We respected and loved each other and the mutual support made the situation tolerable. For my mother wanted to die herself now, and contrived many ways to end her life in subsequent failed suicide attempts.

The emergency calls to hospitals became more frequent as she was snatched from the jaws of death at the very last minute. Deterioration set in, the prolonged sojourns in psychiatric wards continued, returning home with a battery of pills to make her sleep, to wake her up, to cope with depression, to subdue mania. But through it all my tiny mother, rapidly reducing in stature now, retained a girlish sweetness. The rare and precious flashes of brilliance and sly humour still sparkled like sunshine behind stormy skies.

I loved her so much now, much more than before. I felt that I should say sorry for all the stuff that went on between myself and her husband when I was so small. I yearned to unburden myself, to receive a kind of pardon for dishonesty and deceit. But the transference of guilt would have been unthinkably cruel. Her frailty could not have withstood it. I was doomed to a soothing silence, whilst my own spirit was in absolute torment.

A psychiatrist who happened to be a friend, spoke of his child abuse case histories long before I'd broken my silence to my sister. He claimed that the mother always knows in these circumstances, if there is sexual abuse between father and girl-child. Her failure to protect her own small daughter, leads to dreadful inner conflict, mixed with jealousy and hatred. And that usually because it is too terrible and painful for her to confront, she does nothing at all but take refuge in mental illness of a prolonged nature for the rest of her life.

It reinforced my own guilt, hearing that. I took it to mean that I had caused my own mother's madness. How could I ever recompense her for that? And how could I find enough ways to punish the male race for making me the way that I had become?

All my friends were going out with young men their own age. When I told them about my older ones, they were at first incredulous, and then faintly derisory, but by the end, brutal. They were only trying to steer me onto the straight and narrow, into the normal way of behaviour. They called me eccentric and asked what the sex was like. Non-existent, I'd explain. I wasn't interested in sex. Though, later of course, I couldn't complain of the joys that I had experienced with my film star.

They said it was sick to be so preoccupied with the elderly and to make certain I didn't return to the film star, or take up with another 'grandpa', as they snidely referred to them.

Following the death of my father, they began bombarding me with party invitations and coaxing me to functions full of young men to partner me, to convert me. They were just trying to be helpful. But I wasn't ready for a social life of that nature, not just yet. I did what Elizabeth always does when she's dejected; I took to the shops.

But Elizabeth Taylor had no need to go out shopping, now. Her life had become fraught with debts as the wife of Michael Wilding. He failed to find suitable roles of any kind in the film business there. His career had come to a complete standstill. In 1956, when we were both twenty-four, the year my father died and I ended my big romance with James, her marriage to Michael Wilding was in its own death-throes. She had met the man who would become her third husband, the flamboyant film producer and entrepeneur, Mike Todd.

He showered her with gifts from the moment they met, practically. He was determined to make her his wife, although she was still somebody else's at the time. Nobody before and certainly nobody since indulged her craving for jewels, couture clothes, shoes, handbags, perfumes, finery, luxury, and heady extravagance on a superhuman scale, as Mike Todd indulged Elizabeth Taylor when 1946 edged into 1947. Now the shops were coming to her, as her financial situation spun into complete reversal. No need to get out to them.

And I was in luck with my own shopping too: the January 1947, post-Christmas Sales were in full swing. And there were lots of cut-price bargains on offer. I headed off to Fenwicks, the New Bond Street mecca for all career girls, keen on budget-price glamour. And without even looking further than my nose 'the frock' simply fell into my hands, literally walked into arms.

It was what could be called an 'interesting colour', that not everyone would be able to get away with. So the Fenwick sales assistant told me. Not to put to fine a point on it, a lay-person might term it khaki. The same colour as a shipment of army clothing. But the crucial difference was in the fabric.

This divine garment was in taffeta, shot taffeta. It was woven from two seperate strands of colour, two disparate threads. One sludge-brown, the other toad-green. On an artist's pallette we would be referring to Raw Sienna and Olive or Sap Green.

Spot-lit, it mirrored my own eyes. In shadow it was several tones darker. Whoever designed this apparition must have had me in mind. That was the opinion of the sales assistant and I agreed with her whole-heartedly. She even called over several of her colleagues to take a look.

Apparently they'd had this particular garment in stock for simply ages and the price had been lowered dramatically through the changing seasons. They had almost given up on ever selling it, so they said. Obviously, as they explained, it needed an extra-special personality to wear it, somebody a little outside the normal approach to fashion. An original thinker, with a style of her very own. And here I was, the perfect one. That's what they all agreed. There was no question of not buying the creation after that.

When I slipped it over my shoulders, I knew there and then where I would wear it later that very day. I'd been invited to a party off Baker Street. The reason I had been unenthusiastic about going was simply that I couldn't think what to wear. And my hair needed reshaping. But with the cash that I'd saved from the reduced price of the dress, I could afford to go and have a really good cut.

It was Saturday. I planned my day carefully, no work of course that day. I fitted everything in and by the evening was on the London Underground train to the party. Even though I say it myself, I did look pretty spectacular.

The bare-armed cocktail dress, with plunging decollete, could have been considered more appropriate for a summer occasion. But this was precisely why it was reduced in price. I could keep my coat on in the party, if I felt chilly.

My shorn tresses, termed The Italian Cut by the salon in Earls Court, was so avant garde that the ignorant may have assumed that I'd been treated for head-lice. My eye make-up, an arresting concoction of mauve and deep puce, with ink-black eye-liner and sooty mascara, combined with my pallor caused a concerned fellow traveller on the train to enquire if I was all right.

I was wearing the scarlet overcoat, which had been dyed funeral black expressly for that purpose, for the funeral of my father. I looked, probably to those kindly eyes of the motherly woman, much like a refugee who had fled from a violent husband.

But I sailed into the party feeling absolutely splendid. The hush as I entered confirmed this conviction. Others were wearing pleasant tweed dresses and in some cases, twin sets and pearls. Poor things. They had no idea how to dress for special occasions.

I married the first young man who asked me. He fitted my mother's stated requirements. Public schoolboy. Oxford University. He was my own age, several months older. I was ready to be normal, ripe for falling in love like all my friends. So I did, I allowed myself to be swept off my feet, as Elizabeth Taylor was so fond of doing.

We married in Chelsea, enjoyed the reception in Belgravia. I gave birth to two beautiful blonde daughters. And then we divorced.

Within five years I had married again. I lost our baby when I was thirty-nine in a miscarriage. We divorced.

I was married for about twenty-two years, counting both

husbands. Those years were serene, tempestuous, violent, rewarding, highly creative, mutually satisfying, frantically social, calm, philosophical and heartbreaking towards the end when both marriages simply ran out of steam.

I ended them both because life is too short for boredom. But each time I suffered the loss of the marriage and had second thoughts, but didn't act upon them. I believe that all three of us, me and both husbands, have led happier lives than if we had remained together. It sounds like a threesome. But it wasn't.

I could go into far greater detail about each of those forays into the joys and drawbacks of matrimony. But I won't. In my wisdom I have learned loyalty and do still retain a love for those men who were my husbands. I've never regretted for a moment that I married them. Married sex is still the best I ever enjoyed, that was my own glorious experience.

I think somewhere in all ex-partners there remains a kernel of love. It's a tiny distillation of all those hopes and dreams in the first heady years of colliding together when the future beckons, bright and rosy as a sunrise. What tragedy it would be to go throughout life never having experienced the madness of love, the mind-whirling exaggerations of all that it means to be utterly lost in another person.

But the man I miss most of all, who enters my dreams and remains until dawn when he brings me to orgasm, is James. He died without us ever meeting again, but it doesn't matter. We always knew that we'd be in each other's hearts forever.

He is the one I thank for making me the woman that I am today. Our love was a sacrificial passion, it may have appeared to perish in flames from the past, but in fact has flourished independently all through the years to this very day. I believe that, and it is enough.

Nothing has compared with what we had together, the warmth and the shared wit. The sexual attraction so potent that we could never keep our hands off each other. The mutual affection. The never seeming to get enough of each other's company. The difficulty of achieving sleep when lying next to each other in bed because sleep would seem to take us away from each other.

I see him often on digital television on various film channels. His beautiful face fills my screen. His laughing eyes sparkle when he sees me, he knows I am watching. Sometimes he winks behind the director's back, it wasn't in the script that wink. But neither of us ever much cared for direction. We made everything up as we went along.

Most, except a few, of my lovers have died. Victims of the heady sixties, perished by their own hand or simply expired from drink or drugs or gruelling hard work or just giving up the ghost when the creative juices ceased to flow. But I feel their presence, they are all awaiting my arrival when my earthly journey is done. And some are too impatient, and are already with me. I feel them every day.

By 1958, at the tender age of twenty-six, Elizabeth Taylor was a widow. Her husband Mike Todd had been killed in a terrible plane crash. She couldn't accompany him on the trip because of ill health. He tried repeatedly to leave the house, embracing her and showering her in farewell kisses, leaving, then returning moments later to repeat the ritual.

It was as if he sensed that they would never be together again. That is how it has been reported anyway.

The young and tragic widow was devastated. Sooner than anybody would have expected her to, sedated and yet word-perfect, punctual, thoroughly professional, she returned to the film she was making, *Cat on a Hot Tin Roof.*

She played Maggie the Cat, shades of my Welsh Auntie Lizzie the Cats. The production was completed to everyone's wonderment, on time. Her performance was sublime. She looked on screen better than she had ever looked, if that was possible. Highly-strung, piteous, alluring, seductive, feisty.

Her entire wordrobe had to be altered, taken in to fit her. Though she spent most of the time in a revealing petticoat in the bedroom, trying to seduce her impotent husband, Paul Newman. She had lost so much weight over the tragedy of losing the one man that she appeared to be supremely happy with. Indeed, even Richard Burton, whom many perceive as the love of her life, claims that she would never have broken up with Mike Todd, that they were as perfect as it was possible to be, together as a married couple.

She was comforted through the sudden loss by her dead husband's best friend, the next door neighbour, singer Eddie Fisher. Debbie Reynolds supported the generous amount of time that her husband was spending with Elizabeth at that time. They had spent much time as a foursome, when Mike Todd had been alive. This seemed the neighbourly act of compassion.

Until she began to be suspicious. And with good cause, as it transpired. Eddie Fisher and Elizabeth Taylor were having an affair. He was to become her fourth husband.

The sympathy of the world press switched from that to venom, overnight. From being perceived as the tragic widow she was now reviled as a scarlet woman.

It was quite difficult even for me to leave the house because of my resemblance. One woman hissed, 'Hussy!' to me, baring her teeth as I boarded a bus. I was wearing a striped sailor, navy and white top, my hair in a rumpled, curly Poodle Cut. I couldn't think what had riled her so.

But Elizabeth Taylor was on the cover of all the newspapers that morning, I saw on the newsstand when I got off the bus. She had announced her engagement to Eddie Fisher. Alongside was a snap of the betrayed and discarded loyal wife, Debbie Reynolds, a toddler at her knee, a baby in her arms. Elizabeth had exactly the same Poodle Cut hairstyle as mine. That was probably what had caused the woman's aggression. She was confusing the two of us.

It has never, ever, been my practice to jump from one man to another. When a love affair or a marriage is over I like to take a breath and play the field. I enjoy luxuriating in being alone again, I actually relish the single state. In fact I much prefer it to being one half of a couple. It seems to me that is when you truly come into your own, when you are face to face with yourself. When that sublime state is reached and it is not given to all, for it is a narrow path to follow, then there is no such thing as loneliness.

I wonder if Elizabeth has reached that place yet? I hope so. For it seems to me that a life lived for love affairs and marriages to men, is ultimately an empty shell for a woman. As looks fade and time withers the facade, the competition grows fiercer for males, the majority of whom will always be drawn to youth. For a sublime actress like Elizabeth Taylor, fêted as a beauty, the parts became scarcer. Katherine Hepburn and Bette Davis acted on-screen until the end of their days, but these roles have not been offered to Elizabeth. Though she would have taken them between her teeth and savaged the hell out of them. The studios refuse to see her as the serious actress she actually is, capable of all roles. They have always compartmentalised her, as they did Monroe, as a sensuous femme fatale, eternally young. More fool them.

But she has resilience and a genuine concern for humanity. Her work and struggles for her Aids Foundation have elevated

Elizabeth to the status of sainthood amongst homosexual communities all over the world. To have had her at the helm has helped their cause immeasurably in getting financial backing for medical research and support for the suffering.

But all this was far ahead, in the future, in 1959. At the death of Mike Todd, she couldn't bear to be alone and without a man by her side. She flung herself into the waiting arms of Eddie Fisher. But no sooner had she married him than she had to confront the fact that she had made an appalling mistake. Really the only thing they shared, the one thing they had in common, had been their love and loyalty to Mike Todd.

After continuing delays, not least the very real threat of death, with viral pneumonia and a deadly congestion in her throat which required a last-minute life-saving operation, she prepared for the colossal screen role of Cleopatra. Elizabeth was unaware of it then but her fifth husband, a married man again, with children and a long-suffering, faithful wife (a familiar scenario) was already waiting in the wings.

Richard Burton was born and reared right at the bottom of our Welsh valley. I was surrounded by his type, growing up myself. My cousin, a miner, could have knocked spots off him for looks and the swaggering Don Juan, irresistible-to-women-everywhere appeal. It's dyed in the wool Welsh valley boyo flirtatious stuff-strutting, nothing uncommon at all. Very Celtic.

The deep-chested, broad-shouldered physique, the magnetic voice, the dark hair and transluscent eyes are all standard Welsh, handed out at birth. But take it out of the valley and it becomes something very special. Place it in Hollywood with a background of stage presence and Shakespeare on the tip of the tongue and you've got a star. Much has been written about Burton's raw impact on the London stage and the effete theatrical coterie of the times.

At the happening of the miners' strike in Thatcher's reign when the Coal Board announced plans to close so many mines (all in my valley), I arranged to meet up with my close miner friends and join in with the protest to Parliament Fields. The march was re-routed, many of the coaches from collieries all over Britain who were showing support for each other, were refused entry to inner London on police authority. But when the Welsh contingent came singing over Blackfriars Bridge my heart burst with pride. What energy. What strength. What animal magnetism. What maculine virility.

Easy to see what Elizabeth Taylor saw in Richard Burton. They were two birds of the same feather. Not too difficult to understand why Richard Burton was magnetically drawn to Elizabeth Taylor. Apart from her beauty, the sensual appeal, all the physical attributes matching his own. A mirror image. The most beautiful, in the same way as her, men she had played opposite before had been gay. Montgomery Clift. Rock Hudson. James Dean. They were amongst her very closest friends, but she was their shoulder to lean on. Burton needed the shoulder, too, but not merely to lean on. The passion between them was all-devouring. To see them together was to gasp at the chemistry.

I saw them dining at Sardi's, the theatrical restaurant in New York. The place was humming with beauty, the cream of the New York theatrical best. But all eyes were turned upon them. He was riding the crest of the wave at that point.

His *Hamlet* was the toast of the season.

They were involved with each other to the exclusion of everyone else. He looked fit and tanned and undeniably handsome. She looked super-humanly heavenly.

But I was delighted to note with eagle-eyes that the collar of her black satin creation (I guessed Balenciaga, maybe Givenchy) was besmirched with dandruff. I could have told her that satin of any colour, but particularly black and oddly enough white when it resembles particles of snow has always been a bastard for dandruff. She wouldn't have cared less, I imagine, even if somebody had pointed it out. As if anyone could have been that presumptuous. You can't carp in the presence of a goddess.

This critical eye of mine, call it envy, was not limited to Elizabeth Taylor's dandruff. I was as delighted to note the snow-stains up the back of Grace Kelly's stockings, accumulated on the short walk from her limousine into Jaeger's shop in Regent's Street, one Christmas when snow-sludge was thick on the ground.

And on another occasion, my taxi drew level with another at the traffic lights. I was intrigued to see Ursula Andress inside sobbing, her mascara running in two black rivulets over her famous cheekbones, right the way down to her equally famous chin. It was not long after she had stepped, like something from outer space in a white bikini, from a mediterranean ocean in the James Bond movie, *Dr No*.

Am I the only one, surely not, to note the feet of clay of our exorbitantly-paid and idolised screen-queens?

But I did wish the Burtons well, both of them. I held my breath with the nation, if not the entire globe, when Burton, inebriated, made regular anouncements claiming that, though he had separated from his wife, he had no intention at all of marrying Elizabeth Taylor.

I found it extraordinarily insensitive and boorish behaviour. I couldn't for the life of me understand why on earth the glorious creature would have remained with such an oaf. Not when the entire universe would have given their very life to whisk her off her feet. I can only deduce that she enjoyed the challenge of finally getting what she wanted, marriage to him, even if he didn't want it. Just by hanging on in there she eventually achieved her goal. That is single-minded persistence.

Richard Burton had always been a womaniser. So had Mike Todd who, I was shocked to learn from the writings of Evelyn Keyes, had planned to continue his affair with her after he had ensnared and married Elizabeth Taylor. Keyes had been living with Mike Todd for three full years, when she was unceremoniously dumped by him in his pursuit of Elizabeth. Yet he was mystified then furious at her refusal, and apoplectic when she went on to marry Artie Shaw. She was a much sought-after lady, who had already been married to such towering directorial talents as Charles Vidor and John Huston. Why should she hang around as second best for Mike Todd?

Richard Burton had been habitually unfaithful to his wife, the sainted Sybil. She had tolerated the pain and public humiliation because she loved him and cherished his talent so much, certain in the conviction that he would always return to her. Which he did, except in the case of Elizabeth Taylor.

The Taylor/Burton affair lasted two years, from 1962 to 1964. Following their marriage in 1964 he remained faithful for seven years. But he was restless under the gimlet eye and constant guard of his fiercely jealous wife, Elizabeth, who didn't trust him once out of her sight.

He was the first of the two to betray the beloved spouse, who by that time was proclaiming, in drink, that she would be glad to see the back of him and wished that 'he'd get the hell out of her life'. But she didn't mean it.

Between them they consumed copious oceans of alcohol. Burton had the problem long before the two had got together, though Elizabeth enjoyed a drink enormously, also. But it had never interfered with her work before. She had always been and was proud to be the absolute professional and remained sober throughout a day of filming.

Burton by contrast would have already consumed Bloody Marys for breakfast and looked forward to alcoholic reinforcements over long lunch breaks. On the set of *Cleopatra*, their first film together, she adopted the habit as enthusiastically as a duck to water. Afternoon filming took expert lighting and make up to conceal the results on both leads.

But nothing could cloud the electricity sizzling between the two, onscreen and off. No chemical could dilute that, in fact quite the reverse. When the director, Joseph L. Mankiewicz, called 'Cut', the kissing continued. Audiences, worldwide, flocked to the cinemas to sit through *Cleopatra*, despite critical thumbs down. Nobody cared, they just couldn't get enough of the most publicised lovers of the century.

Elizabeth's total income from the film exceeded $7,000,000. In 1963, the highest paid American business executive earned $650,000, and President Kennedy, $150,000. Elizabeth Taylor received at least $2.4 million.

In their next co-starring venture, *The V.I.P.s*, she was paid a million dollars and Burton a half of this. But with their percentage of the profits, they waltzed off with more than $4,300,000. But her appearance in that empy and cynical vehicle was lifeless and glum. It was one of her very worst performances. Richard was taking every opportunity to disappear off to his wife, Sybil and his daughters at weekends, leaving Elizabeth behind in the Dorchester Hotel. He was still announcing to reporters, who would listen and then avidly write it up in the popular press, that he had no intention of marrying Elizabeth. This and his behaviour caused her real distress. It was clear to her closest friends and collegues that he was the one calling the tune in their relationship at that time.

By the time the famous couple finally became man and wife in 1964, I was living the high life of a single woman again and I loved every minute.

Everybody seemed to be having a sensationally sexy time in the sixties. Money appeared to flow like champagne and there was certainly plenty of that around. Life in Britain was like a bubble, waiting to be pricked but with no sign of subsidence yet.

I drove around town in a yellow four-seater Morgan sports car, sprayed yellow to match the frontage of my Chelsea house. Soon it would be joined by an enormous vintage Rolls Royce, sprayed the same colour. Teenagers would knock at the front door asking for autographs of whichever pop star lived there.

The Rolls was a present from an ardent aristocratic admirer, a gift that the family persuaded me to accept, just for the fun of it. But I turned down his offer of marriage. There was no way that I would swap the good times on the town for a crumbling mansion and acres of greenery in the shires.

He became a devoted family friend instead, an escort for my mother, who was nearer his age than I was, anyway. They attended auctions at Sotheby's and Christie's together, which would have bored me to distraction. I would probably quite enjoy them now, given the affluence. Everything is a question of timing.

I jumped from one high-flying career as a succesful painter of landscapes in the Abstract Expressionist manner, to another really glamorous one as Fashion Editor, on *Nova*, *Harpers*, and finally *The Sunday Times*. I won plaudits for all three, but my heart was never in it.

Nevertheless, the newspaper post turned me into a journalist, which led to my next career as a writer, a novelist. I published ten comic-erotic bestsellers in the next following years. The money was flowing in. I had married my second husband. At the end of twelve years we divorced and I was happily single again.

My fourth successful career presented itself to me. I was already a recognisable face from the television. Now I went on stage with my One Woman Show. I was in essence a stand-up comedienne, with a basic set-piece of risque poems and raffish repartee which I wrote myself.

My material basically was the life I had led up until then. It played to packed and appreciative audiences two years in succession at the Assembly Rooms in the Edinburgh Festival. Then I embarked on a nationwide tour over two years. That was enough. My own alcoholic intake was now taking its toll. My chain-smoking habit, up to one hundred a day by the end was affecting my voice. I performed heroically with a crucifying sore throat and bronchial lungs. The stage show is never the end of the evening. Fans clamour for autographs at the stage door. There are invitations to parties and clubs, the night stretches out seductively until dawn. Lovers abound. More than once I entertained entire teams of Welsh rugby players, far from home, looking for fun and needing the motherly touch. That's how I choose to view it.

Meanwhile the Burtons were going from strength to spectacular strength. From 1967 onwards they embarked on an orgy of conspicuous spending. Together, over the decade they earned more than $88 million. And spent more than $65 million of it.

They invested in real estate all around the world: Ireland, England, Switzerland, Mexico, the Caribbean. They bought a fleet of Rolls Royces, a yacht with fourteen bedrooms and quarters for a crew of nine. It cost them $192,000, but they sold it soon after for $6 million. They purchased paintings by Monet, Utrillo, Picasso, Vincent van Gogh and Rembrandt. They booked entire floors of luxury hotels. They bought aeroplanes and helicopters and furs and precious gems. Plenty of those because they had been Elizabeth's favourites from childhood.

But as the Burton's conspicuous consumption soared out of control, so did their professional lives suffer. Elizabeth drank and ate to excess and was hooked on pain-relieving drugs, to relieve an excruciating earlier spinal injury, which were lethal when combined with alcohol.

Richard had been warned by medical men to cut out the drink, it had already wrecked his liver. To continue would be dangerous. And he tried to stay on the wagon, but Elizabeth didn't care for lunchtime martinis all on her own. She coaxed and cajoled until he joined her for drinks again. She could not provide the support he so desperately needed. Together they were destroying each other.

They were both immensely kind and generous people, massively talented. Those around them were concerned and anxious for both of them. But they were surrounded by their entourage, who overprotected them. Then there was a posse of paid acolytes in attendance, too. The friends who could have advised them, speaking honestly with no bullshit simply couldn't get close enough. They had no intimates except each other.

Boredom, restlessness, the exhaustion that follows various excessive indulgences, a desperate fear of ageing, and becoming old fashioned and losing their public, all these placed greater stress on their neurotic co-dependent relationship.

Burton recorded in his diary at that time that Elizabeth was wildly drunk each night. 'Stoned, unfocused, unable to walk straight, talking in a slow, meaningless baby voice utterly without reason, like a demented child.' Her doctors had already diagnosed serious liver damage. The two of them shared that. Burton however did remain sober when his wife was ill, real or imagined. He lovingly attended to the most intimate nursing duties, and these tasks occupied him whilst he was filming *Anne of the Thousand Days*.

By 1969 and 1970, Richard Burton's diary notebooks expressed his frantic fear over Elizabeth's consumption of drink and drugs. She was falling down constantly, was intolerant with everything, with life itself. She had become semi-literate, and suffered chronic back pain, for which she took increasingly greater numbers of painkillers. She continued to drink, more and more.

The two of them were bickering and quarrelling incessantly now. But try as he would to imagine life without her, Burton could not. She was afflicted by idleness, anxieties about premature ageing although she was only thirty-seven.

But her greatest fear was of being abandoned by her husband. And now she was prone to irrational jealousy, convinced that he was having an affair with his leading lady in this latest film, Genevieve Bujold. Quite without proof or reason.

Their underlying friendship and humour asserted itself on occasions such as their appearance in the popular Lucille Ball television show, when Lucy tries on Elizabeth's enormous diamond ring but can't get it off her finger in time for a press reception.

But life was increasingly onerous for both the Burtons, and equally boring and repetitive for their public who were now beginning to lose interest. The private extravagance was now viewed as mere ostentation, instead of two people having fun on a spending spree. It was out of kilter with the times and the increasing plight and poverty of the beleaguered nations of the Third World.

Audiences dropped, now disinterested in their films. They felt cheated by the lack-lustre performances and glassy-eyed lack of vitality of both Burtons in the inferior material which followed such a seminal work as *Who's Afraid of Virginia Woolf?* This was released in 1966. In 1967 came another joint acting venture, *The Taming of the Shrew*. Burton revelled in his role, making use of his magnificent Shakespearean oratory. Elizabeth still looked magnificent, but out of her depth. *Doctor Faustus* in 1967 was a pretentious flop.

Reflections in a Golden Eye, in 1967, without Richard Burton, brought Elizabeth back into public and critical favour. She played her finest sultry self, with an edge of empty-headed vulgarity, opposite a strangely wooden Marlon Brando. Directed by John Huston, in this screenplay from the novel by Carson McCullers, Elizabeth Taylor actually acted the rest of the cast off the screen, including Brando and Julie Harris.

From there it was downhill all the way, in professional terms. In 1967, came and went *The Comedians*, with both Burtons and an estimable cast which included Alec Guinness, Peter Ustinov, and Lillian Gish.

In 1968 came the excruciating *Boom*, directed by Joseph Losey, with the Burtons in appallingly self-indulgent form and Noel Coward inexplicably playing the Witch of Capri. Audiences stayed away in droves.

The less said about *Secret Ceremony*, 1968, the better. Kinder not to mention Elizabeth, or Mia Farrow, Robert Mitchum, Pamela Brown, or Peggy Ashcroft. Difficult to imagine how a flop could come from such a cast. But the director, Joseph Losey, managed it.

It is tragic to record that twenty years after George Stevens had coaxed such an exquisite performance from Elizabeth Taylor in *A Place in the Sun*, he or she or the script led to such a bitter travesty of all their talents in *The Only Game in Town*, co-starring Warren Beatty who was the heart-throb of the moment then. The less said the better.

In 1972 came more of the dismal same for Elizabeth, starring with a fine cast again. Michael Caine, Susannah York, Margaret Leighton, X, Y, and Z, promised great things with a screenplay written by Edna O'Brien but it turned out to be a hollow exercise. It was a great disappointment to O'Brien, who deplored the constant and savage cuts and rewrites to her original script.

Hammersmith is Out, 1972, with Peter Ustinov directing himself and both Burtons, must have looked pretty good on paper, but failed to make the grade on-screen.

Night Watch in 1973 with Elizabeth Taylor, Laurence Harvey and Billie Whitelaw was as abysmal as another film in the same year starring Elizabeth and Henry Fonda, *Ash Wednesday*. She was simply going through the motions, he just looked utterly wretched. Others followed, too depressing to even mention.

How could it be that these two charismatic stars, the Burtons, had no advisers to suggest what they should accept or refuse when all this rubbish was offered to them? Or perhaps they did and by that time they just weren't listening. Their personal problems had taken over; there wasn't that much energy left over for anything else.

Elizabeth was involved in violent verbal disagreements with her mother. After years of discomfort and bleeding she underwent an operation for haemorrhoids. The recovery threw her back on the drugs which she was trying so hard to escape. But her recovery re-ignited an abundant sexual appetite. Unfortunately, for the first time ever in their marriage, her husband was unable to respond to her demands. His new found sobriety had left him without an appetite for sex, which can happen. But for Burton this was a new thing.

By 1972 however, when his wife turned forty, Richard Burton was drinking again to drown his sorrow at the death of a beloved brother. He rediscovered enough sexual desire to embark on an affair with a beautiful young actress appearing in his film *Bluebeard*. The infidelity took place in Budapest, the first so he claimed in his eight-year marriage to Elizabeth.

'Once I started being attracted to other women,' said Burton, 'I knew the game was up.'

The game for Elizabeth Taylor and Richard Burton was truly up, though they divorced, subsequently remarried and divorced a second time. They remained in constant touch however and were linked right through to his death, by which time both had married and divorced other partners.

At the time of his death at fifty-eight, from a massive stroke, Burton was married yet again and living in Switzerland. Elizabeth had undergone treatment for her dependence on alcohol and drugs. She was engaged to be married to a Mexican lawyer. But this ended at the news of Burton's demise. She was too devastated to make any plans.

The greatest romance of the 20th century had finally, and this time definitely, drawn to a close. Now we could all get on with our own lives at long last.

When Michael Jackson requested the pleasure of the invited one hundred and sixty guests to the marriage of Miss Elizabeth Taylor and Mr Larry Fortensky, at Neverland in 1991, my own small world turned to me in anticipation. But I was already prepared.

'No! no! no! no! I am NOT following the path of my Almost Astral-Twin this time. I refuse to comb the building sites of Britain, for a blond-highlight, bouffant-haired, treble-chinned, perma-tanned construction worker as a husband.'

At fifty-nine, I was the same age as my chosen alter-ego. I had no problem with the age thing. Her age or his, thirty-nine. Twenty years difference between couples is nothing these days, something to celebrate indeed when the man is much younger. More stamina, harder erections, greater appetite, all that stuff. For however long you're into all that.

More to the point, thinking ahead, younger men these days are so much sweeter, kinder, more compassionate and less-macho than they used to be. Their post-feminist mothers have seen to that.

So useful, later down the line, for scrubbing the dentures, back-fastening the brassiere, making the breakfast, emptying the bedpan, mending the telly, pushing the wheelchair. And let's face it, still earning the wage when the older woman is well past it.

Nor had I any difficulty at all with the fact that she had chosen a fellow recovering alcoholic. They would be working the inspirational Twelve Step Programme together. That was enough of a guide of how to live a mutually rewarding life for any couple.

She was the one who had steered my own life away from the booze. I'd seen her talking to Oprah about winning her own battle with it and I thought, if Elizabeth can do it, so can I. I approve of her choice from that point of view, despite the two of them flouting the Recovery Rooms unspoken rule of not getting into romantic attachments in the first year of sobriety. If I had not paid attention myself to that one, I'd have been back and forth to Reno countless times in my initial twelve months.

Any chap only had to smile at me from the other side of a meeting, and my head would be whirling. How would he get on with my kids? Would we live in his home or mine? Where would we hold the wedding? Would it be an intimate one or full-on? These thoughts would be teeming in one return of the smile.

Then I'd look the other side of the room. Another, quite different man, would flash his molars. My sister wouldn't approve of this one, but I was going to marry him anyway. And who cared what the kids thought. It was time I made my own choices where men were concerned, instead of all this people-pleasing. I'd been doing for years to keep everyone around me happy.

I'd get married in black leather, with biker boots, too. Absolutely, why not?

So, yes, my thoughts held some concern for Elizabeth. Why marry this one? If you're up for any animal, don't lock the farmyard gate. There's variety out there, girl, and plenty of it. Especially in sobriety, it's all a very different ball game to so-called living spontaneously. You can still jump in at the deep end, but now you make sure that the water's there, and plenty of it. Looking before you leap, real-life stuff like that.

But right! Now you've done it, you're back from the honeymoon.

Please, please, don't hole yourself up in the mansion, munching Southern Fried Chicken and Extra Peach Ice-cream. Or get snapped in a diner hogging on burgers and fries. It's just not, well, *sexy*, Liz!

The way to a man's heart, our mothers may have told us in the 'fifties, is through the stomach. But that was way back then when we'd only just emerged from the Ark, when domestic goddesses still ruled the roost. It doesn't apply today.

Oh dear, oh no! This one is not going to go the distance, for sure! So, her eighth marriage lasted from October, 1991, through to August, 1995. She'd returned to the prescription drugs, pain killers, for her new hip operation. He was back on the booze with rumours of infidelity. Bastard!

Elizabeth announced that the two of them were separating after marginally less than four years together. During that time she had launched her perfume, 'White Diamonds'. I made certain to be there in the advertised Selfridges shindig on London's Oxford Street.

Queuing downstairs in the Ladies beforehand, I waited behind two senior citizen shoppers, watching the video of Elizabeth urging us to buy the perfume. A hot news notice ran at the bottom of the screen, heralding her presence for the Press Launch up on the 5th floor, amongst carpets. She looked utterly exquisite, taut, lithe, youthfully radiant, narrow as a knitting needle, on the video. I couldn't wait to see the goddess, my own personal deity. This would be the inspiration of a lifetime.

'Can we be bothered going up?' one senior citizen asked the other.

'No, I'm not fussed.'

'Nor me. She won't be looking like that, not in the flesh.' A dismissive thumb jerked towards the video. 'You can bet she won't. They have ways to make these celebs look better on those contraptions. It's like they do with photos, retouching and carving off pounds round the edges. My grandson's in the business, he was explaining it. In person she'll be looking just like the rest of us.'

'Yep,' chuckled the other. 'Fat and over forty, well past our sell-by date! Frothy coffee and a cream cake in the snack bar, instead?'

'It had been as much as I could do not to give a vicious jab on the shoulders of both these ignorant dolts and say something like, 'Excuse me, but show some margin of respect, you're talking about a myth here, an icon. Elizabeth Taylor, The Ultimate Enduring Hollywood Legend.'

I seethed up to the 5th floor instead, fighting for a seat as near the front as possible. I'd only just got there in time for the grand entrance. There wasn't one.

If it hadn't been for the sudden clicking of cameras, I wouldn't even have realised that this stout, pleasant but very ordinary indeed person who'd walked on was her and not just another sales assistant on Selfridges Carpets, Fifth Floor.

The celestial blue of the eyes was still catching the light, and the luscious lilt of the lower lip was in place. But the size on her! What had happened? And the unflattering clothes! Surely she hadn't chosen this matronly outfit, and the crap wig, for surely it was a wig. And the little girl voice, and inappropriately flirtatious behaviour in front of the cameramen, for this was being televised. God help her! Pity coursed through me. I was reminded, and I pushed the hateful thought away, of Bette Davis in *Whatever Happened to Baby Jane*.

She was asked about Larry, her husband. And she wriggled and blushed like a bashful schoolgirl, saying, that yes, of course, he was with her. But in the little girl voice that she'd employed to such great breathy effect in *National Velvet*, when she was a little girl.

Elizabeth, our idol, you're in sight of your sixtieth birthday and we all love you more with each passing year. You don't have to be young anymore, we're not. Please STOP IT!

This was going from worse to worse. Why hadn't anyone the guts to enquire about the size of her vastly expanded girth, considering that she'd so recently published a book about becoming as slim as her, which was meant to help everyone? Then, she'd been displaying her own surreal weight loss on the telly with Oprah, which was presumably when the perfume promotion video had been shot.

Well, I could have asked, but I didn't. Why spoil her day and mine? There was something vulnerable there, a need to be accepted just as she was now. Perhaps she was sick of the pedestal we'd put her on for so long. But we'd been faced with the reality of seeing the legend in the hefty flesh, that was a shock for us when all the packaged promotion had been of a different image.

If they had promoted her as she looked now, like the rest of us, as the two women downstairs had rightly said, they might have sold far more perfume. But the beauty industry doesn't work like that.

They dropped the gorgeous daughter of Ingrid Bergman, Isabella Rosselini, the seductive star of *Blue Velvet*, when she hit forty. Estee Lauder cosmetics dumped slinky Liz Hurley's face as she aged from the fey safety-pinned, Versace filly on Hugh Grant's infidel arm.

Elizabeth Taylor has meant so much more to us, particularly me, me, me, than these fleeting celebrities. We will always stick with her, through thick and thin.

But just what was the point of this tawdry personal appearance, anyhow? This still orbiting star, advertised down in ablutions, then up on the fifth floor slotted between piled Axminsters and scullery mats. The P.R. deserved to be slaughtered. Now I was indignant and protective of my idol, on her behalf.

Why, oh why, couldn't she have stayed happily indoors with Larry, pigging away at the trough of room service, on their own? Then rolling together in the hay of the Dorchester Hotel, overlooking the sylvan glades of Hyde Park.

Why couldn't she just have allowed the ethereal video image to do it all for her? Or simply, if the lure of a live audience still cannot be resisted, have made more of an…effort!

Whatever the size, where was the salty language and sense of being a free spirit? That was what we all loved, quite apart from the face.

Had she been advised against her shimmering kaftans simply because it was in the middle of the day? Any one of those would disguise a hundred Southern Fried Chickens and Double Malt Butterscotch Shakes.

I'd visited, with my sister, the display of Elvis Presley's spectacular outfits in Graceland, growing progressively more vast as he took to his grub. Certainly no diminishing glamour there.

Had Fortensky, the construction worker, drained the poetic gypsy from Elizabeth's personality in the way a dubious choice of partner can do? One had only to recall how utterly mundane she looked with husband number four, Eddie Fisher. And, if possible, even more appalling than that after Burton, with that politician, Warner. Words fail!

Perhaps the American executives of her perfume company had put their oar in, misjudging the British public, playing for safe with her appearance, with profits from scent sales uppermost in mind.

Alas, frothy coffee and cream cake may well have been the better choice, those two senior citizens were wiser than me. If I saw them downstairs over my own frothy coffee and cream cake now, I'd bloody well tell them that they were right.

But they weren't there and I skipped the frankly calorie-laden snack.

I needed to get home and reflect seriously on today's experience, sensing a change of direction, a massive upheaval in my life. How would I exist in the time allotted to me, meaning the rest of my days, without Elizabeth Taylor central to my life? What becomes of an ageing Almost Astral Twin when the once enviable mirror-image appears no longer enviable? I was being forced to re-evaluate my role model now. It was clearly time to uncover who I actually was and what exactly I wished to become.

All but the first twelve years of my life had been consumed by envy. It had begun at the age of twelve when I first beheld Elizabeth Taylor on the silver screen. Discovering the accident of our almost identical birthdays, I deluded myself into actually believing that we were uncannily linked. I convinced myself that our mutual existences were following the same path.

Throughout my adolescence and adulthood, I would refer to myself as, 'The Woolworth Edition of Elizabeth Taylor', whenever people remarked on our striking physical resemblances.

At the age of seventeen I'd smirk with pride as I said it, in a self-congratulatory sense. Mine wasn't a modest response, quite the opposite. I'd actually preen, pulling back my shoulders and elbows so that ogling folk could get a faceful of proud frontage, 36C. I had yanked my bra-straps so high they were nearly cutting into the bone.

And I emulated Elizabeth's legendary miniscule waist measurement by ordering extra holes to be punched along all my broad leather belts, at the shoe repair shop since they were the only ones with the equipment.

Each month I set myself the goal of achieving the next hole, strangulating my intestinal digestive system until my mother called the doctor to my nightly colic. He suggested mildly that she burn all my belts. He had seen me running for a bus the previous week and feared that I would snap in two. My silhouette then was that of a wasp.

But why would I have demeaned myself, by actually believing in my heart and soul that I was the copy, cut on the cheap? Me, the inferior mould. The mere shadow of a splendiferous statue.

My father failed in raising the funds to fly us both to Hollywood when I was eleven. He had learned that Errol Flynn, the top screen idol then, had a penchant for young girls, the younger the better. If we had gone, I could easily have become Elizabeth's understudy, for by the age of twelve the likeness was remarkable. But this is to presume that she, not I would have been the star. Why shouldn't it have been the other way around, so that Elizabeth would have ended up as my understudy?

She was good at Art. She enjoyed writing very much. She could easily have turned her back on the acting career, as a mere understudy. Many times, as a star, she expressed the wish to do so. Each time she married she claimed to be looking forward to a life of pure domestic bliss. Given my life she could have become instead, the painter and writer that I became.

Studying in London she could have met Richard Burton when he was making his way. She might have been an art student at St Martins Art School, slap-bang in the middle of theatreland. They could have bumped into each other in Soho, the haunt of high bohemia. That was in itself enough glamour for a Welsh-born boy. They needn't have bothered with Beverly Hills.

As a writer she would have encouraged his own, and found that her existence would have been much happier without all those other certain men in her life, and all that spectacular wealth and those possessions weighing her down.

It was not until my first honeymoon that I came to understand that the penis is not actually permanently erect. That had been my girlish experience in the presence of the opposite sex on dance-floors and dates.

But a rigid erection can be a threatening presence. A flacid penis offers playful pleasures, like toying with warm plasticine. As pliable as my present, elegantly-empty, breasts.

I had taken the number 22 bus home after waiting at the bus-stop in a kind of loved-up daze. I felt like a teenager flashing my Senior Citizen Free Pass, leaving my lover and the opulence of the Ritz Hotel behind me. Our long-running affair had always been conducted in luxurious settings. But we chose currently unfashionable ones such as the London Ritz where we would be unlikely to bump into people we knew, or be spotted by the press. He was still in the dregs of his fifth marriage, and I was still recognisable to hovering paparazzi. We neither of us needed that sort of publicity.

I went back home, to World's End.

I love this new home of mine, more than anywhere I've ever lived in London. I mostly appreciate the multi-cultural aspect of getting into the elevators to meet faces from every conceivable nation. I smile at them, they smile back at me. These are instant friendships, next time we see each other in the streets we wave. If we shared the same language we could enjoy conversations. But for now we are content with the contact of mutual recognition. I say 'have a good day', a charming American habit I learned from living in the Chelsea Hotel, that bastion of Bohemian depravity in New York City way back in another life with one of my husbands. They nod, not understanding, but smile anyway, uttering their own greeting in their own language. I laugh at my own incomprehension, so do they. Language isn't important. It's the feeling flowing betweeen you that counts.

My place, now all painted up in Mexican colours, is as stylish as anywhere I've ever lived. And with a garden of my very own too.

The very first week I moved in an inebriated fellow-resident, an old wino with a hell of a whiff, lurched into the lift. I warmed instantly to him. He was what I would have become if my boozing had continued for much longer. He could have become my constant companion if I was still at it.

'Good morning, sir.' I flashed my new dentures in true film star style. They'd taken some bloody getting used to, these false teeth, but it had been worth the effort. Though at first it had felt as if I was balancing the entire contents of the British Library above my tongue.

The dentist advised removing the bastards at night, and drowning them in a glass of water by the bed. I'd pray for shrinkage in my dreams. And even resorted to furtive outings with a polo necked sweater pulled up over my mouth, my teeth in my pocket. They hurt so much, pressed against the swollen upper gums still leaking gore from the six recent extractions.

What kind of sadists these young males must be to choose dentistry as a legal profession behind which to lurk, indulging their perverted need to inflict pain. They had probably been abused as children. It makes you wonder what kind of home life they suffered.

'It is amazing just how many people my age actually don't bother to wear their teeth when they're out and about,' I'd ventured bravely at my next fitting. 'I've been noticing.'

The dentist snapped back, rudely, I thought. 'And did you notice how many more do?'

But I'm definitely pleased now that I stuck with them and made the effort. My pearlies now pull the punch of the white keys on a grand piano. My smile had never had this much impact. I now wish that I'd taken my frankly below par tombstones out much sooner, the whole lot of them, instead of forking out fortunes for porcelain caps, which barely survived the passionate onslaught of tongue-lashed kisses, let alone the violent cut-and-thrust punches of married life.

Having said that I graciously declined the offer of National Health lower dentures as well as upper. I don't feel I have the horse-power any more, keeping grip on two sets of plastic intruders in the same orifice. I really don't know how other people do it. Though my sister claims that the lower set sits in very nicely, thank you, due to the force of gravity.

The smile this morning wasn't having the expected effect. Seeing me the old wino's eyes filled with tears.

'You've gorn an' ruined me day now, you 'ave, seein' you 'ere.'

'I'm sorry,' I responded cheerfully.

'You was an icon, you was. A proper star. I heard you was moved in. S'not right. You shouldn't be living in this dump. It's only fit for the likes of me.'

The stench was ripe enough to make me thankful that I was getting out at the first level. But his unshaven chin was wobbling with emotion. I recognised the maudlin stage of an on-coming hangover, when everything turns to tears and later to thoughts of suicide. That piercing yearning to end it all.

'Oh no, I can't agree with that. I love it here already. Where do you think I should be living then?' I humoured him.

'Up with the nobs in some swanky place fit for stars.'

'Bless you,' I laughed. 'Have a good day.'

I squeezed his stinking shoulder and gave him a kiss. That's what he needs, I thought I knew. But when I turned to wave goodbye before the doors of the lifts closed, I glimpsed fresh urine staining his front and spreading down around his shabby shoes over the floor as he frantically fumbled to undo his trouser zip. Too late.

A timely reminder for gratitude, I thought as I was walking away. Back amongst the living instead of cosseted in luxury, existing in ivory towers.

For all my mansions in the past, I've never felt so much a part of the daily ritual, or felt so utterly at home. My neighbours rarely communicated with each other before. People took pride in respecting the privacy of those around them. They kept themselves to themselves, as if this was the best way to be. There was an innate suspicion of strangers. This had been the shock for my parents when they moved away from our valley to live in the seedier suburbs of London because they couldn't afford better. There was no chatting over the garden wall, no exchanging of gossip or sharing of problems whilst pegging out clothes on the washline.

The English as a race practice a reserve which I had never got used to. And still haven't.

My housing estate when Christine Keeler moved in had already come to be regarded as one of the more dangerous ones of the inner city. Drug dealing and a criminal element had run riot. Dangerous, it may have been. But we have our own police system in place now, with regular patrols by policemen in pairs, combined with constant security checks. And in my case, in sheltered accommodation a series of cords, seven in all, placed strategically in the kitchen, the bathroom, the bedroom, the sitting room, for easy access in case of the first coronary, or signs of break-in, or should one slip, slide, break a limb, sustain an injury or an assault, panic buttons for emergencies.

On my first night in my new place I had inadvertantly pulled one of the cords assuming it to be a light. A click. Then a loud, loud voice blared from the walls as if from a high volume speaker.

'Are we to bring the paramedics now?!'

My single friends envy me my latest home, living alone as they do, widowed or divorced, wondering what will happen to them in practical and financial terms when they become enfeebled. All this is taken care of for me. I'm assured that this is to be my home for life, until I die, as the 24-hour warden delicately pointed out.

I made my very first friend on my first evening. I'd arrived back after midnight having had dinner with my daughters. They escorted me back to the building. I assured them I was perfectly capable of taking the lift up to my floor and kissed them goodnight.

I was however filled with early trepidation, not knowing whether violence may occur on the way up. It was only because I was on unfamiliar territory. There was then, and ever since, nothing to be concerned about at all.

Leaving the lift I turned into my corridor, the walkway

overlooking the communal courtyard off Kings Road. It was partially lit, beautifully so, like a horror film by Hitchcock. Several bulbs had failed but there was one spotlight working and in the gloom this light lit up what I actually saw to be the ghost of my mother, standing still as a statue, dressed in the sheer cream nightdress that had been her favourite.

'Hello,' I greeted her softly. I love seeing my mother. It had been twenty years since we'd embraced in the flesh and I still ached as much for her earthly presence as I had when gazing into her coffin.

The loss of a much loved mother is like no other.

Now here she was come to greet me, with that growing mischief dancing around her mouth and the still beautiful eyes beginning to sparkle.

But it wasn't my mother and she wasn't a ghost nor earthly apparition, simply the one-hundred-and-three-year-old neighbour who lived two doors along the corridor from me. She was usually there, wandering, whatever time I arrived home. The nightgowns would vary but the welcome remained. We became best friends, but those were the only times we met. It was only ever late at night or in the early hours of the morning.

Then, returning from a trip to India that first winter, financed by my family, I missed her presence. The warden explained that she'd been taken to hospital on medical advice. I said eagerly that I'd like to visit her. We had really formed a bond with each other. On the first meeting she had asked how old I was. I'd told her my age—seventy years old. She had burst out laughing and touched my cheek.

'A mere child,' she'd said soothingly and she'd told me hers. One hundred and three. It had inspired me then to make the most of things from then on. That I could have over thirty years left to be a joy to myself and an inspiration to others.

'She died in hospital,' the warden said. I was so sad, I really missed her corridor presence there in the shadows. But we were meant to meet, if only for those few brief months.

'Is this cash enough to get you home, darling girl?' My lover had passed me a wad of folded notes, before I left him in the Ritz.

'I'll go home on the bus.'

'My darling girl will be doing no such bloody thing! What an extraordinary suggestion! Public transport! I don't think so. I can't have you despoiled by sub-human dross, you exquisite creature in your delicious finery. Allow me to call you a car, a taxi, any vehicle other than a BUS. Please!'

I suspect that this particular lover has had the wrong idea of me all along. My witty mix of jumble sale, charity shop, couture special items, has always misled many to believe there's more in the bank than there ever has been. Even the Official Receiver got it wrong at the time of my bankruptcy.

'We'll be taking your jewels.'

'I have no jewels. Mine are all cheap junk. I'm too careless a person to own the genuine stuff. I lose things.'

'We'll be taking your antiques.'

'I have no antiques. I'm a modernist. I prefer plastic.'

'Well, we know you own a house here in Wales. We'll be having that from you for certain.' A note of triumph.

'But that's my home. Where will I live?'

'Somewhere else!' There was spite in his voice and immense satisfaction.

I could do little but burst into laughter. 'I hadn't thought of that.'

End of brief conversation. I had been declared bankrupt.

These days I dress in post-menopausal, geriatric art student style, which turns heads, probably in derisive disbelief, who knows. Who actually cares! I never look back. My lover had been surrounded by high-born English Tory ladies his entire life. The Camilla Parker Bowles type who look great on a horse or striding in tweeds. I had always been his piece of exotica. His piece of Celtic rough, if we're to be brutally honest, not overlooking my gypsy blood. The attraction of opposites was why we always sparked each other off so satisfactorally. Neither of us was in awe of the other. It had always been a meeting of equal minds. I enjoyed his pomposity. He admired my irreverence.

A chauffeur was waiting outside the Ritz to whisk him to the helicopter, which would take him to Heathrow. He was flying back to his Sarah Lawrence-educated young wife this morning, back to her inherited billion dollar business in the States. As if he didn't have enough wealth and status of his own.

'Cheers, darling!' I said, 'I've adored every minute.' I pocketed the wad of notes, I have no false pride these days. This would save me going to the post office for my income allowance and state pension, which totalled one hundred and five pounds per week exactly.

Fare money doesn't count as earnings on the side. I wasn't breaking the law, as far as I knew. I'd have to check with Social Services on that one. They can come down on you like a ton of bricks if they think you are diddling them.

He nodded and clinked his flute of champagne, satisfied. It was only nine in the morning and he'd already drained almost a bottle. It wasn't for me, after years of sobriety, to say anything. It wasn't my business. But this would be the cloud, this and the chain-smoking habit, which would shadow our continuing relationship. I knew it with a sinking heart.

He hadn't got an inkling when it came to finance, he appeared as useless as me when it came to totting things up. He'd come from vast wealth and astute investors had multiplied that many times over. One nought extra, or less, didn't seem to register. The super-rich are extraordinarily immune to amounts. If I had mentioned any amount of cash he would have summoned it on the spot. But I'm not his kept mistress or an occasional call girl, I've never been that and it was too late to start now. You can't be a call girl at 70. Or can you? Why not?

Earlier in the bath together, I'd told him I was living on a council estate now, in sheltered accommodation. He'd no idea what the hell these places were. His expression was totally blank. It was like talking to an android from another planet.

'It's where Christine Keeler lived when she was totally down and out, after the Profumo scandal. When she was at her lowest ebb.'

'Ah, Christine Keeler, beautiful breasts. Not a patch on yours, of course.' He leaned forward and gave them a tweek. Strange how he hadn't even noticed that they were grazing the ground now. That Profumo business crucified the MacMillan government though. Tories never the same since then, alas. Paved the way for that ghastly grammar school gal, Thatcher, brought up on shop premises.

'Like me,' I said, meaning Keeler and Thatcher. 'One down and out and the other a grammar school girl brought up in her dad's shop.'

He burst out laughing. 'You're devilish lefty, always have been. I know I'm an old fuddy-duddy, stick in the mud, dyed in the wool Conservative, but you've always kept me on my toes.' He aimed the giant sponge at my nose, I flung it back at his. We flooded the bathroom floor.

We were more like naughty schoolchildren than lovers, now. At one time this bathtime would have taken place under the power-shower instead and we would have spent the entire time experimenting on the various possibilities of genital insertion. Not anymore. But our sedate ways now were just as pleasurable, full of fondness and fun. We enjoyed each other's company so much, that it felt like the old intimacy even when we were fully dressed and not even touching.

The phone was ringing back home, when I put my keys in the door. I reached it in time. His voice was forlorn, full of longing, full of alcohol. He was ringing from the airport. A helicopter took less time to reach Heathrow than it took me on the bus to get through ferocious traffic conditions from Piccadilly to Chelsea. That's what money buys. Speed. Impatience is indulged when you are wealthy. There is no need to wait for anything.

'I'm missing you already. I want to shower you with red roses. You didn't give me your address.'

'Don't do that, please. This isn't that sort of place.'

'What on earth do you mean?'

'I know your romantic gestures, you don't do things by halves and hundreds of red roses could put my income support at risk. The neighbours snoop and report. It will look as if I have a wealthy admirer.'

He exploded! 'Wealthy admirer be fucked. I feel like cancelling my flight. I can't leave you. We haven't as much time as we once had. We should always have been together, I want to spend the rest of my life with you.' He sounded urgent now. 'Will you marry me? I'm going back to get a divorce. When will I have the answer? Darling girl, make it "yes".'

'I'm thinking about it. I promise I'll let you know soon,

very, very, soon.'

'Shall I send a helicopter for you now? Or shall we meet in an hour's time back at the Ritz. Or, for a change what about taking a flight to Paris, we haven't been there in years…'

'He wants to get a divorce and marry me,' I told my sister on the telephone.

She responded with her usual sound opinion. 'Be sensible for once in your life. You still love him, you always have. This affair has been going for over forty years now. He's right, you know he is, you should always have been together. Why would you even hesitate, eh?'

'I don't know. It's just that I enjoy life on my own so much now.'

'I'll give you a really good reason to marry him.'

'Yes?' I brightened. My older sister always had the answer.

'You're totally broke. He's made of money. That's reason enough. You'd have to be blind not to see it.'

'I'm not totally broke. I manage very well indeed. Why would I get married? I don't need to. And perhaps the affair lasted this long because we're not tied to each other's apron strings. The sex is not what it once was, not any more.'

'Be realistic, we're none of us teenagers. Some may say that you're lucky to get anything. What's up? What's all this palaver really about?' My sister is patience itself.

'The booze.'

'Mm. Serious problem?'

'Serious for me. And the chain-smoking, too. That's worse. I can't even lip-read, there's always a cigarette in his mouth, with all the smoke that goes with it. The passive smoking alone, chokes me up. The only way would be to join in and be like we used to be. He would much prefer that, I know. But I don't want to go down that road, not again. I'd love him to give up both, they're no good for his health. He certainly shouldn't be smoking, not with his heart condition, it's madness. But you know how stubborn some people can be.'

'Put it on standby. You don't have to decide now, he still has his divorce to get through. He's waited this long, he can wait that much longer.'

Two weeks later I read my lover's obituaries in the newspapers. A sudden death, but not unexpected. Heart. I closed my eyes to seal the tears. Images of us as lovers came to me. We were our youthful selves in Venice, jubilant at being together again. The sex was rude and rough and raunchy and continued every night until dawn. Dining out became a sensual experience, limbs entwined beneath the tables. Meals would be left unfinished, desire took precedence over hunger. He couldn't pass windows displaying jewellery, without lavishing it on me. Farewell kisses were hungry and heartbreaking, with feverish plans to meet up again within the month. The embraces were tearful and tender at parting.

I opened my eyes and smiled out of the window, the obituaries had already slipped to the floor. Death does not obliterate memories. Only two weeks before at the Ritz we had re-filled each other's hearts, secure in mature and much weathered mutual devotion.

Love has its seasons. Who knows whether or not we'd have married? My most enduring love affair of so many in my life was finally over.

There was no need for any answer now.

I am sitting at the centre of a straggling row of 10-year-olds in the large Assembly Hall of my primary school in North London, clutching my raffle ticket between the palms of both hands. My ragged fingernails, bitten to the quick, are pressed together just below my chin. I can feel the pounding of my heart beneath the sleeve of my home-knitted woollen cardigan. Every other pupil but me is gazing expectantly up at the platform, where the winning ticket is about to be drawn by the headmaster. But my eyes are screwed together so tightly that my eyebrows are almost touching my cheeks.

An onlooker may have assumed, and rightly so, that I was praying. This would have been frowned upon by my teachers, certainly by the headmaster. Praying as fervently, not to say ferociously, for my raffle ticket to be picked, for me to be the winner, would not have been considered generous in spirit, given the circumstances. This raffle was to support the national war effort, the proceeds going to our boys at the Front, fighting the Huns, as they called the Germans.

My father had helped us win the First World War, serving as an officer in the airforce. He claimed this to have been his hour of glory and that life had taken a downward slant ever since. I told everyone he was a pilot, because it sounded more glamorous. And the photographs of him in his uniform did back that up, with the peaked cap over one eye, and the silver-tipped stick under his arm.

'He looks just like Cary Grant, that's who your father looks like,' my best friend, Myra would say. 'And your mother looks a cross between Vivien Leigh as Scarlet O'Hara and Joan Fontaine in *Rebecca*.'

'I know,' I'd answer proudly, swelling with pride. Though I hadn't seen either of those films yet. But I knew what the stars looked like, from Myra's *Picturegoer Magazine*.

'I wonder if their good looks will ever pass on to you, perhaps when you grow up?' She'd study me closely. 'There's not much sign of it so far. Your eyes are like a pair of pale green grapes, your fringe is too long and you're skinny as a snake. Never mind. You've got other things to make up for the lack of looks.'

'Like what?' I never ceased to enjoy this part, however many times she told me.

'You've got a bright mind, a good vocabulary for someone your age, you paint lovely pictures. Yes, and you've got a cheeky grin and a lucky streak and all of those could take you a long way. Beauty alone isn't what it's cracked up to be. Look where it's got me.' And she'd sigh.

Myra, a singer and dancer, had been kicked out of E.N.S.A. (Entertainments National Services Association) for getting pregnant after a dance, by a soldier who'd walked her home. She never saw him again, he simply disappeared.

'He might have been unexpectedly posted overseas and killed in action on very the first day.' I'd said this to make her feel better, less abandoned.

'Could be, mm.' She'd rolled her blue eyes, then she'd shrugged as if it made no odds anyway. I didn't think Myra was in love.

Now she was living back with her parents, two doors along from us. They were respectable people, I heard my mother saying to Mrs Marsden, our very next door neighbour. And it must take a lot of doing to hold their heads up, given the disgrace of the circumstances.

'Cross fingers it will never happen to your daughters, given time,' Mrs Marsden said pointedly. 'You never know with girls.'

My mother's voice shook with emotion. 'God willing, that should happen. It would be the death of us all if it did. We protect our children's innocence as long as long as is humanly possible.'

'You need to keep that younger girl of yours away from that Myra, then. She's a bad influence, if ever there was one. I've seen them getting chummy.'

'Over my dead body.' My mother was grim now. I could expect another thrashing, that was for sure.

Myra had a miscarriage and started losing the baby on a Saturday in the snuggery of the Bull and Bush. This was the vastly popular public house behind Willesden High Road, much frequented by servicemen on leave. Now she was working in Munitions, like a lot of girls and women, at the factory the other side of the railway track and she'd got her figure right back to what it was before.

There was no denying that Myra was beautiful. With her blonde Veronica Lake pageboy harnessed in her hairnet, just the frothy fringe tumbling over her forehead, the rest wrapped in her emerald headscarf, I thought she looked the image of Lana Turner. I couldn't stop gazing at her. That's how smashing she was.

I was as proud to be considered her friend, despite the eight years between us, as I was to have a beautiful mother and a handsome father, both as good as any film star. But I never let on about how it was at home. Never ever, not even to Myra, and there were plenty of chances because we kept our friendship up on the sly, behind everyone's back.

On the sly, keeping things secret, so Myra said, was the best way with everything. It was the most exciting way to live, she giggled then. And that would have been the very moment to tell her about my father, but I didn't.

She was right about my lucky streak though. Right as right, as anything. And I was thinking about Myra saying that whilst I was in the school Assembly Hall. I shut my eyes tight, and pressed my raffle ticket even tighter between my hands. I must have been praying for almost ten minutes by now, without moving my lips. My time was almost up. God must have read my thoughts by now.

Please God! Let it be me! Let it be me! Let it be me!

The entire school, including the staff, rose to their feet and applauded as I approached the stage to collect my prize. There was silence as the headmaster shook my hand and congratulated me.

'You are a lucky girl, well done. Your father will be very proud to receive this.' He handed me a lacquered oak letter-rack. My heart sank to the pit of my brown crepe-soled Clarkes sandals. I could already see my mother's expression, bordering on tears of disappointment.

'And where was her prize?' she'd pout.

Then relief flooded through me as the Head reminded everyone to save up their pocket money for next month's raffle ticket. I'd be able to win something for her then. I knew how to do it now. God was backing me up. I wasn't just the little girl with the lucky streak.

My mother was more than pleased with her prize. The raffia

sewing basket, with cottons and silken threads, scissors, needles, pins, and a silver thimble was exactly what she'd always wanted.

She was proud of me, she said, and gave me a rare hug. I should have been proud of myself, but something was wrong somewhere. I couldn't have explained it.

The applause hadn't felt as enthusiastic as it had the month before, when I went forward to collect the prize for a second time. In a strange way I felt as if I'd been cheating and hadn't deserved to win again. My prayer had been answered, but it didn't feel good. Was God trying to tell me something that I didn't want to hear?

Worse was to come. I also won the next month. And this time I hadn't even prayed. I'd kept my eyes open all through the headmaster's ritual of choosing the winning raffle ticket.

When he read my name out, it was greeted with total silence. I could sense the hostility and even heard a hiss as I walked up to the platform. But there was no prize in his hand this time. Instead the Head put his arm around my shoulder and laughed.

'Well, well, well! You're on a winning streak, young lady! I think we all agree it is only fair for someone else to have a crack of the whip this time, eh? Would you care to pick the winner?'

I nodded numbly, but only to show that I understood what he was saying, that the shiny blue and red Oxford Dictionary should go to someone else, not me. But this was the only prize that I actually really, really, wanted. I loved words, I could never get enough of new words, or looking them up, ever since I'd learned how to use a dictionary.

We didn't have one at home. Nor did we know anybody else who had one. Except my Auntie Dilys, the head mistress, but she lived back down in Wales, with the rest of our family.

'Do I have to give up the prize? I don't want to and I'm sorry, but I'm not going to.'

I heard my own voice, and the intake of breath from the entire school. I heard the Head clear his throat. I saw the change of expression first, then the surprise, and finally an icy coldness in his eyes.

I didn't care. The Oxford Dictionary was mine, it was meant to be mine. I had won it fairly and squarely this time. I hadn't prayed for it.

That was what God was telling me, not to waste his precious prayer time on winning prizes. He'd given me the winning streak for that in the first place. That was his gift to me, one that was meant to be used.

My prayers were there for more important things like praying for our soldiers and sailors and airmen to be kept safe. Praying for my own family and those of our neighbours, to the right and the left of us, to come unharmed through the air raids of the Blitz, which we had to put up with every night now. Three houses had been bombed to the ground with five people killed and three on the danger list, including two children from our school. That had happened just a street away from us only the week before.

My shrapnel collection was the biggest in my class now, the envy of my friends, because I'd arrived at the scene before any other child the next morning and collected all the best bits.

There was already serious talk of the entire school being evacuated to the country. With luck I may be sent back to the safety of the Welsh valley where I was born, to be with my kind and gentle grandmother and grandfather who neither looked nor acted like film stars, with their moods and play-acting, and scenes of jealousy. And worse.

That's what I must start praying for now, to be back in the Welsh chapel. And to put a prayer in for the enemy, who according to my Granny, are all God's children, too. People forget that, she says.

My Oxford Dictionary lasted all through my childhood, my children's childhood, and my grandchildren's too.

Myra got killed in a daylight air-raid, buying high-heels in Bond Street with an American G.I.

I inherited my parents' good looks when I grew up.

My winning streak is still with me to this day.